Six Plays for Children
by Aurand Harris

Six Plays for Children

by Aurand Harris

Biography and Play Analyses
by Coleman A. Jennings

University of Texas Press, Austin & London

Library of Congress Cataloging in Publication Data

Harris, Aurand.
   Six plays for children by Aurand Harris.
   CONTENTS: Androcles and the lion.—Rags to riches.—
Punch and Judy. [etc.]
   1. Children's plays. I. Jennings, Coleman A.,
1933-   II. Title
PN6120.A5H3588   812'.5'4   77-655
ISBN 0-292-70325-2

Androcles and the Lion, copyright, 1964, by The Children's Theatre Press (now
Anchorage Press); *Rags to Riches*, copyright, 1966, by The Anchorage Press; *Punch
and Judy*, copyright, 1970, by Anchorage Press, Inc.; *Steal Away Home*, copyright,
1972, by Anchorage Press, Inc.; *Peck's Bad Boy*, copyright, 1974, by Anchorage Press,
Inc.; *Yankee Doodle*, copyright, 1975, by Anchorage Press, Inc.
   Reprinted with permission of the publisher, Anchorage Press, Inc.
   Caution: Producers are hereby warned that these plays, being fully protected by
copyright, are subject to royalty, and anyone presenting the plays without consent of
the publisher will be liable to the penalties provided by the copyright law. Also, no
part of this text may be reproduced in any form. Applications for play-books and
performing rights may be made to:

   Anchorage Press, Inc.
   4621 St. Charles Ave.
   New Orleans, Louisiana 70115

To my wife, Lola,
whose encouragement
made this work possible

Contents

Foreword

by Lowell Swortzell

My first recollection of seeing a play by Aurand Harris was an occasion that might have been a playwright's nightmare. The Children's Theatre of Washington, D.C. observed International Theatre Month with the world première of *Simple Simon* performed by local children in a large theatre seating fifteen hundred persons. As if the producers were not already courting disasters enough, they also decided to make the event a benefit for Korean War orphans and Israeli Youth Services and to invite as guests of honor youngsters from Washington's many embassies. Just about every child from every embassy turned up on that colorful afternoon a quarter of a century ago. They came costumed in native dress, carrying flags and banners, singing national anthems and performing folk dances. Speeches in many languages greeted the capacity crowd, and parades proceeded up and down the aisles, as each country was recognized and applauded. How, I wondered, could this or any play compete for attention with the kaleidoscope of kimonos, kilts, and kaftans contributing to the juvenile united nations surrounding us? Yet when finally allowed its moment, *Simple Simon* cut through the heavy sense of ceremony and quieted the house. Soon its humor lowered language barriers as it developed a language of its own, spoken in action by characters who could be understood by everyone. After its laughter had fully dispelled the burden of official protocol, its themes, personified in a hero whose large ears made him different from everyone else, emerged dynamic and significant. The play's message, that we should think less about ourselves and more about others, rang through the auditorium in both word and deed, convincing the assembly that mutual trust is possible, at least onstage and therefore perhaps beyond. And now, not as representatives of forty nations but as one group, a children's theatre audience, we shared the common experience of a lively play earning its deserved measure of life in performance. Harris, by taking hold of the interest of his audience, transporting it into his own theatrical kingdom, and uniting it in spiraling adventure, made this matinee more truly international than could all the flag-waving pageantry in the world.

Two sequences proved we were in the presence of a real playwright, even if he was a dramatist few in the audience had heard of before that day. Early in the first act Simon gives the King a shave, complicated by the fact that he is not a barber and that he is being watched by an Executioner who will take him off to prison if he cuts the King and not his whiskers. Taking a deep breath, Simon raises his razor just as the King enters into a prolonged sneeze. The ensuing close shave is worked out in merry detail worthy of comparison to Figaro's in Beaumarchais's *The Barber of Seville*. It is physical, funny, and fully realized. Later, in another scene, from a clothes basket a nightshirt, a dress, and a set of long underwear come to life as speaking characters in a Fellinilike dream-dance; they hover above the sleeping Simon, imparting courage to him to break the silence of the night with the declaration: "The Queen—is a tyrant!" This passage of magic and mystery ends with a tree growing out of the ground, its leaves constantly whispering, "The Queen—is a tyrant!"

Both scenes possess pure dramatic ingredients of comedy and fantasy, shaped and proportioned to deliver the results they promise: laughter and enchantment. They also reveal something even rarer, and that is style. Moments such as these, emerging with that precise vision and voice which persuade audiences to see and hear exactly what the author intends, bring children closest to plays and to playwrights. Harris from the beginning could write them, and, as this volume ably demonstrates, has continued to do so ever since.

Throughout his career Harris regularly has widened the boundaries of his theatrical kingdom to extend far beyond the fairy-tale locations of his first plays. For not only did he early develop a style of his own, but he also began to explore styles of other periods, places, and persons, and to employ them as sources for his plays. His range of subjects spreads from fable and fiction to folklore and fact. His historical scope includes among other periods the Renaissance, Victorian England, and two hundred years of American life. His geographical latitude orbits from India to Indiana and encompasses the Orient and Europe, as well as mythical spots not found on any map. His interest in people has led him to write plays about Buffalo Bill, Pocahontas, and the many Yankee Doodles celebrated in his musical revue. Among authors who have caught his attention and influenced his work are Shakespeare, Molière, Collodi, and Kipling. Each new play takes him into another region of research and style of presentation, as he continues to expand his own interest in past and present forms of production, and to introduce them to young people. These theatrical forms, sampled here in impressive variety, take playgoers from *commedia dell'arte* and traditional "Punch and Judy" shows to ragtime musical melodrama and the sparse cinematic flow in which he dramatizes the story of two runaway slaves escaping along the Underground Railroad. Style, in both content and form, governs the ever-growing theatrical kingdom of Aurand Harris and illuminates the pleasure to be gained in reading, studying, and producing the plays in this collection.

Harris has been praised for many qualities other than the ones I have singled out to salute here. Coleman Jennings in his exellent examination of the plays calls attention to these, including the playwright's respect for his audience that is evidenced in each of his texts. Certainly, Harris deserves special commendation for ignoring passing trends such as "camp," the device that has done so much to cheapen the quality of children's theatre in the last ten years. Tongue-in-cheek spoofing, burlesques, and television-inspired lampoons hold no place in his work because he regards the material on which he builds his plays with the same high respect that he accords to his audience. Other of his artistic trademarks I esteem include his abilities to dramatize stories in straightforward plotlines, to structure short scenes within the attention spans of youngsters, to prune dialogue to dramatic essentials, and to make scenes immediate and playable. Producers, directors, and actors will list additional attributes they discover in performing these texts and sharing them with children.

Over the last twenty-five years youngsters in many parts of the world have articulated the appeal of these plays through their laughter, applause, and letters of appreciation. During this time the playwright determinedly has remained in close touch with his audiences, claiming that what he likes in the theatre is what children like. It is in the twenty-four plays of Aurand Harris that young people have discovered most to like, for, more than any other contemporary playwright for children, he has created a true theatrical kingdom in which they may grow in wonder and flourish in experience.

The Playwright and the Plays

The Playwright

Even before the age of seven, when James Aurand Harris wrote his first "dramatic piece," he knew that he was going to "do something" in theatre. Certainly his life in Jamesport, Missouri, was conducive to guiding him into a career in the arts. Almost from the day of his birth, July 4, 1915, his mother, Myrtle Sebastian Harris, drama teacher, play director, and amateur actress, focused his life for a career in theatre, starting him at an early age in special classes of dramatic art, music, and dancing.

James Aurand, the only child of Myrtle and George Dowe Harris, a respected Jamesport physician, made his not entirely successful debut in the theatre at the age of four as a bumblebee in a local school operetta. Harris remembers the incident clearly: "During the performance, my short white underwear, which all little boys wore, began to fall from its place beneath my brief, black and yellow striped tunic. The more the audience laughed, the more I buzzed, and the more the underwear slipped. I was quickly yanked offstage."[1]

Today, Aurand Harris, author of twenty-four published plays for children, is America's most-produced children's theatre playwright. His scripts have had more than eleven thousand performances in the United States and thirteen other countries. His plays, which have been constantly produced since the late 1940's, have enormously enriched the literature of American children's theatre. Harris has been honored as the recipient of numerous playwriting contests and awards (see Appendix 2). In 1944–1945, his *Once upon a Clothesline* won an award in the Seattle Junior Programs nationwide competition for new children's plays. Thirty-one years and seventeen awards later, Harris, in 1976, received a Creative Writing Fellowship from the National Endowment for the Arts to create a children's play based on the American Toby Shows.

Harris's dramatic talents, enhanced by an outgoing personality, were evident from his early childhood. His dramatic play and a desire to perform led him to attempt theatrical activities involving neighborhood children. Since, of all the children, young Harris was the most disposed toward presenting plays, it was he who engineered the proceedings.

[1]This and all subsequent quotations are from a series of interviews with Aurand Harris, made over a two-year period, 1972–1974, in New York City.

The Harrises owned a large home with an adjacent barn and smokehouse. The smokehouse porch had supporting pillars which formed a proscenium arch. Between them Harris hung curtains discarded by his grandmother, and the porch became the stage for his first neighborhood productions. With the cement steps for audience seating, his outdoor amphitheatre was complete.

Next came the task of creating the material. Harris does not recall where he got the idea that he could write, but the desire to act and to present plays was the necessary motivation. For the other children the play-acting was just another childhood activity, and, if someone suggested a more exciting game, they were quickly diverted. There were few "finished performances" of his childhood plays, but his personal involvement in writing and preparing the plays continued, and that was more important and satisfying to him than actually performing for an audience. Harris recalls presenting one play, which had not been very well rehearsed. Before it was over, the entire audience of five or six had left.

> I was crushed. It was not that we were playing to an empty house, but because the play had not been the perfect performance which I had visualized in my imagination. Perhaps it was just as well that the audience left, as we had never rehearsed the third act.
>
> Today, if I have anxieties when working on a script I often dream that I am acting in or directing a play which has no final act. As the audience waits I search for a script—but there is none. I'm certain this relates to my childhood experiences.

From a very early age Harris attended his mother's play rehearsals. His own melodramatic childhood productions, which he remembers as "plays with maids, butlers, much dramatic action, and no motivation," were often based on incidents from the scripts she was directing. Later, during Harris's early teen-age years, his introduction to the plays of Shakespeare was with a theatrical rather than a literary approach, for he first read the works from his mother's Northwestern University textbooks, which were filled with her acting and directing notes.

Because the constant demands of his mother's career often took her away from home during Harris's childhood, he spent much of his time at his Sebastian grandparents' house. Harris remembers going to traveling medicine shows with his grandmother, sitting on the front row each night the show was in town, and being fascinated by the patter of the medicine seller. "Perhaps," recalls Harris,

"I learned something about how to hold an audience from these shows."

As a child, he frequently saw films, many of them silent. Harris believes that he must have stored in his mind plots, characters, dramatic situations, comedy routines, and especially the need for action to tell the story.

Several summers of his early childhood were spent with his parents in Chicago, where his father took special medical courses and his mother studied at the Bush Conservatory or the Columbia School of Expression. While in Chicago, Myrtle Harris also saw that her son's cultural life was improved by taking him to the theatre, ignoring the reactions of more conventional people who were shocked to see such a young child at evening performances.

Although Harris remembers himself as a "fat little square—and a poor sight reader," as he matured he had quite a dramatic flair. Myrtle Harris saw in her son the potential for a professional actor, so she began to include him in her various drama classes and plays. She taught the Curry method of acting, which was based on Stanislavski's theories combined with techniques to project a role. Her understanding of acting became an integral part of her son's way of life. As he remembers those years, he realizes the extent of that influence: "I took it for granted that everyone in a family learned how to emote and to speak fairly well. Growing up with acting, I learned to believe, to think, to feel, so I could be other people. I still follow this pattern when I write a character in a play." Harris's careful observation of human nature, sense of language, understanding of dramatic action and empathy with children and adults were later to become important resources for creating his dramatic works.

Assisting the local high school English teacher, who received the official credit, Myrtle Harris helped direct the Jamesport drama students. Throughout their high-school years, Harris and Faye Wiles, another student, played the leads in all of the one-act play competitions, winning at the county, district, and state levels.

The summer after their sophomore year, Harris and Wiles went to Kansas City to attend the Horner Conservatory. They were the only teen-agers in the program, which was designed for semiprofessional adult actors. The experience was less than satisfactory for Harris because the instructors were unable to adjust their methods to meet the needs of such young people.

The following summer Harris's mother took them again to Kansas City, this time to audition for "The Opportunity Revue." The revue, under the aegis of a Hollywood promoter and R.K.O. Studios, was a vaudeville show which was produced with local and professional talent in many of the larger cities throughout the United States. Primarily a publicity venture, the show was ostensively designed to discover new talent for the motion-picture industry. From the crowd of aspiring movie stars who auditioned, the two young actors from Jamesport were selected to perform in comic double-entendre vignettes.

"The Opportunity Revue" was presented at the Kansas City Main Street Theatre between the showings of Frank Buck's *Bring 'Em Back Alive*. For the fifteen-year-old Harris, playing four times a day in a professional theatre and having the opportunity of watching experienced vaudeville actors at work was a memorable experience. He returned to Jamesport that fall of 1931 and finished his last year of high school. The year was filled with theatrical activities, and he was named the best actor and the best orator in the state of Missouri.

Myrtle Harris had hoped that after graduating from high school her son would go to Boston to study the Curry method of acting, but the financial hardship of the Depression prevented his leaving home. Even so, his parents never doubted that he would attend college.

After his first semester at Trenton (Missouri) Junior College, Harris was permitted to take the advanced course in "narration," for which he wrote a one-act folk tragedy, *The Grind of Death*. It was the first play Harris remembers consciously plotting. Based on the lives of an outcast family of Jamesport, the tragedy included actual events and hearsay relating to a poor old woman and her two moronic children, who traveled around in a wagon selling homemade brooms. The boy spent much of his time grinding an ax, which he used at the end of the play to murder his sister.

The English teacher was impressed with Harris's writing and entered *The Grind of Death* in a playwriting contest. The play did not win, nor did Harris keep a copy of the script, which he remembers as "a self-conscious tragedy, painfully and sorrowfully written . . . with everything dramatic." At that time Harris thought that to be a real playwright one had to write a tragedy.

Although not as morbid, Harris's next play also had a serious theme. Written the summer after his freshman year at Trenton, *Dusk* dealt with the problems of a son and daughter as they decided to take their mother to an old people's home.

His mother thought *Dusk* was a good script, and the next summer she directed it for the annual Jamesport Fox Hunt. For years the Fox Hunt was the most important summer activity in Jamesport. The week-long celebration, originally begun as a Chautauqua summer entertainment, included fox hunting, picnics, carnival events, and free stage presentations each evening in which a variety of performers appeared—radio personalities, bands, fiddlers, and local actors who presented plays. The shows were performed in an outdoor pavilion, filled to capacity, with many standing outside the enclosed seating area and some even sitting in the trees.

Performing for the large Fox Hunt audience was difficult. The spectators had the reputation of wanting only comedies for their entertainments, but they were attentive to Harris's *Dusk*. A one-act hillbilly farce was also presented the same evening. Harris appeared in both plays, as the son in *Dusk* and an old man in the comedy.

His next script was *The Ghost House*, which he wrote while continuing his education at the University of Kansas City. The three-act comedy had two featured character roles: a continually frightened maid and a stuttering gardener. Harris speculates that he took many of his ideas from the movies of the time, and certainly his stuttering character was based upon Rosco Ates, the motion picture actor who specialized in playing comic stutterers. "I was too naïve then," recalls Harris, "to realize the negative aspects of satirizing such a physical handicap."

After his junior year the play was presented for the Jamesport Fox Hunt audiences, with Harris and Faye Wiles playing the gardener and the maid. He admits that "we dominated the entire play, although it was not about us. I just kept padding our parts. It played surprisingly well." His acting in these productions with hundreds of people in attendance taught him the necessity of using "theatricality in writing and acting—the need to create characters and situations which are larger than life and capable of being projected honestly to an entire audience." As an actor Harris learned how to use comic timing during these early years: ". . . you quickly recognized how far you could take a joke. Most of my comic roles, although primarily for adult audiences, were in a child's vein—unsophisticated, but with a simple, rustic universality."

During his undergraduate years at Trenton and Kansas City, Harris acted in many theatrical productions. These acting experiences were, however, no longer so rewarding as most of his previous work had been, because the college productions were not very well staged, especially when he compared them to those his mother had directed.

Harris graduated from college in the spring of 1937. Unable to obtain a teaching position, he decided to continue his studies at Northwestern University and earned a master's degree in speech and theatre in 1939. As a graduate student Harris was totally saturated with drama, including an introduction to the specialized fields of children's theatre and creative dramatics in the elementary school. Although Harris had never been concerned with young audiences and was not at that time primarily interested in child drama, he was greatly influenced by the creative dramatics and children's theatre pioneer Winifred Ward. Harris worked on several technical crews for Ward's children's theatre productions, directed a one-act play for her at an Evanston school, and later became one of her creative dramatics leaders in the elementary schools. After Harris began writing plays for children, Winifred Ward became a close friend, evaluating his plays and continually encouraging him to develop his playwriting talents. He took no playwriting courses at Northwestern, for he was planning to be an actor or director.

At the nearby Goodman Memorial Theatre in Chicago, Charlotte Chorpenning was writing and directing her children's theatre plays. Harris did not work with her, but he saw many of her productions, which he considered well directed and technically excellent. For the first time at Goodman he discovered the joy of being part of a child audience.

"I was at the right place at the right moment, when especially exciting things were happening in child drama—when Chicago was the center of children's theatre," recalls Harris. Winifred Ward's ideas about creative dramatics and children's theatre had gained national attention with the publication in 1930 of her first book, *Creative Dramatics*. Charlotte Chorpenning's plays were being made available nationally, and producers looked to the Goodman Memorial Theatre for scripts and production techniques.

While at Northwestern, Harris worked with fellow graduate students Geraldine Brain Siks, Kenneth Graham, and Walter Kerr, who were to become national leaders in the fields of creative dramatics, children's theatre, and dramatic criticism, respectively. During that time children's theatre specialist Campton Bell was also at Northwestern, working on his doctoral degree. He and Harris became good friends, and later Bell was instrumental in Harris's writing of *Buffalo Bill* and *We Were Young That Year*. George Eells, another student acquaintance from Northwestern, later editor of *Theatre Arts Magazine*, entertainment editor of *Look* magazine, and a biographer, became a lifelong friend who still serves as advisor and critic of Harris's plays.

His graduate studies completed, Harris began his teaching career in September, 1939, in the Gary, Indiana, public schools, which encompassed an innovative educational system that had originally been conceived by William Wirt. The work-study-play plan had reached a crest of popularity before his death in 1938, and his work was continued by his wife and coworker, Mildred Harter Wirt. An essential part of the Gary Plan was the popular "auditorium class" of music and dramatic lessons. The pupils participated either as performers or as spectators in programs which were an educational and artistic integration of their curriculum. Harris was hired as a studio teacher in dramatics at Horace Mann High School.

To Harris, teaching drama within the Gary Plan at the high school was "a baptism by fire." He recalls, "On paper the Gary system looked perfect: work, study, play—eight hours a day, ten months a year—keep the students occupied and off the streets. Wirt had created a good school system, but there were problems."

In the Gary system every pupil, kindergarten through high school, went to auditorium one hour each day: the first half was devoted to choral singing or music appreciation, the second half to a stage presentation. Every classroom teacher was expected to sponsor an assembly program each semester which demonstrated the studies of the class. The studio teachers, such as Harris, dramatized this classroom material and rehearsed the students. He wrote a dozen playlets a month. Every three weeks he had to have a show ready for the stage, and each time with a different group of students. The twelve half-hour drama classes each day, with thirty students each, meant that he always had twelve different plays in rehearsal. Harris also directed the freshman and sophomore class plays and taught the classes in stagecraft which mounted all the productions.

After one semester at the high school level, which he found chaotic, Harris's teaching assignment improved, as the enrollment warranted a "half" teacher in the high school and a "half" teacher in the elementary school. Harris at his request "became the two halves." He remembers this solution as a pleasant one: "Working with the little ones was a glorious experience. We did creative dramatics and little shows on the stage."

The next year he was assigned to the newest school in the system, where he continued his studio teaching duties in addition to supervising the school entries in the system-wide speech, interpretation, and drama events. In these monthly events the most interested and talented children represented the school.

One month, Harris entered a production of his own dramatization of a brief segment of Collodi's *Pinocchio*, which he had entitled *Pinocchio Pays a Penny*. Winifred Ward, who often evaluated the citywide drama assemblies in Gary, thought Harris's one-act play was one of the best presented, "but was afraid that it was a little more Harris than Collodi." *Pinocchio Pays a Penny*, Harris's first playlet for children, subsequently entitled *Pinocchio and the Fire-Eater*, was published almost thirty years later with minor revisions for classroom use.

The two years Harris spent in Gary, although mentally and physically exhausting, served as an invaluable experience in preparing him for his later writing, because he had the chance to see innumerable child audiences responding to what they saw and heard on the stage.

In September, 1941, Harris became the head of the drama program at William Woods College, a junior college for girls in Fulton, Missouri. He taught several drama classes, directed the adult productions, and initiated the presentation of a special play for young audiences. Hundreds attended the annual children's theatre production, including students from the local State School for the Deaf.

Having his own base of operations, Harris was able to experiment with many of his playwriting and production ideas, and, for his second children's theatre presentation, he wrote the script. Using the basic idea of clothespin characters from a puppet play which he had outlined while in Gary, Harris created the fantasy *Once upon a Clothesline*. Under his direction the première performance was given in December, 1943, at the college.

Harris entered *Once upon a Clothesline* in the Seattle Junior Programs Second National Playwriting Contest in 1944–1945 and won second prize. He remembers thinking: "This is it. I enjoyed writing the script, it played well, and now others like it." His euphoric state continued to increase as Row-Peterson published the play. *Once upon a Clothesline*, his first published script, is still in print and has remained a frequently produced children's theatre piece.

During his three years at William Woods College, Harris wrote one other play: *Ladies of the Mop*. Very brief and intended for presentation on a bare stage by four women, *Ladies of the Mop* is actually a skit rather than a play. Harris wrote the piece as a teaching device for his college acting class, using the doggerel rhyme to illustrate basic principles of rhythm. The skit was extremely well received when first presented for an audience at William Woods and is even now used as a comic "stunt" for high school groups as an interlude between other short plays. Although not written for a young audience, *Ladies of the Mop* foreshadowed a style of rhyming dialogue which Harris later used in several of his children's theatre plays.

After his third year of teaching at William Woods, he went to New York to enroll in a summer playwriting course being offered at Columbia University by the Pulitzer playwright Hatcher Hughes. After reading Harris's manuscripts, Hughes was convinced that the young playwright could become a professional and encouraged him to remain in New York to continue his writing. Harris remembers, "All I needed was for someone to tell me to stay in New York, for I loved the stimulation of the arts and the city."

In New York City, where he has continued to live ever since, Harris accepted an elementary teaching assignment at Grace (Episcopal) Church School in Manhattan. Even though he would not be teaching drama as he had originally hoped, Harris chose the Grace Church School position because it was a small school with an understanding headmaster and a situation which allowed him much free time for writing and seeing plays. His choice proved to be a good one, and he has remained on the faculty there for over thirty years.

While teaching the first year, Harris, having no idea that the Grace Church School position would become a permanent one, sought and received an interview with Clare Tree Major, the head of the long-established Clare Tree Major Children's Theatre of New York. During the school winter recess of 1946, Harris was employed by Major to "touch up the scenery" for her production of *Peter Pan;* to take two replacement actors to the *Old King Cole* company playing in Wisconsin; and to see that the company met a West Virginia engagement as scheduled.

During his first visits to Clare Tree Major's palatial home in Chappaqua, New York, and before seeing one of her productions, Harris seriously considered taking a permanent position in her organization. After observing the uneven quality of her children's theatre shows and realizing some of the managerial problems, he lost interest in continuing. Clare Tree Major, who was nearing retirement age, saw in the young, energetic Harris a possible successor. In discussing his contact with this controversial playwright, director, and producer of professional children's theatre productions, Harris says:

> At one time Clare Tree Major was an important figure and a motivating force in children's theatre. When I met her, however, it was in the later years, when her artistic integrity, in which she prided herself, was beginning to wane.
>
> Clare Tree Major was extremely nice to me during my brief association with her. It was a "moment" of being in contact with an established person that might have led to something. Certainly had I joined her organization I would have had a completely different life.

Years later Harris had a brief encounter with Edwin Strawbridge, another established children's theatre professional, who directed a national touring dance company performing for children and youth. Strawbridge asked Harris to adapt Grimm's *The Brave Little Tailor* for his company. His dance version was soon completed but was never staged because of Strawbridge's untimely death in 1957. Four years later Harris converted the original dance drama into a children's theatre play.

Harris continued to study playwriting with Hatcher Hughes, and during that time theatrical producer John Golden established a playwriting contest open to students of Columbia University. Harris's *Circus Day*, the only children's play entered, was one of the ten winners of that first John Golden Playwriting Contest in 1945.

The winners were to meet weekly with Golden in his office above the St. James Theatre to have their work criticized. They met only rarely, Harris remembers, when the producer had time for them.

> Sometimes Golden entertained us in a private room at Sardi's, but mostly we met in his office. He sat in his barber's chair surrounded by eager playwrights, and said: "I always wanted to be a king and now I feel like one."
>
> I recall he asked us to state the theme of our plays in one sentence, but mainly the discussions were not about playwriting, but of his past successes, his stars, his life—all of which was quite interesting, but of little help to a practicing playwright.

One of Golden's expressed purposes in sponsoring the contest was to find scripts which he could produce on Broadway, but none were found, and of the winners that year only Harris had his play published.

After studying with Hughes at Columbia, Harris became the private pupil of S. Marion Tucker, whom the young playwright had met as a visiting professor at Northwestern University during his last year of graduate work. Harris later returned to Columbia to study with author and drama critic Barrett Clark, who was then editor of Dramatists Play Service and president of the Dramatists' Guild, the union of professional playwrights. He found Barrett Clark's approach to theatre intellectual and literary, in sharp contrast to Hatcher Hughes's approach, which had been from a more practical point of view. As a playwright, Harris believes that he benefited greatly from his exposure to both methods and philosophies.

During this time Harris was teaching playwriting and history of theatre as a part-time instructor at the Katherine Dunham School of

Arts and Research, a professional program of dance and theatre in Manhattan. Even though he held teaching positions at the Dunham School and at Grace Church School, he still found time to write an adult play, *Missouri Mural*. The play, originally entitled *The Woods Colt*, was a folk drama of northern Missouri about an illegitimate child. Although the play won the Stanford University Miles Anderson Award for playwriting in 1948, it was never produced or published.

While working with Tucker, Harris also enrolled in the much-publicized playwriting course being taught by the dean of American drama, John Gassner, at the New School of Social Research. Harris submitted *Circus Day* to Gassner, who thought the play amusing but without social significance. While in the class, Harris began writing *Lo and Behold*, a script about an eight-year-old boy who, during dramatic play, imagined that he was Jesus Christ and played the role for several days to the embarrassment of his family and community. Harris says: "I remember Gassner's mood and general reactions, if not his exact words, as he read to the class at random from my script. 'Here is a charming play with believable dialogue. I can read from any part of the script—you don't have to know what it is about to appreciate the delightful conversation.'" Gassner, nevertheless, thought that Harris should change his light comedy into a thesis drama with "important overtones." The intense seriousness of the students and their obsession with social message plays was of little interest to Harris, who was primarily concerned with writing optimistic comedies. Combined with the solemn mood of the large class was the lack of individual contact with the instructor, which Harris considered essential for his development as a writer. Withdrawing from the course after one semester, Harris ended his formal study of the art of playwriting.

Harris's interest in children led him to write two adult plays in which the main characters are children: the eight-year-old boy in *Lo and Behold* and a nine-year-old girl in *Hide and Seek*. The roles of the child characters were drawn sensitively, with great care for realistic detail. In fact, the roles were so challenging that finding young actors capable of creating them was not easy. "These two plays were written," Harris explains, "before I realized how difficult it is for young children to play such demanding roles, to sustain an entire adult play."

About the same time, Harris also created *Madam Ada* for the adult theatre. The subsequent productions of *Madam Ada* and *Hide and Seek*, and especially the staging of *Hide and Seek* by the Theatre Guild, were influential in pointing the direction of his playwriting career. *Madam Ada*, a traditional well-made comedy, had its first production at the Try-Out Theatre in Seattle, followed by the official première, under Harris's direction, at the Bennington Drama Festival in Vermont, during the 1946 summer season. A play scout from Samuel French, a company which had recently published a Harris script for the high school audience, was at the opening performance of *Madam Ada* and purchased the amateur rights to it after seeing only the first two acts. Harris remembers their conversation: "'But you haven't seen the third act!' 'No matter,' replied the publisher's representative. 'Madam Ada is our kind of play and we are going to publish it. Come into the office when you return to New York.'"

At Samuel French, Harris was greeted warmly by the editor, Garrett Leverton, whom he had first known as the chairman of the Northwestern University School of Speech. As a graduate student Harris had been in Leverton's play-directing courses. When Harris first came to New York he had considered contacting his former professor, but "was afraid to call him as he was such an awesome, famous personality." After the publication of *Madam Ada*, Leverton published two other Harris plays before his sudden death in 1949.

Although *Madam Ada* was never produced on Broadway and only occasionally by community theatre groups, the nostalgic comedy was presented successfully on television by the Matinee Theatre in 1957 as one of their "Broadway plays." Harris's next and last adult play, *Hide and Seek*, was also shown on national television, under the title *Party for Jonathan*, by the Kraft Theatre during the 1954 season.

Prior to its television adaptations, *Hide and Seek* was selected by Lawrence Langer of the Theatre Guild for a pre-Broadway tryout at the Guild theatre in Westport, Connecticut, during the summer of 1955.

Harris was encouraged and excited during his initial conference with Langer and thought him "the greatest promoter in the world and so convincing." His enthusiasm began to decrease as Langer obstinately insisted upon casting Jessie Royce Landis in the leading role, which, according to Harris, was one of the major reasons that the play was unsuccessful at Westport. *Hide and Seek*, a sensitive psychological study of loneliness, became in the Guild production a forced melodrama. The original version of the play contained more fantasy than Langer thought audiences would accept. Harris had purposely created an ambiguous but dramatic situation, concerning an eccentric spinster who might or might not have had a brother for whose return she had been waiting for twenty years. Harris was extremely discouraged by the changes Langer requested in the script and, finally, by Landis's "ludicrous interpretation of the leading character." He continues: "I sat there every night for a week—seeing a play I had not written being performed under my name. If the play had been properly performed it might have been a success on Broadway . . . never a major hit, but a successful first play. A Broadway production would have encouraged me and I would have continued to write adult plays, trying each time to improve." Harris was bruised by the Theatre Guild experience, and the production of *Hide and Seek* became a climactic turning point in his career. After the Westport summer, he no longer wanted to write an adult play. This attitude persisted even though *Hide and Seek* was televised nationally and later selected as the winner of the Marburg Prize at Johns Hopkins University, where it was staged in 1956. Since then, Harris has not written another adult play. He says: "I have little interest now in writing an adult play. Certainly the odds are against you in trying to get a hit on a dying Broadway. William Inge once said, when approached to write a children's play, 'I have nothing to say to children.' Well, perhaps I have nothing to say to adults."

During the ten-year period from 1946 to 1956, Harris experimented with a variety of plays. He had been writing not only for audiences of adults, but for teen-agers and children as well. For the high school audience, in addition to *Ladies of the Mop*, he wrote three originals which were immediately published: *The Moon Makes Three, The Doughnut Hole*, and *We Were Young That Year;* and a dramatization of Sylvia Dee's novel, *And Never Been Kissed*, which he later rewrote as a musical.

Harris was writing for teen-agers at the end of an era in which plays written for high school production were very unsophisticated and "pure, with no profanity, no sex, no alcohol, no smoking, and no social issues." His four published high school comedies with the familiar subject of first-love-in-the-high-school were no exception to the prevailing fashion. This type of playwriting, in which Harris enjoyed dramatizing many of his own high school memories, developed his skill in constructing plots.

Harris's interest in writing for the adult and high school theatre waned, but his urge to write for children continued. During the decade of his interest in creating plays for high school and adult audiences, Harris had also completed seven scripts for children: *Seven League Boots* (1948), *Circus Day* (1949), *Pinocchio and the Indians* (1950), *Young Alec* (1950, unpublished), *Simple Simon* (1953), *Buffalo Bill* (1954), and *The Plain Princess* (1955). By the summer of 1955 the six published scripts were being produced throughout the United States. Of the six, *Simple Simon* was the most widely acclaimed. Before the highly emotional Theatre Guild experience, Harris did not consider himself exclusively a children's theatre playwright, but afterward he began to "see everything only in terms of what would make a good children's play."

He liked writing for youth, and, with the publication of *Simple Simon* and *Buffalo Bill* by the children's theatre specialty publisher, Anchorage Press (formerly Children's Theatre Press), Harris's reputation as a playwright for young audiences was established. By 1962, he was hailed by George Freedley, then theatre curator of the New York City Public Library and drama critic of the New York *Morning Telegraph*, as "the most important children's theatre writer to appear since the late Charlotte B. Chorpenning of the Goodman Memorial Theatre."

Writing for children provided Harris with opportunities which were unfettered by the naturalistic limitations usually expected by adult audiences. Because children are imaginative and willing to accept any theatrical form if it is honestly presented, he found great satisfaction in writing for them: "I have enjoyed the creative freedom of writing a lyrical play, an historical epic, a *commedia dell-'arte* caper, a realistic slice-of-life drama, an audience participation romp, a musical melodrama, and, in still a different style, *Punch and Judy*, a dark comedy." Furthermore, the encouragement of both publisher Sara Spencer and her assistant, Polly Colgan, of the Anchorage Press, was an important factor in his continuing to write. As Spencer published and often personally publicized his plays, Harris's name became associated with children's theatre. He is convinced that without her publishing company there would have been no future in his writing plays for children.

Harris was particularly encouraged to write *Buffalo Bill*, his second children's theatre play published by Spencer. Campton Bell, then chairman of the theatre program at the University of Denver, was planning a European tour of American children's theatre productions. He asked Charlotte Chorpenning to write a Johnny Appleseed mime and Harris to write a play about Buffalo Bill. After lengthy research Harris found it an arduous task, trying "to make a national hero of such a contradictory character, whose claim to fame was killing off one of our natural resources—the buffalo." Nevertheless, he wrote his version of *Buffalo Bill* and took the manuscript to an annual convention of the Children's Theatre Conference of the American Educational Theatre Association. In a crowded hotel room, Harris read the play to Campton Bell, Sara Spencer, and Charlotte Chorpenning. Harris remembers being pleased that Chorpenning was especially complimentary about the play. Moved by the script and the playwright's reading of it, Spencer contracted to publish it, and Bell planned to include the play in the European tour. *Buffalo Bill* was published in 1954, after the première production given by the School of Drama at the University of Washington, but the European tour never materialized.

After the printing of *Buffalo Bill* and *Simple Simon*, all but four of Harris's children's theatre plays have been published by Spencer's Anchorage Press.

Since the publication of his first children's script, Harris's plays have been performed throughout America by college and university theatres, community theatres, municipal recreation programs, and professional regional theatre groups. In addition his plays have been presented in Canada, England, West Germany, Denmark, Israel, Nigeria, South Africa, Lebanon, Belgium, Norway, Czechoslovakia, New Zealand, and Midway Island. Contrasted with the remarkable number of regional and foreign performances is the fact that only two of his plays, *Androcles and the Lion* and *Buffalo Bill*, have had New York professional productions. Harris attributes this uneven development of children's theatre to the fact that "in New York most children's theatre is financially unfeasible." The producer is beset by problems unique to the city which regional groups do not encounter, such as staggering production costs and the difficulties of finding a convenient time to perform and of transporting audiences of children in the heart of the city. Most professional children's theatre productions in New York, says Harris, "operate on very limited budgets, without the subsidy found in many regional theatres, which means that they can seldom afford to present proven, royalty scripts."

Androcles and the Lion and *Buffalo Bill* were produced and directed by Stan Raiff as major off-Broadway productions. The musical *commedia dell'arte* version of the Androcles legend opened at the Forty-first Street Theatre in New York City in December, 1963. Several weeks after the opening, the production was moved to the Theatre DeLys, another off-Broadway theatre, for the duration of its performances. Almost two years later, in November, 1965, Harris's *Buffalo Bill* opened for nine weeks of performances in the DeLys before touring metropolitan and suburban elementary schools. For this particular production Harris and composer Gil Robbins adapted the play into a musical.

During more than thirty years in New York City, Harris has had a mutually beneficial dual career as a playwright for children and an elementary school teacher. His appreciation and understanding of theatre has shaped his teaching, and that, combined with his thorough sense of knowing how to teach children, makes his philosophy and methods seem deceptively simple.

> I just teach. I'm in the classroom to teach the children what they should learn at a particular age level, and I try to do it the best way I know how.
> The classroom needs a bit of theatricality. I give it that. I find that fairness, honesty, and a sense of humor usually succeed more than reprimands or impersonal rules. Sarcasm has no place in teaching.
> The "praise and encouragement" method of creative dramatics is most effective. To succeed I must feel a mutual and healthy rapport with each student. And I listen!

Just as his teaching is enriched by his knowledge of drama, his writing has been directly influenced by his being in close touch with children.

> Teaching has kept my focus on children and has helped me with my writing. I have learned the way a child thinks; how they react to various situations; what their interests are; how long you can hold their attention; what things they think are funny that are not amusing to adults; what behavior-reactions to anticipate in the classroom and auditorium; how to open up their imaginations.

During his years at Grace Church School, Harris has worked with all elementary grades in dramatic activities. He has led the younger children, up to twelve years old, in creative dramatics, an informal, improvisational drama created by the children and never destined for an audience. The eighth-year class, however, he has directed in formal productions. The scripts presented by the thirteen- and fourteen-year-olds have often been selections which Harris adapted from such theatre classics as *The Romancers, A Midsummer Night's Dream, She Stoops to Conquer, Scapin,* and *Ralph Roister Doister.*

> I think there are many adult comedies which, when properly adapted, will play for children. Certainly some are more suitable than others.
> For the eighth-grade students I always take an adult play that has elements which children like: comedy, action, fun, beauty. My adaptations consist mostly of cuttings to make the script better suited for their age level—just a shortened version— eliminating long passages which children of this age are not

able to comprehend and enjoy. It's always an adult show designed for younger people.

Harris's adaptations of the classics have been questioned, because some educators are not enthusiastic about presenting shortened versions of dramatic masterpieces for younger students. He refutes this objection by pointing out that

> If you give an entire Shakespearean play to children, most get bored before it is over. They will like scenes, but there will be great sections that they will not understand—which are dull to them. But if you give them the highlights in keeping with their interests, they will have a delightful time and will start thinking that Shakespeare is a pretty good writer. As they grow older they will read more and more Shakespeare because of this positive experience. I wouldn't think of expecting a child to read the Bible, but I would give them children's Bible stories to read. It's the same idea when presenting adult classical theatre pieces.
>
> If the classics can be adapted so that the spirit of the original is retained without distortion, but in a form entertaining to younger people, the adaptations can serve as a valid introduction to the plays.

Harris considers his many adaptations of adult plays a "good exercise" in playwriting. Occasionally, as in the instance of his version of Molière's *A Doctor in Spite of Himself*, the script has been published.

Harris's work with young actors, especially in his versions of the classics, has taught him the necessity of making all of his scripts as "actor proof" as possible, even though they all are written to be performed primarily by adults for the child audience.

A very important aspect of the underlying total educational philosophy of Grace Church School is the affirmation of the basic tenets of the Christian faith, but for Harris formal religion has never been a major factor in his life. As a child, however, he did attend a Methodist church and even wrote a playlet for his Sunday School class to perform. He remembers: "All the religious materials they sent us to read about foreign missions, drinking, and parables, were rather stilted and dull, so I wrote a play about a little serving girl who had been mistreated. The moral of which was not to preach so much, but to *do* while preaching." There are no surviving copies of Harris's brief "human-rights" playlet, but his concern for others has remained an integral part of his writing. For example, themes which assert the importance of the freedom and dignity of all humankind appear in his plays *Simple Simon, The Brave Little Tailor, Androcles and the Lion,* and *Steal Away Home.* Even though the development of his own ethical convictions was not directly related to his being involved with formal religion, the ceremonies of the church interested him by providing an extra dimension to his appreciation of theatre.

As the church extended his understanding of theatre, the opportunity to teach college classes in creative dramatics provided him with the necessity to thoroughly evaluate and analyze his methods as a teacher and creative dramatics leader. The occasion came in 1953, when he was invited to join the faculty at Teachers College of Columbia University, where he taught creative dramatics for five summers. During this period Winifred Ward lectured at both Columbia and Union Seminary. In coordination with many of Ward's lectures, Harris led a group of children in creative dramatics demonstrations. During the 1955–1956 academic year, Harris was engaged to initiate creative dramatics at Hofstra University. He believes that the combination of teaching college students and elementary school children has enriched his own development as a teacher and playwright.

> The college teaching helped me clarify certain concepts I had about creative dramatics and playwriting for children.
> My classes were large and consisted of graduate students from many different regions of the country who had worked with a variety of children. These classes helped broaden my view of the American child. The students brought in materials which they had used with children. It was a mutual sharing of successful techniques and ideas.

Even though an educator of both children and adults, Harris considers himself primarily a playwright and director. "I have enjoyed my teaching, but if I had not simultaneously had the theatre work I would have been very frustrated. My major interest is the theatre."

For many summers, Harris has also directed plays for young audiences at the Harwich Junior Theatre in Massachusetts, which presents plays drawn from a wide range of works for children and youth. There he has directed his own scripts as well as those of other playwrights.

Harris finds it a continual stimulus to his own growth and a source of enjoyment to write in a variety of dramatic forms, using material from different settings and historical periods. Although he has developed his own method of writing plays, Harris is reluctant to discuss the philosophical rationale from which he works. "Too much philosophizing can lead to static, lifeless plays. I'd rather be doing—writing—than philosophizing." Harris's "doing" begins with his view of children. "I consider children young adults—individuals. Since they lack the background and experience of adults, it is my job as a playwright to lead them into this world of make-believe on a slightly higher level."

"Often, I'm told, 'How wonderful that you don't write down to children.' This never occurs to me, as I don't know how to 'write down' to a child. I never try to be 'childlike.' I write to please myself as an adult." Harris emphasizes the fact that he likes what children like in the theatre, that is, a good story, interesting characters, excitement, suspense, fantasy, beauty, and fun. Correspondingly, he is opposed to patronizing attitudes toward children. "It is unfortunate that children are often exposed to 'cute,' 'camp,' condescending plays. It never occurs to me to be 'cute' with children in the classroom or the theatre. I write for children who are at the theatre to be entertained, pleased, excited on an honest, emotionally mature level—yet not so far above them that they cannot comprehend the meaning of the experience." If the material is dramatic, Harris believes that a play "will find its own age level." He does not attempt to write for a specific age or grade. "It is true that in children's theatre there are age differences which must be considered, but many good children's plays appeal to a wide age range. The nine-year-old and the young teen-ager often like the same script, but for different reasons. In a successful play, children of many ages as well as adults can find something that is satisfying for each of them."

Harris does not believe anyone can really teach a creative process or even explain exactly how he or she creates. Playwriting, for him, is a very personal, intrinsic process, full of trial and error. His process, however, does form a general pattern.

First of all, Harris is constantly searching for new material, for he believes children should have the opportunity to see many types of plays with subjects and forms adapted from all periods of theatrical history. Once interested in a story or idea with dramatic possibilities, he researches the topic extensively.

Because experiencing a play in the theatre can become a lifelong memory for a child, Harris carefully evaluates the subject matter and inherent ideas. The thought underlying the play must be of enduring positive value that makes it worthy of keeping in mind. But, although universal truths inherent in a story are important and to be preserved, the subject must certainly have the possibility of being theatrically entertaining if it is to become a successful script.

Harris evaluates the material in a second way: the subject must lend itself to dramatization without dependence on technical tricks or production. The resulting play must stand alone, telling the story with a minimum of necessary scenic effects and properties. At this point, Harris relies on his comprehensive training and experience in the theatre to decide how well the material will shape into a script that will then transfer to the stage. "One must know what will and will not work in the theatre and what one can reasonably expect of actors, directors, and designers."

As he continues to think about the dramatization, he asks himself similar questions to those he asks of children in creative dramatics, such as: "What is it about? What happens? Can you show it as well as tell it? Will the story hold our attention? Why? Can the story be told by action and dialogue? Is there a unity in the story? Does the action progress to a rewarding final conclusion? Are the characters interesting? What makes them believable human beings or animals?"

As the characters begin to take form in his mind, he outlines the course of the plot and prepares a detailed notation of the various scenes, with possible high points of action, crisis, and climax. After the major scenes are established he then decreases the total number of roles by discarding or combining all unnecessary characters. This initial planning stage of the writing is one of the most difficult for Harris.

With the outline intact and characters solidified, he begins to write the dialogue. He becomes the characters, saying their words and listening to the sound and rhythm as he writes. Revising, changing, reversing, rewording, Harris reads the words aloud many times. If he really knows the characters and exactly what they must do in a scene, the dialogue comes easily. If the scene is primarily one of exposition or transition, the task is more challenging. He writes every line that comes to mind, knowing that from these he will select only a few at most, and these few will surely be revised.

The result of many sessions of rewriting, the play is finally completed. Harris then asks someone whose judgment he respects to read and react to the play. The constructive criticism of an objective advisor can be extremely helpful, and he welcomes it. In instances in which he does not understand or agree with the reader's suggestions for changes, Harris remains true to his original concept.

The real test of the script naturally comes in performance on stage. The question is not "How well does it read?" but "How well does it play?" If necessary, during the preparation for the initial production, Harris continues to revise lines of dialogue in terms of greater clarity, intensity, or brevity.

With some scripts, he has waited months, even a year, for the right theatre group to present the première production. The wait, however, has always proven advantageous to both playwright and publisher. A good director and cast will add their own creative touches to the play. If these improve the play by clarifying a situation, character, or mood, Harris incorporates them into the final version of the script. Having a second production with a different cast and director is ideal, for, if there are weaknesses apparent in the script, Harris can more accurately analyze and correct them.

Titling the plays, which may come at any step during his script development, is usually a problem for Harris. The title is a key factor in attracting directors, producers, and audiences, so it must be selected with care.

Harris is intensely involved while writing a script, and the creating becomes his "whole life for a little while." During the months he is working on it, every play seems to him to be his best one to date. After his script has been produced and published, however, he usually remembers few specific details about its creation and can assess the effectiveness of the work more objectively. In some instances, upon rereading certain scenes from his previous plays, he scarcely recognizes his own work. Harris's thoughts are elsewhere once his expectations for any given script are met and his creative urge is satisfied. He has already begun searching for his next play.

The Plays

To write successful plays for children's theatre, an author must appreciate and understand the youthful audience with the same depth and thoroughness that he knows the techniques of playwriting. An audience comprised of children of various ages, representing many stages of maturity with widely differing interests and abilities to concentrate, presents an extra dimension of challenge to the playwright. Children are sensitive, perceptive, and quick to react overtly and honestly to whatever they see and hear. Aurand Harris's sensitivity to child audiences, desire to create plays of high quality which adults perform for youth, and thoroughly practical knowledge of all aspects of theatre have made him the respected professional playwright he is today. A complete list of Harris's plays to date can be found in Appendix 1.

The content of Harris's children's plays is derived from four sources: original stories, fairy tales and legends, historical personages, and published literature. Harris wrote three original plots, but creating new stories has obviously been of secondary interest to him, as twenty-one of his twenty-four published children's plays to date are dramatizations of existing material. For example, fairy tales and other legends have been a fertile source throughout his career, but especially for his earlier plays; and the lives of actual personages of American history have provided him with material for four of his scripts. The source which Harris has preferred above the rest, however, is the diverse category of published literature in which may be included adult plays, fiction for children and youth, and a narrative published in a series of newspaper columns.

Regardless of the source, Harris has always been favorably disposed to stories, subjects, or characters which have not already been dramatized. He has chosen with an eye for the unusual, but always weighing his choice against his belief that directors are often hesitant to produce totally unknown titles because parents of young audience members are much more likely to take their children to productions with recognizable titles.

Certainly Harris's selection of content is a central factor in his writing, but of even greater importance is the way he has learned to shape the content. As his craftsmanship has steadily increased throughout his career, so has the range of maturity in the audience for whom he writes. In his later plays he has broadened his approach to include older youth, even as he continues to command the attention of the younger audience members. The six plays selected for this collection are representative of his mature work and exhibit several types of dramatic form unusual for a children's theatre playwright.

In writing each of the plays, Harris has re-created a dramatic form from the adult theatre with adjustments that make it suitable for a child audience. His selection of form—a comedy in the style of *commedia dell'arte*, a late-nineteenth-century melodrama, a comedy with sober overtones, a dramatic chronicle, a light-hearted farce, or a musical revue—is determined by the presence of intrinsic qualities which appeal to children. His adaptation of the form is then governed by his knowledge of his audience, their interests and levels of understanding.

Theme, plot, character, dialogue, song, and spectacle are ingredients of dramatic form through which a playwright creates a play. An analysis of these elements in Harris's work reveals how he has specifically employed them to write plays for the young audience.

The thematic statement, the foundation of the script, expresses either a universal truth or a moral value of society which is within the grasp of a child audience. The forceful and forthright message, always clearly evident in the opening scene, becomes the source for the prime dramatic question motivating the course of the plot and pervading the entire play. The resolution of the play answers the question and affirms the theme.

Because children respond and are attentive to action, the themes chosen are those which can be expressed through two or more characters in verbal and physical conflict with one another. The message is further emphasized by its explicit and repeated statement, in speech or song, from the leading character, who deeply believes it and whose characterization may symbolize it. Because the spoken or sung thematic statement is always embedded in the action, the plays transmit their obvious, underlying messages effectively without being didactically moralizing.

Plot is the single most important factor in Harris's plays for children. His selection of both the type of dramatic form and the theme is usually made with the consideration that a carefully constructed plot will be the key element. The core is physical action, which tells the story of the conflict and is enhanced by speech and song.

Harris's plots are built with a series of events so closely intertwined that the result of one is often the cause of the next. The main plot may be heightened by a concurrent subplot, and, if so, the two are connected by the hero's presence in both. Complications caused by the unexpected appear at regular intervals, helping to create scenes which mount to exciting conclusions. The highest peak or climax precedes the dénouement, which completely and rapidly resolves all questions of plot.

To catch the immediate interest of the audience, the opening scene of each play is skillfully crafted to begin with action which asks the major dramatic question, reveals the characterization of the leading character, presents essential exposition briefly, establishes the type of dramatic form and locale of the play, and includes song if that is inherent in the form.

To maintain the attention of the children, Harris has created increasing tension with suspense, comic suspense, foreshadowing, and anticipated outcomes. Quick changes of mood and tempo within and between the short scenes release the spring of the audience's concentration and simultaneously begin tightening it anew.

The prevailing tone of each play is bright, happy, and optimistic. Even when the play is not a comedy in form, many comic scenes are interwoven into the plot. The serious, contemplative moments are usually shorter than the preceding and following livelier scenes of comedy, again in consideration of the needs of the young audience.

Harris's characters have also been fashioned for the child audience. All the characters have been drawn with unambiguous clarity so that the children can quickly appraise them and their place in the all-important plot. They are very straightforwardly presented, with little emphasis on either personality growth or introspection. Characters are present as part of the story. Each one is primarily revealed by actions, and then by lines in dialogue and song. Occasionally a character is sharpened further by what others say about him or her.

The leading character is usually a hero with whom the children can readily identify. He is a youth of the middle teen years, several years older than the average age of the child audience member. His virtues and wit often solve a difficult situation, especially when an adult or authority figure is floundering. The hero has a *joie de vivre* and a penchant for mischief common to most youth, and his characterization may also embody the theme.

Secondary characters are important in presenting a range of carefully defined human relationships with which children are familiar. The basic relationships, parent-to-child, authority-figure-to-pawn, friend-to-comrade, and protagonist-to-antagonist, are variously portrayed. Often they involve the hero and a secondary character. In rare instances, a lover-to-sweetheart relationship has been included when necessary for the plot, but, because of children's usual disinterest in such a relationship, the interpretation is treated briefly and lightly, and the hero is never one of those involved.

If the particular dramatic form of the play, such as nineteenth-century melodrama, demands the presence of certain stock characters such as the villain and the helpless victim, they have been drawn in harmony with the accepted formula to preserve the authenticity of the form. Harris, however, has added his own distinctive touches to give them traits which are particularly interesting for children.

Sentences or phrases in the dialogue of Harris's plays are usually concise so that the meaning will be immediately communicated to the child audience, whose attention span for talk is short. The consistently brief lines propel the movement of the play quickly forward and simultaneously reveal characterization. Longer speeches, which are used sparingly to provide necessary exposition or to foreshadow an important event, are often interrupted by meaningful action which augments the monologue.

Though he has practiced great economy in his use of words, Harris has never sacrificed the type of dramatic form in which the play is written. In each play its type has influenced the construction of the dialogue from the figures of speech to the choice of words and the use of rhythm and rhyme. Harris's familiarity with the nature of his audience's sense of humor has been invaluable in creating comedy through language which children understand and consider amusing. There are jokes and riddles, plays on words, double meanings, and misuses of words. The dialogue has been written with a vocabulary of common words that children comprehend instantly, especially in the essential revelations of plot development. However, when the meaning of the lines is conveyed simultaneously by the action, Harris has included many words that may be beyond the immediate literal understanding of many in the audience, but not beyond their ability to appreciate subconsciously the lively shifting patterns of rhythm and rhyme that the words create together.

The songs in each play enrich and underline plot, characterization, and mood. Because the lyrics are always an extension of the dialogue, they either relate necessary exposition, reveal characterization, or move the plot forward. Together the lyrics and the music are consistent with the dramatic form of the play, reinforce the mood of a scene, and may also emphasize the high points of the action. Furthermore, the combination of singing interspersed with spoken lines produces aural variety which helps maintain the interest of the audience.

The required visual element in the plays is quite simple, because Harris's scripts have been written in many short scenes which are designed to succeed each other rapidly. Spectacle never deters the necessary pace of the plot; multiple locales are to be merely suggested to facilitate their change. The only effects of spectacle recommended within the stage directions are those which would further stimulate the children's involvement in the unfolding action.

Because the six elements of dramatic form are so closely interdependent in these plays of Aurand Harris, the works exhibit a vital theatricality to which young audiences respond. Furthermore, each play, unified and satisfactorily resolved, has a unique quality of its own because of the playwright's desire and ability to expand the horizons of American children's theatre.

Androcles and the Lion

Based on an old fable, *Androcles and the Lion* is written in the *commedia dell'arte* tradition. The cast, a group of strolling players, set up the stage and then become stock characters from the *commedia* who enact the tale. Since the comic story is presented by characters who are immediately established as actors, the script is a play-within-in-a-play, a form which is maintained from beginning to end by devices directly from the *commedia* tradition. In addition to the strolling players who become the stock characters of Pantalone, the *innamorati* (Isabella and Lelio), the Captain, and Arlequin (Androcles), there are several references by the actors to a scenario on a scroll posted onstage, instances of direct address to the audience, and the setting of some locales by actors' pronouncements immediately preceding the scenes. Other devices derived from the *commedia* are broad, physical comic action, chase scenes, and use of the slapstick.

The theme, the bedrock of the play, is simple, direct, and unmistakable: "Every man must be free to be." The subject of attaining freedom dominates both the main plot about Androcles and the subplot about Isabella.

The six characters of the play are developed on three levels: the most fully drawn are Androcles and the Lion; the next most completely portrayed are Pantalone and the Captain; and the least developed are Lelio and Isabella. The Lion is the only character not from the *commedia* tradition, but he is integrated into the group of stock characters by his first playing the Prologue, who is the spokesman of the players.

Androcles is the center of the plot because all the events are his adventures. Willing to befriend those in need even though he fears the severe punishment he risks by doing so, he is an honest, occasionally mischievous underdog whose tricks are amusing rather than malicious, and justified because of the circumstances. He fools only the gullible Captain and Pantalone, whose stupidity and cruelty to others makes them deserving of their lot. It is young Androcles with whom the audience identifies.

Far more man than beast, the Lion has a friendly gentleness that is evident in his first appearance, as he sings about the glories of roaring. He exhibits a range of human emotions and reactions, but he remains a lion because of a device used in his speeches. Even though he understands everything that is said by the human characters of the play, the Lion never uses words to communicate with the characters who speak to him, but answers with roars, noises, pantomime, and facial expressions. He does, however, speak directly to the audience in lines and song.

The second pair of characters, Pantalone and the Captain, are foils for Androcles, the Lion, and Isabella. Their foolishness creates the humor which appeals to the young audience. Pantalone, the prime antagonist of the piece and an old miser, obviously cares nothing for others. The Captain, the more empty-headed of the two, is a brash braggart who never tires of describing his impossible exploits. His courage is only empty boasting, and, whenever faced with real danger, he wilts.

Isabella and Lelio are revealed simply as young, in love with each other, and loyal to Androcles. Instead of being important as individual characters, they are primarily devices for the plot. There is one romantic scene, but the comic treatment keeps the scene in harmony with the dramatic form and the interests of the audience.

Adversaries in the conflict of the main plot are Androcles, the slave, and Pantalone, his owner. Pantalone is furthermore the antagonist of Isabella in the subplot. From the opening scene of the story, the two plots are skillfully woven together. As Isabella flees to her lover from her tyrannical guardian and Androcles follows to help her, Pantalone and the Captain chase them both in hasty pursuit. The plot is soon complicated by the appearance of the Lion, who frightens them all and immediately injures his paw. Androcles overcomes his fear and stops to help him, thus forging a friendship that results in the freeing of both man and beast in the dénouement.

Comic suspense is a frequently occurring device for intensifying a sense of anticipation in the audience. For example, Androcles must trick the Captain so that Isabella may escape. In a moment alone with her, Androcles explains his plan. They will gull the captain into removing his cape, hat, and sword, and she will wear them, pretending that she, not he, is the Captain. Wondering if the incredible plan could possibly succeed, the members of the audience, watching the ruse actually materialize, find it doubly satisfying and funny because of their anticipation of it.

Although the predominant tone is that of a bright, fast-moving comedy throughout the play, slower, more serious moods relieve the excitement and preserve the audience's interest, such as Androcles' lone lament of his lot as a slave immediately following an intense build of activity among several characters in the opening scene.

In one instance, the audience participates to thrust the story forward at a crucial moment. Androcles' request for assistance is genuinely motivated by the circumstances and, hence, deserves a response. Furthermore, the use of direct address from actors to audience has already been well established.

The chief characteristic of the dialogue is its clean spareness, in which a few words say much. Sometimes the lines are reduced to an exchange of single words, through which excitement and humorous tension mount, as when Isabella and Androcles trick the Captain into believing the day is too hot to wear his cape, hat, and sword.

Another technique which creates a humorous effect is the use of rhyme. The end of one character's short line rhymes with that of the next to speak. The comedy is produced not only by the sudden occurrence of hard rhyme in the dialogue but by the unexpected combinations of rhymed words which come within rapid exchange between characters, and sometimes even within a single line.

Dialogue also sets locale. Early in the play an actor simply announces that the scene is laid in ancient Rome. After the plot is underway and the actors have become characters in the story, the locale is set either within a conversation, or by a character thinking aloud.

Song is subtly woven into the structure of the play. Each character's song is an expression of personality and feelings and occurs logically within the plot. In the three instances of Androcles, Isabella, and the Lion, the characters introduce themselves in song, and the lyrics thus become a mode of exposition. Although Lelio's song does not introduce him as a character, it is a logical development within the single love scene. In keeping with the treatment of romantic love in the plot, the length of Lelio and Isabella's song is minimal, even briefer than the already short ones of the other characters.

Song and music intensify the entire play. Song heightens important events of the plot, as when Androcles removes the thorn and the Lion, unable to contain himself, sings exuberantly. Musical sounds enhance mood and create atmosphere: trumpet calls add majesty to the implied presence of the Emperor; drums bring excitement to the confrontation in the arena; and cymbals, bells, flute, and drums suggest the gaiety and brightness of entertainment by strolling players.

The setting is simplicity itself, for spectacle is to be improvised. The play opens on a bare stage which the actors prepare by selecting items from a trunk of properties and pulling a painted backdrop across the stage. The four shifts in locale are managed swiftly by the performers within the dialogue and action.

Androcles and the Lion, a fast-moving comedy of wit and good humor, is arbitrarily divided in two acts, for the dozens of minor events overlap one another to create a continuous movement forward to the final resolution of the closing scene.

Androcles and the Lion

Adapted by Aurand Harris

A play for the young, based on the Italian tale of "Androcles and the Lion," and written in the style of Italian *commedia dell'arte*

Original music by Glenn Mack

The première production of *Androcles and the Lion* was presented in December, 1963, at the Forty-first Street Theatre,
New York City.

Androcles

Pantalone

Isabella

Lelio

Captain

Lion and Prologue

SCENE

The improvised stage of a *commedia dell'arte* troupe of strolling players. Sixteenth century, Italy.

An intermission is optional.

Androcles and the Lion

ACT ONE

(The curtains open on a bare stage with the cyclorama lighted in many colors. There is lively music and the Performers enter, playing cymbals, flute, bells, and drums. They are a commedia dell'arte group.

Arlequin, dressed in his traditional bright patches, leads the parade. Next are Lelio and Isabella, the romantic, forever-young lovers. Next is Pantalone, the comic old miser. Next is the Captain, the strutting, bragging soldier. And last is the Prologue, who wears a robe and who later plays the Lion.

After a short introductory dance, they line up at the footlights, a colorful troupe of comic players.)

PROLOGUE. Welcome!
    Short, glad, tall,
    Big, sad, small,
    Welcome all!

(Actors wave and pantomime "Hello.")

We are a troupe of strolling players,
With masks, bells, and sword,

(Actors hold up masks, ring bells, and wave sword.)

A group of comic portrayers
Who will act out upon the boards
A play for you to see—
A favorite tale of Italy,
Which tells how a friend was won
By a kindness that was done.
Our play is—"Androcles and the Lion."

(Actors beat cymbals, ring bells.)

The players are: Arlequin—

(Arlequin steps forward.)

Who will be Androcles, a slave.

(Arlequin bows, steps back, and Pantalone steps forward.)

Pantalone, stingy and old,
Who thinks only of his gold.

(Pantalone holds up a bag of gold, bows, steps back; and Isabella and Lelio step forward and pose romantically.)

Isabella and Lelio, two lovers
Whose hearts are pierced by Cupid's dart.

(They bow, step back, and Captain marches forward.)

It is the bragging Captain's lot
To complicate the plot.

(Captain waves his wooden sword, bows, and steps back.)

There is one more in our cast—
The Lion! He, you will see last.
Set the stage—

(Actors quickly set up small painted curtain backdrop.)

Drape the curtains—raise the platform stand!
Here we will make a magic circle—
Take you to a magic land—
Where love is sung, noble words are spoken,
Good deeds triumph, and evil plots are broken.

(Holds up long scroll.)

Our story is written on this scroll which I hold.
What happens in every scene here is told.

(Hangs scroll on proscenium arch at L.)

Before we start, I will hang it on a hook
So if someone forgets his part
And has the need, he may have a look
And then proceed.
All the words in action or in song
We will make up as we go along.
All is ready! Players, stand within.

(Actors take places behind curtain.)

For now I bow and say—the play—begins!

(He bows.)

In ancient Rome our scene is laid,
Where the Emperor ruled and all obeyed.

(Points to curtain, which is painted with a street in the middle and with a house on either side.)

A street you see, two chariots wide,
With a stately house on either side.
In one lives Pantalone—rich, stingy, sour,

(Pantalone leans out the window flap on the house at R and scowls.)

Who counts and recounts his gold every hour.

(Pantalone disappears.)

With him lives his niece Isabella, who each day

(Isabella leans out the window.)

Looks lovingly—longingly—across the way

(Lelio leans out the window of the house at L.)

At the other house, where Lelio lives, a noble sir, who looks across lovingly—longingly—at her.

(Lelio sighs loudly. Isabella sighs musically, and they both disappear. Androcles enters from R, around the backdrop, with broom.)

And all the while Androcles toils each day.
A slave has no choice but to obey.

(Prologue exits at R.)

ANDROCLES. *(Music. He sweeps comically, in front of the door, over the door, then down the "street" to footlights. Sings.)*

Up with the sun,
My day begins.
Wake my nose,
Shake my toes,
Hop and never stop.
No, never stop until I—
Off to the butcher's,
Then to the baker's,
To and from the sandalmaker's.
Hop and never stop.
No, never stop until I—
Spaghetti prepare
With sauce to please her.

Dust with care
The bust of Caesar.
Hop and never stop.
No, never stop until I—drop.

Some masters, they say, are kind and good. But mine . . . ! He cheats and he beats—he's a miser. Never a kind word does he say, but shouts, "Be about it!" And hits you a whack on the back to make sure. I'm always hungry. He believes in *under* eating. I'm fed every day with a beating. I sleep on the floor by the door to keep the robbers away. My clothes are patched and drafty because my master is stingy, and cruel, and crafty! When —oh when will there ever be a Roman Holiday for me!

(Sings.)

Will my fortune always be,
Always be such drudgery?
Will hope ever be in my horoscope?
Oh, when will I be free?

PANTALONE. *(Enters around R of backdrop, counting money.)*

. . . twenty-two, twenty-three, twenty-four, twenty-five . . .

(Androcles creeps up behind him, and, playing a trick, taps Pantalone on the back with broom. Pantalone jumps.)

Who is there?

ANDROCLES. Androcles.

PANTALONE. Be about it! Be off! Go! Collect my rents for the day. Everyone shall pay.

(Androcles starts R.)

Lock the windows tight. Bolt the doors.

(Androcles starts L.)

My stool! Bring me my stool.

(Androcles exits R.)

Lazy stupid fool! There will be no supper for you tonight. Oh, I will be buried a poor man yet—without a coin to put in my mouth to pay for ferrying me across the River Styx.

(Androcles runs in R with stool.)

My stool!

ANDROCLES. *(Places stool behind Pantalone and pushes him down on it roughly. Pantalone gasps in surprise.)*

Yes, my master.

PANTALONE. Go! Collect my rents. Make them pay. Bring me—my gold. Away!

ANDROCLES. Yes, O master. I run!

(He starts "running" to L at top speed, then stops, looks back impishly, and then slowly walks.)

PANTALONE. *(Brings out bag and starts counting.)*

Twenty-six, twenty-seven, twenty-eight, twenty-nine, thirty . . .

ISABELLA. *(At the same time, she leans out the window, calls, stopping Androcles.)*

Androcles . . . Androcles!

(He runs to her UR. She gives him a letter.)

For Lelio. Run!

(Androcles nods and smiles, pantomimes "running" to painted house on curtain at L, pantomimes knocking. There is music during the letter scene.)

LELIO. *(Appears at his window, takes letter.)*

Isabella!

(Androcles smiles and nods. Lelio gives him a letter. Androcles "runs" to Isabella, who takes letter.)

ISABELLA. Admired!

(Gives Androcles another letter. He "runs" with leaps and sighs to Lelio, who takes it.)

LELIO. Adored!

(He gives Androcles another letter. He "runs," enjoying the romance, to Isabella, who takes it.)

ISABELLA. Bewitched!

(She gives him another letter—they are the same three sheets of parchment passed back and forth—which he delivers. This ac-

tion is continued with a letter to each lover, and with Andro-cles "running" faster and faster between them.)

LELIO. Bewildered!

ANDROCLES. And she has a dowry. The gold her father left her.

("Runs" to Isabella with letter.)

ISABELLA. Enraptured!

LELIO. Inflamed!

ISABELLA. Endeared!

(Holds letter.)

LELIO. My dear!

(Holds letter.)

ANDROCLES. My feet!

(Androcles sinks exhausted to ground. Isabella and Lelio dis-appear behind the window flaps. Music stops.)

PANTALONE. *(Picks up the dialogue with his action, which has been continuous.)*

. . . one hundred three, one hundred four, one hundred five, one hundred six . . .

(Bites a coin to make sure.)

one hundred seven . . . one hundred . . .

LELIO. *(Enters from L, around backdrop.)* Signor Pantalone.

PANTALONE. *(Jumps from stool in fear.)* Someone is here!

LELIO. A word with you, I pray.

PANTALONE. *(Nervously hides money.)* What—what do you wish to say?

LELIO. I come to speak of love. I come to sing of love!

(Reads romantically from a scroll he takes from his belt.)

"To Isabella."

PANTALONE. My niece?

LELIO. "Oh, lovely, lovely, lovely, lovely flower,
Growing lovelier, lovelier, lovelier every hour . . .

Shower me your petals of love, O Isabella,
I stand outside—with no umbrella."
Signor, I ask you for Isabella. I ask you for her hand in marriage.

PANTALONE. Marry—Isabella?

LELIO. *(Reads again.)*

"My life, my heart revolve around her;
Alas, I cannot live without her."

PANTALONE. *(Happy at the prospect.)* You will support her?

LELIO. I ask you—give me Isabella.

(Pantalone nods gladly.)

Give us your blessing.

(Pantalone nods eagerly and raises his hand.)

Give her—her dowry.

PANTALONE. *(Freezes.)* Money!

LELIO. The gold her father left her.

PANTALONE. Gold! It is mine—to keep for her.

LELIO. But hers when she marries.

PANTALONE. How did he find out? No. She shall not marry you. Never! Part with my gold! Help! Androcles!

(Androcles runs to him.)

LELIO. Part with Isabella? Help! Androcles!

(Androcles, between them, runs from one to the other as their suffering increases.)

PANTALONE. My heart is pounding.

LELIO. My heart is broken.

PANTALONE. Quick! Attend!

LELIO. Lend!

PANTALONE. Send!

LELIO. Befriend!

ANDROCLES. *(To Lelio.)* There is hope.

PANTALONE. I am ill.

LELIO. Amend!

ANDROCLES. *(To Lelio.)* Elope!

PANTALONE. I have a chill!

LELIO. *(Elated with the solution.)* Transcend!

(Exits around L of backdrop.)

PANTALONE. I will take a pill!

(Exits around R of backdrop.)

ANDROCLES. *(To audience.)* The end!

(Comes to footlights and sings.)

They are my masters and I obey.
But who am I? I often say.
"Androcles!" They ring.
"Androcles!" I bring.
But who am I?
A name—I am a name they call,
Only a name—that's all.

(Speaks simply and touchingly.)

My father's name was Androcles. We lived on a farm by the sea.
Free to be in the sun—to work the land—to be a man. One day
when my father was away, a ship came in the bay. "Pirates,"
my mother cried. I helped her and my sisters hide, but I was
caught and brought to Rome—and sold—for twenty pieces of
gold. I thought I would run away! But when they catch a slave
they decree a holiday. The Emperor and everyone come to
watch the fun of seeing a runaway slave being beaten and eaten
by a wild beast. Personally I don't feel like being the meal for a
beast. So I stay . . . just a name . . .

(Sings.)

"Androcles!" They ring.
"Androcles!" I bring.
But who am I?
If I were free
Who would I be?
Maybe . . . maybe . . .
A doctor with a degree,

A poet, a priest, a sculptor, a scholar,
A senator—emperor with a golden collar!
I want to be free
So I can find—me.

PANTALONE. *(Calls off, then enters UR.)* Androcles! Androcles!

ANDROCLES. You see what I mean.

PANTALONE. Androcles!

ANDROCLES. Yes, my master.

PANTALONE. Quick! Answer the bell. Someone is at the gate.

(Androcles picks up stool and crosses to R.)

Then come to me in the garden by the wall.

(Holds up a second bag of gold, different colors from the first.)

I am going to bury—to plant—this bag of—stones.

ANDROCLES. Plant a bag of stones?

PANTALONE. Be off! To the gate!

(Androcles exits DR. Pantalone holds up bag, schemingly.)

Ah, inside this bag are *golden* stones! It is Isabella's dowry.

(There is a loud crashing of wood off R, announcing the entrance of the Captain.)

Who is at the gate? I have forgot.

(Hurries to scroll hanging by the proscenium arch, reads–announcing in a loud voice.)

"The Captain enters!"

CAPTAIN. *(He struts in DR, wooden sword in hand. His voice is as loud as his look is fierce.)* Who sends for the bravest soldier in Rome? Who calls for the boldest Captain in Italy!

PANTALONE. I—Pantalone.

(Goes to him, speaks confidentially.)

I will pay you well—

(Looks away. It breaks his heart.)

—in gold—

(Then anxiously. Androcles peeks in at R.)

to guard my niece. I have learned today she wishes to marry. You are to keep her lover away. Stand under her window. Station yourself at the door. Isabella is to be kept a prisoner forever more.

(No reaction from Captain.)

ANDROCLES. A prisoner? She will be a slave—like me.

PANTALONE. What do you say?

CAPTAIN. *(Pompously.)* I say—she who is inside is not outside.

ANDROCLES. *(To audience.)* I say—no one should be held a slave. This is treachery!

(Exits UR around backdrop.)

CAPTAIN. *(Struts.)* I have guarded the royal Emperor. I have guarded the sacred temple. I can guard one niece—with one eye shut.

(Shuts one eye and marches L.)

PANTALONE. No, no. The house is over there.

(Points R.)

And that is her window.

(Isabella leans out of window.)

CAPTAIN. Someone is there! Death to him when he tastes my sword!

(Advances with sword waving.)

PANTALONE. No! No! It is she! *(Whispers.)* It is—Isabella.

ISABELLA. *(Sings happily.)*

Oh, yellow moon,
Mellow moon,
In the tree,
Look and see
If my lover
Waits for me.

PANTALONE. *(Softly.)* Keep watch. Keep guard. She must not meet her lover.

(Captain salutes, clicks his heels, turns, and with thundering

steps starts to march. Androcles slips in from around backdrop UL and listens.)

Sh!

(Captain marches with high, silent steps to window and stands at attention. Pantalone speaks to audience.)

I must go to the garden! In this bag is the gold her father left her. I gave my oath to *keep* it—for her. To keep it safely—and for me. I will bury it deep, deep in the ground. Never to be found.

(He hurries off DL.)

ANDROCLES. *(To audience.)* More trickery that's wrong. The gold belongs to Isabella.

ISABELLA. *(Aware someone is outside.)* Lelio?

CAPTAIN. *(Laughs.)* Ha ha ha—no.

ISABELLA. Oh!

CAPTAIN. I am the Captain!

ISABELLA. Oh?

CAPTAIN. I guard your door. You cannot come or go.

ISABELLA. Oh.

CAPTAIN. Do not despair. I will keep you company. Observe how handsome I am—fifty women swooned today.

ISABELLA. *(Calls softly.)* Lelio . . . ?

CAPTAIN. Know how brave I am—on my way to the barber two dragons I slew!

ISABELLA. Lelio . . . . . ?

CAPTAIN. Hear what a scholar I am—I say, "He who is sleeping is not awake."

ISABELLA. Lelio-o-o-o.

(Cries daintily. Captain makes a sweeping bow to her.)

No!

(She disappears, letting the flap fall.)

CAPTAIN. She sighs.

(Louder crying of musical "o's" is heard.)

She cries. Ah, another heart is mine! Fifty-*one* women have swooned today!

(Poses heroically.)

ANDROCLES. I must do something! She cannot be put in bondage. No one should be. Everyone should be free. But how—

(Beams with an idea, looks at scroll by proscenium arch and points.)

Ah, look and see!

(He quickly reads scroll at side.)

ISABELLA. *(Appears at window, sings sadly.)*

Oh, lonely moon,
Only moon,
Do you sigh,
Do you cry
For your lover
As—as I?

ANDROCLES. Yes, here is the plan I need!

(Clasps hands and looks up in prayer.)

Oh, gods of the temple, please give me the courage to succeed.

(Makes a grand bow to Captain.)

Signor Captain!

(Captain jumps.)

It is said you are so fierce the sun stops when you frown.

CAPTAIN. That is true.

(Makes a frightening frown, turns, and frightens Androcles.)

ANDROCLES. And that the tide goes out whenever you sneeze.

CAPTAIN. That is true.

(Screws up his face comically, puffs up and up his chest, then sneezes.)

A-a-a-achew!

ANDROCLES. *(Circling in front of Captain, going to R, toward win-*

dow). Oh, brave and mighty Captain, I shake before you.

(Bows, back to audience shaking.)

CAPTAIN. Yesterday I swam five hundred leagues.

ANDROCLES. I heard you swam one thousand.

CAPTAIN. One thousand leagues I swam into the sea.

ANDROCLES. I heard it was into the ocean.

CAPTAIN. The ocean! To meet a ship—

ANDROCLES. A fleet of ships.

CAPTAIN. To meet a fleet of ships!

(Captain suddenly huffs and puffs as he starts pantomiming how he swam in the ocean, his arms pulling with great effort.)

ANDROCLES. *(At the same time, whispers to Isabella.)* I have a plan to set you free; listen—carefully.

(Whispers, pointing to Captain. Pantomimes dropping handkerchief and fanning himself.)

CAPTAIN. *(Suddenly starts coughing and waving his arms.)* Help! Help! I am drowning! Drowning!

ANDROCLES. *(Rushes to him, hits him on back.)* Save him. Throw out a rope. Man overboard!

CAPTAIN. *(Sighs in relief, then dramatically continues with his adventure.)* I was saved by a school of mermaids—beautiful creatures—and all of them swooned over me.

ANDROCLES. Then you swam on and on—

CAPTAIN. *(Swimming on L, comically.)* And on—

ANDROCLES. *(Pushing him to exit.)* And on—

CAPTAIN. And on—

ANDROCLES. And on—

CAPTAIN. And on—

(Exits L, "swimming.")

ANDROCLES. *(Quickly speaks to Isabella.)* Do as I say and you can escape. We will trick the Captain. Wave your handkerchief. Get his attention. Then say the night is so warm—fan yourself. As

he becomes warmer, he will shed his cape and hat and sword—
and you will put them on. You will be the Captain.

ISABELLA. I?

ANDROCLES. *(On his knees.)* Try.

ISABELLA. The Captain's cape and hat will cover me, and I will be
free to go—to Lelio.

CAPTAIN. *(Re-enters at L.)* After I had sunk the fleet of ships—

ANDROCLES. And brought the treasure back.

CAPTAIN. Treasure?

ANDROCLES. You awoke.

CAPTAIN. Awoke?

ANDROCLES. And found—it was but a dream.

*(Isabella waves her handkerchief, then drops it coyly. Captain
sees it and smiles seductively.)*

CAPTAIN. Ah! She signals for me to approach. Signora—your ser-
vant.

*(Androcles, behind him, motions for Isabella to begin the
trick.)*

ISABELLA. *(Accepts handkerchief with a nod.)* The night is so warm.
The air is so still, so stifling. There is no breeze.

CAPTAIN. I will command the wind to blow a gale.

ISABELLA. The heat is so oppressive.

CAPTAIN. I will command the wind to blow a hurricane!

ANDROCLES. My nose is toasting.

CAPTAIN. I will call the wind to blow a blizzard!

ANDROCLES. My ears are roasting.

ISABELLA. The heat is baking.

*(Captain, between them, looks at each one as each speaks.
Captain becomes warmer and warmer. The dialogue builds
slowly so the power of suggestion can take the desired effect on
the Captain.)*

ANDROCLES. Sweltering.

ISABELLA. Smoldering.

ANDROCLES. Simmering.

ISABELLA. Seething.

(Captain begins to fan himself.)

ANDROCLES. Stewing!

ISABELLA. Parching!

ANDROCLES. Scalding!

ISABELLA. Singeing!

(Captain takes off his hat, which Androcles takes, as Captain mops his brow.)

ANDROCLES. Scorching!

ISABELLA. Smoking!

ANDROCLES. Sizzling!

ISABELLA. Blistering!

(Captain, growing warmer and warmer, removes his cape and sword, which Androcles takes.)

ANDROCLES. Broiling!

ISABELLA. Burning!

ANDROCLES. Blazing!

ISABELLA. Flaming!

CAPTAIN. Help! I am on fire! Blazing! Flaming! I am on fire!

(Captain goes in a circle, flapping his arms, puffing for air, fanning, hopping, and crying, "Fire! Fire!" At the same time, Androcles quickly gives hat, cape, sword to Isabella.)

ANDROCLES. *(Comes to Captain, who is slowing down.)* Throw on water! Throw on water!

CAPTAIN. *(Stops, dazed.)* Where am I?

(Isabella, dressed in Captain's hat, cape, and sword, marches from R and imitates Captain with comic exaggeration.)

ANDROCLES. *(Salutes her.)* Signor Captain! What is your philosophy for the day?

ISABELLA. *(Poses and speaks in low loud voice.)* I say—he who is outside—is not inside.

ANDROCLES. Yes, my Captain.

CAPTAIN. Captain?

ISABELLA. I am off to fight a duel. Fifty-four I slew today. Fifty more I will fight—tonight!

ANDROCLES. Yes, my Captain.

CAPTAIN. Captain? Captain! *I* am the Captain.

(They pay no attention to him.)

ANDROCLES. Your horse is waiting.

(Pantomimes holding a horse.)

Your horse is here. Mount, O Captain, and ride away.

(Isabella pantomimes sitting on a horse, holding reins.)

CAPTAIN. I am the Captain!

ISABELLA. Did you hear the wind blow?

CAPTAIN. I am the Captain!

ANDROCLES. *(Listening and ignoring Captain.)* No.

ISABELLA. I will ride a thousand leagues—

ANDROCLES. Two thousand—

ISABELLA. Three—

CAPTAIN. I am the Captain!

ISABELLA. Is that a shadow—there?

(Points sword at Captain.)

ANDROCLES. A shadow . . . ?

(Takes sword and slashes the air, making Captain retreat fearfully.)

No one is here . . . or there . . . or anywhere.

CAPTAIN. *(Almost crying.)* But I am the Captain.

ANDROCLES. To horse! Away—to the woods.

ISABELLA. To the woods!

ANDROCLES. But first, a bag of stones—by the garden wall, yours to take before you go.

ISABELLA. And then—to Lelio!

ANDROCLES. Yes, my Captain.

CAPTAIN. *(Crying comically.)* But I am the Captain. Look at me. Listen to me.

ISABELLA. To the woods!

(Starts pantomiming riding off L.)

Ride, gallop, trot, zoom!

ANDROCLES. Hop, skip—jump over the moon!

(They "ride" off UL.)

CAPTAIN. *(Crying.)* But I . . . I am the Captain.

(Then, horrified.)

If that is the Captain—then—who—who am I?

PANTALONE. *(Enters DL.)* Captain . . . Captain.

CAPTAIN. Someone calls. Oh, Pantalone . . . Pantalone! Can you see me?

(Waves his hands in front of Pantalone, then shouts in his ear.)

Can you hear me?

PANTALONE. Yes.

CAPTAIN. Am I . . . I here?

PANTALONE. *(Peers at him.)* Yes.

CAPTAIN. Ah, I live. I breathe again.

(Breathes vigorously.)

I am the Captain.

(Struts.)

Look on my hat and shudder. Look at my cape and shiver. Feel my sword—

(Realizes he has no hat, cape, or sword.)

It is gone! Ah, your slave took it. Androcles! It was a trick of his. After him!

PANTALONE. My slave? Ha ha, a trick on you.

CAPTAIN. And another one dressed in my clothes!

PANTALONE. *(Laughing, stops immediately.)* Another one?

CAPTAIN. One who came from your house.

PANTALONE. From my house?

(Runs to house UR, then turns.)

Isabella!

CAPTAIN. Ha ha, a trick on you.

PANTALONE. *(In a rage.)* Fool, stupid, simpleton! You have set Isabella free!

CAPTAIN. I set Isabella free?

PANTALONE. Fathead, saphead, noodlehead! It was she who left the house in disguise—and is off to meet her lover. Stop them! Which way? Which way?

CAPTAIN. He said—

(Thinks, which is difficult.)

to the woods!

PANTALONE. Bonehead, woodenhead, blockhead! Quick! Save her! Before she is wed! To the woods!

(Starts R.)

CAPTAIN. He said—

(Thinks.)

first, take a bag of stones by the wall.

PANTALONE. A bag of stones—the gold! Muttonhead, pumpkin head, cabbage head! To the garden! Before he finds it.

(Starts to L, as Captain starts R.)

Forget Isabella. Save the gold!

(Pantalone exits DL. Captain salutes and marches after him. Lights may dim slightly. There is music as the Wall enters DR

and crosses to C. Wall is an actor (Lion) with a painted "wall" hanging on his back and short enough to show his feet. The back of his head is masked by a large flower peeping over the wall. He stands at C, feet apart, back to audience. He puts down a bag of gold and then puts a rock over it.

Androcles, followed by Isabella, tiptoes in UL. They circle around to DR. Androcles starts feeling for the wall.)

ANDROCLES. The gold is buried—by the wall—

(Flower on the Wall nods vigorously.)

buried under a stone—

(Flower nods again.)

Look—feel—find a stone—a stone—a stone—

(Wall stomps his foot, then puts foot on top of stone, but Androcles passes by it.)

ISABELLA. *(Wall again taps foot and points it toward stone. Isabella sees stone and points to it.)* A stone!

ANDROCLES. Ah, I see it! Pray that this will be it!

(Slowly lifts stone.)

Behold!

(Holds up bag.)

A bag of gold!

(Jumps up, sings, and dances.)

We've found it! We've found it! We've found the gold! Yours to keep! To have! To hold!

ISABELLA. Sh!

ANDROCLES. You are free—go! Off to Lelio, who implores you— adores you. Quick, do not hesitate. Run—before it is too late.

ISABELLA. Thank you. Some day may you be set free, too.

(Kisses her finger and touches his nose with it.)

Goodbye.

(Exits DL.)

ANDROCLES. *(Thrilled that she has touched him.)* Fly—arrivederci.

(Sees he has the gold.)

Wait! The gold! Isabella forgot the gold! Isabella! Isabella!

(He exits after her DL. At the same time, Pantalone, followed by Captain, tiptoes in UL, circling DR, where they stop.)

PANTALONE. *(Peering and groping.)* It is so dark I cannot see.

CAPTAIN. *(Also peering and groping.)* Wait . . . wait for me.

PANTALONE. The gold—by the wall—under a stone—find—find—

CAPTAIN. You look in front. I'll look behind.

PANTALONE. *(He turns R, Captain turns L. Each peers and steps in the opposite direction on each word.)* Search—scratch—dig around it.

CAPTAIN. *(Still peering, they now step backward toward each other on each word.)* Feel—touch—crouch—

(They bump into each other from the back.)

PANTALONE. Ouch!

CAPTAIN. *(Grabs and holds Pantalone's foot.)* I've found it! I've found it!

PANTALONE. Knucklehead of soot! You've found my foot!

(Kicks free and creeps toward C.)

Here . . . there . . . oh, where . . . where is my gold? The stone . . . the stone . . . where has it flown? Quick . . . on your knees . . . search . . . find . . . use your nose . . . and not to sneeze.

(He and Captain, on their knees, comically search frantically.)

Pat . . . pound . . . comb . . . the ground . . . chase . . . race . . . find the place.

(He finds stone.)

I have found it! Ah, to gods in prayer I kneel. The stone is here. My gold is back.

(Reaches between feet of Wall, then freezes in panic.)

What do I feel? There is no sack!

(Rises in a frenzy.)

I have been robbed! Thieves! The gold is gone!

CAPTAIN. *(Rises.)* It was the slave who took it! Androcles!

PANTALONE. He is a robber. He is a thief! He will pay for this—with his life!

CAPTAIN. I will find him . . . bind him . . . bend . . . make an end of him!

PANTALONE. He has run away! To the woods! Catch him! Hold!

(Captain stomps to R.)

To the woods! Before his tracks are cold.

(Captain stomps to L.)

Follow! Follow! My bag of gold!

(Pantalone exits DL. Captain salutes and follows him. Wall picks up stone, then he pulls the street scene curtain to one side, revealing another curtain behind it and painted like a forest. Over his shoulder, back still to audience, Wall announces, "The forest," and exits quickly at R.

Chase music begins. Isabella and Lelio run in from L, look about.)

ISABELLA. The forest paths will guide us.

LELIO. The forest trees will hide us.

(They exit UR around the backdrop.)

ANDROCLES. *(Runs in from L.)* Isabella! Lelio! I cannot find you. You have left the gold behind you.

(Exits off UR around backdrop.)

CAPTAIN. *(Enters DL.)* After them! I say—follow me! This way!

(Exits UR behind backdrop.)

PANTALONE. *(Enters, wheezing, trying to keep up, from L.)* We are near him. I can hear him—and my gold.

(Pantalone exits UR around the backdrop. Isabella and Lelio run in UL from behind the backdrop, start to R, but suddenly stop, frightened at what they see offstage R.)

ISABELLA. Oh, what do I see?

LELIO. It is a—quick! We must flee!

(Isabella and Lelio exit UR behind the backdrop. Captain enters UL around the backdrop, starts to R.)

CAPTAIN. This way! This way! Follow me! Onward to—

(Stops, horrified at what he sees offstage R.)

What is that behind a tree? It is a—Oh, no! We must never meet. The order is—retreat!

(Captain runs off UR behind backdrop. Pantalone enters UL around the backdrop.)

PANTALONE. Find him. Fetch him. Catch him. My gold has run away.

(Stops and looks offstage R.)

What is that? Can that be he?

(Starts to call.)

Andro—No! It is a—Help! It is a *lion*—coming after me!

(There is a loud roar off R. Pantalone sinks to his knees and, quickly walking on his knees, exits L.

Music of Lion's song. Lion enters at R, a most appealing creature. He dances to C and sings.)

LION. Have you roared today,
　　Told the world today how you feel?
　　If you're down at the heel
　　Or need to put over a deal,
　　Happy or sad
　　Tearful or glad
　　Sunny or mad,
　　It's a great way
　　To show the world how you feel!
　　Without saying a single word
　　Your meaning is heard.
　　"Good morning" is dull,
　　But a roar is musical!
　　Happy or sad
　　Tearful or glad
　　It's a great way
　　To show the world how you feel!

(He gives a satisfied low roar, then looks about and speaks.)

The sun is up. It is another day—

(Yawns.)

to sleep. Hear all! The King speaks. No birds are allowed over my cave—chirping and burping. No animals are allowed near my cave—growling and howling. Silence in the woods. The King is going to sleep.

(Actors offstage imitate animal sounds, loud buzzing, barking, etc. Or actors may in simple disguise with masks enter as animals, dance, and make sounds.)

Silence!

(All noise and motion stops.)

The King says, "Silence."

(Noise and motion increases, Lion becomes angry, puffs up and roars like thunder, stalking about in all directions.)

R-r-r-r-r-roar!

(There is absolute silence. If actors are onstage, they run off.)

You see—

(Sings.)

A roar's a great way
To show the world how you feel!

(He roars and exits majestically into cave—a split in the painted backdrop.)

ANDROCLES. *(Enters from around backdrop UR. He runs to C. He looks around anxiously to R and to L, and calls softly.)* Isabella . . . ? Lelio . . . ? They are lost in the woods. *I* am lost in the woods. I have run this way—I have run that way—I have run—

(A terrible thought strikes him.)

I have run—away! I am a runaway slave! No!

(Calls desperately.)

Isabella! Lelio! Where will I go? My master will hunt me. He will track me down. He will take me back. I will be thrown to the wild beasts!

(Sees bag he holds.)

The gold—my master will say I stole it. A runaway slave—and a thief! No, I was only trying to help.

(Calls.)

Isabella! Help *me*, Lelio.

PANTALONE. *(Off L, loudly.)* Oh, beat the bushes. Beat the ground. Find my slave. Find my gold!

ANDROCLES. My master! What shall I do? Where shall I go? Hide—

(Runs behind imaginary tree R.)

Behind a tree—

(Runs to imaginary bush UL.)

Under a bush—he can see.

(Points at cave.)

What is that? Ah, a cave! I will hide—inside the cave and pray he never finds me.

(Quickly he goes into cave, gives a loud "Oh!" and quickly backs out again.)

It is someone's house.

CAPTAIN. *(Off.)* Follow me. I say—this way!

ANDROCLES. *(Knocks at cave in desperation.)* Please! Please, may I come in? I am—

PANTALONE. *(Off)* I think—I hear him!

ANDROCLES. I am—in danger.

(Androcles quickly goes into cave. Pantalone enters UL, followed by Captain. They are in hot pursuit.)

PANTALONE. *(Crosses to R.)* My gold! Find the slave. Bind him! Bring him to me.

CAPTAIN. *(Circles DC.)* I will look in every brook and nook and hollow tree!

PANTALONE. Fetch—catch my gold!

(Exits DR.)

CAPTAIN. Follow me!

(He exits DL. From inside the cave, a long loud roar is heard, and Androcles calls, "Help!" Another and louder roar is heard. Androcles runs out of cave to DL and cries "Help . . . help!" Lion runs out of cave to DR and roars.)

ANDROCLES. It is a lion!

LION. It is a man! He will try to beat me.

ANDROCLES. He will try to eat me.

(They eye each other. Lion springs at Androcles with a roar. Androcles backs away.)

I am sorry I disturbed you.

(Lion roars. Androcles holds up bag.)

I—I will have to hit you if you come closer.

LION. Hit—hit until he kills—that is man.

ANDROCLES. Leap—eat—that is a lion.

(Lion roars and then leaps on him. Androcles struggles and fights, but soon he is held in a lion-hug.)

Help! Help!

(Lion roars. Androcles gets his arm free and bangs Lion on the back with bag of gold. Lion roars with surprise and releases Androcles. Androcles, thinking he is free, starts off, but Lion holds on to his pants. Androcles, at arm's length, runs in one spot. Androcles gets loose, turns, lowers his head, and charges, butting into Lion's stomach. Lion roars. Androcles runs to L and hides behind imaginary tree. Lion, angry, roars and slowly starts to creep up on him. Androcles looks around "tree," one side, then the other, shaking with fearful expectation. Lion springs at him in front of "tree." Androcles leaps and runs back of "tree." Lion turns and runs after him. Androcles tries to escape, running in figure-eights around the two "trees." They stop, each facing opposite directions, and start backing toward each other. Androcles turns, sees Lion, jumps, then cautiously tiptoes toward him and kicks the bent-over approaching Lion. Lion roars and circles. Androcles laughs at his trick. Lion comes up behind him and grabs him, holding Androcles around the waist and lifting him off the ground. Androcles kicks helplessly. Lion throws Androcles on ground. Lion,

above him, roars, raises his paw, and gives a crushing blow.
But Androcles rolls over and the paw hits the ground. Lion im-
mediately roars and waves his paw in pain. Androcles cau-
tiously slides away and is ready to run. He looks back at Lion,
who, with tearful sob-roars, is licking and waving his paw.)

ANDROCLES. He is hurt. I can run away.

(He starts, but stops when Lion sobs.)

He is in pain. Someone should help. No one is here. No one but
one—*I*—am here.

(Lion roars in frustration. Androcles turns away in fear. Lion
sobs sadly. Androcles looks back at him.)

If I go—I maybe can be free! If I stay—

(Lion growls at him.)

he may take a bite out of me!

(Androcles starts to leave. Lion sobs. Throughout the scene the
Lion "talks" in grunts and groans almost like a person in an-
swering and reacting to Androcles. Androcles stops.)

When someone needs your help, you can't run away.

(Trying to be brave, he turns to Lion, opens his mouth, but can
say nothing.)

I wonder what you say—to a lion?

(Lion sobs appealingly.)

Signor—

(Lion looks at him. Androcles is afraid.)

My name is Androcles.

(Lion roars, looks at his paw, and roars louder.)

Have you—have you hurt your paw?

(Lion grunts and nods.)

If you—will sit still—I will try to help you.

(Lion roars defiantly. Androcles backs away.)

Wait! If we succeed, we will need to—cooperate!

(Lion looks at him suspiciously and grunts.)

You don't trust me—

(Lion roars.)

and I don't trust you. But someone must take the first step—greet the other, or we will never meet each other.

(Cautiously Androcles takes a step sideways, facing audience. Lion cautiously takes a step sideways, facing audience.)

That is a beginning—

(Lion roars. Androcles holds his neck.)

But what will be the ending?

(Each raises a leg and takes another sideways step toward the other.)

I don't want to hurt you. I want to help you.

(He slowly holds out his hand. Lion "talks" and slowly shows him his paw.)

It's a thorn. You have a thorn stuck in your paw.

(Lion breaks the tension, crying with the thought of it, and waving his injured paw.)

I know it hurts.

(Talks slowly as if explaining to a small child.)

Once I stepped on a thorn. My father pulled it out.

(Lion grunts and reacts with interest.)

My father—on the farm—by the sea. I will pull it out for you—as my father did—for me.

(Lion grunts, undecided, then slowly offers his paw. Androcles nervously reaches for it.)

It—it may hurt a little.

(Lion draws back and roars in protest.)

I thought a lion was brave—not afraid of anything.

(Lion stops, then grunts in agreement and with great bravery thrusts out his paw.)

Now—hold still—brace yourself.

(Lion begins to tremble violently.)

Get ready—

(Lion shakes more.)

One—

(Lion shakes both of them.)

Two—

(Lion cries and tries to pull away. Androcles is stern, with pointed finger.)

Don't move about!

(Lion tries to obey, meekly.)

Three!

(Lion steps backward.)

It's out!

LION. *(Looks at his paw, looks at Androcles, then roars joyfully and hops about. Sings.)*

Let me roar today
Let me say today
We feel great!
Celebrate!
Exhilarate!
Congratulate!
It's a great way
To show the world how you feel.

ANDROCLES. *(Lion rubs against Androcles and purrs softly. Androcles, being tickled by Lion's rubbing, giggles and pets him.)* You—you are welcome.

LION. *(To audience.)* He looks tired. I will get a rock.

(Quickly picks up a rock off R and holds it high.)

ANDROCLES. He is going to crush me!

(He starts to defend himself, but Lion shakes his head and grunts, and shows Androcles that he should sit.)

For me?

(Lion nods, trying to talk, and dusts the rock with his tail.)

He wants *me* to sit.

(Lion, delighted, grabs Androcles to help him and seats him roughly.)

Thank you.

LION. *(To audience.)* He looks hungry.

(Roars, shows teeth, and chews.)

ANDROCLES. He is going to eat me!

(Lion shakes his head and "talks," points to Androcles and indicates from his mouth down into his stomach.)

He wants *me* to eat.

(Lion agrees joyfully.)

I am hungry. I am always hungry.

LION. *(Thinking.)* What was for breakfast today? A man's skull in the cave—his liver down by the river—

(Embarrassed at what he has thought.)

Oh, I beg your pardon.

(Roars with a new idea, motions Androcles to watch. Lion hums and purrs lightly as he comically pantomimes picking fruit from a tree and eating and spitting out the seeds.)

ANDROCLES. Fruit!

(Lion, encouraged, purrs happily and hops about pantomiming filling a basket with berries from bushes.)

Berries!

(Lion, elated with his success, buzzes loudly and dances in ballet fashion like a bee.)

What?

(Lion buzzes and his dancing is bigger.)

Honey from the bee!

(Lion agrees loudly.)

Oh, that will be a banquet for me.

LION. *(Speaks to audience.)* A new twist in history! Man and beast will feast together. Celebrate! Sit—wait! I'll be back with cherries and berries for you—and a bone or two, before you can roar —*e pluribus unum!*

(Roars happily and exits R.)

ANDROCLES. *(Sits alone on rock, looks around, smiles, and speaks quietly.)* I am sitting down. I am being served. I am being treated like a person. I—have a friend. This is what it is like to be free. To be—maybe—

(Sings.)

Maybe
A doctor with a degree,
A poet, a priest, a sculptor, a scholar,
A senator—emperor with a golden collar!
I want to be free
So I can find—me.

PANTALONE. *(Off.)* Hunt—hunt—search and find my slave. Find my gold!

ANDROCLES. My master has come. My freedom has gone.

PANTALONE. *(Off R.)* Ah, his footprints are on the ground! I have found him!

ANDROCLES. *(Calls quickly.)* Oh, Lion, I must be off before we have fed. I must run—or it is off with my head!

(He starts DL but sees Captain.)

Oh! The Captain! Where will I hide? In the cave!

(Quickly hides in cave.)

CAPTAIN. *(Enters L with fishing net and a slapstick.)* Beware slave, wherever you are. I shall leap and keep and capture you. In this net—I will get you.

(Holds net out ready.)

PANTALONE. *(Enters R, peering at the ground, crosses to L.)* His footprints are on the ground. Toe-heel, heel-toe. This is the way his footsteps go.

CAPTAIN. *(To audience.)* The trap is set.

PANTALONE. Lead on—lead me to him.

CAPTAIN. Ha, caught in the net!

(Throws net over Pantalone, who has walked into it.)

PANTALONE. Help! Help!

CAPTAIN. You stole my hat!

(Hits Pantalone over the head with slapstick.)

PANTALONE. Oh!

CAPTAIN. My sword.

(Hits him again.)

PANTALONE. No!

CAPTAIN. My cape!

(Hits him again.)

PANTALONE. Let me loose!

CAPTAIN. What?

PANTALONE. You squawking goose!

CAPTAIN. Who speaks?

PANTALONE. *(Pulling off the net.)* I—Pantalone.

CAPTAIN. Pantalone? Oh, it was my mistake.

PANTALONE. It was my head!

CAPTAIN. Where is the slave? The runaway? Where is Androcles?

PANTALONE. He is—with my gold.

CAPTAIN. *(Struts.)* I will drag him back to Rome. The Emperor will honor me—decree a holiday—so all can see the slave fight a wild and hungry beast. And after the fun is done and the slave is eaten, all will cheer the Captain of the Year.

PANTALONE. Before you count your cheers, you have to catch one slave—Androcles!

CAPTAIN. *(They start searching, a step on each word. Captain circles to L and upstage. Pantalone circles to R and upstage.)* Search.

PANTALONE. Seek.

CAPTAIN. Track.

PANTALONE. Trail.

CAPTAIN. Use your eyes.

PANTALONE. Scrutinize!

CAPTAIN. *(Stops.)* Think—if you were a slave . . . ?

PANTALONE. I?

CAPTAIN. Where would you hide?

PANTALONE. Inside.

CAPTAIN. *(Sees and points.)* A cave!

(They tiptoe to entrance, hold net ready, whisper excitedly.)

Clap him.

PANTALONE. Trap him.

CAPTAIN. *(Nothing happens.)* The problem is—how to get him to come out.

PANTALONE. Poke him?

CAPTAIN. Smoke him?

PANTALONE. I have a great idea! You will call to him in a voice like Isabella.

CAPTAIN. I—I speak like Isabella?

PANTALONE. You will cry for help in a soft sweet voice. He will think you are her. He will come to Isabella.

CAPTAIN. *(In a high voice, comically.)* Help! Oh, help me. I am Isabella.

(They look at cave entrance.)

I heard—

PANTALONE. Something stirred.

CAPTAIN. *(Falsetto again.)* Andro-o-cles. Come out, ple-e-ese.

(They look at cave and excitedly hold net ready.)

Ready.

PANTALONE. Steady.

(Androcles, behind backdrop, roars—long and loud!)

It is a lion in the cave!

(Runs DR and hides behind a "tree.")

CAPTAIN. *(Androcles roars again, up and down the scale, louder and louder. Even the backdrop shakes. Captain jumps and runs to Pantalone and hides behind him.)* It is *two* lions in the cave!

(They stand shaking with fright.)

ANDROCLES. *(Peeks out of cave, then comes out.)* They have gone. Ran away from a noise. I have learned that a roar is a mighty thing. No wonder a lion is a king.

(He enjoys another roar.)

PANTALONE. *(Still hiding.)* We are undone!

CAPTAIN. Run! Crawl!

PANTALONE. I cannot move at all.

(Androcles roars again with joy.)

I have an idea. You—you will call in a voice like a lion. He will think you are another lion—a brother.

CAPTAIN. I—roar like a lion?

PANTALONE. Our only chance is to answer back.

(Captain gulps, and then roars.)

ANDROCLES. *(He is startled. He hides behind "tree" at L.)* It is another lion.

(Pantalone, helping, gives a roar.)

It is two lions!

(With an idea, he roars back.)

Ro-o-o-hello.

CAPTAIN. *(He and Pantalone look at each other in surprise. Captain answers.)* Ro-o-o-hello.

ANDROCLES. *(Now Androcles looks surprised.)* Ro-o-o-lovely-da-a-ay.

CAPTAIN. *(He and Pantalone look at each other and nod, pleased with their success.)* Ro-o-o-have-you-seen—ro-o-o-ar-a-runa-way slave?

(Androcles is startled, then he peeks around "tree.")

PANTALONE. Named-Andro—

(Captain nudges him to roar.)

—roar—cles?

ANDROCLES. It is my master and the Captain. They have come for me.

(He roars loudly.)

Ro-o-oar-he-went—roar-r-r-r-that-away.

CAPTAIN. *(They nod.)* Ro-o-o-thank-you.

(He and Pantalone start to tiptoe off R.)

ANDROCLES. *(Too confident.)* Ro—o-ar. You are welcome.

PANTALONE. It is his voice. It is my slave, Androcles.

CAPTAIN. It is another trick of his.

PANTALONE. Nab him.

CAPTAIN. Grab him.

(They start back to get him.)

ANDROCLES. *(Unaware he has been discovered, continues to roar gaily.)* Ro-o-oar. Goodbye. Ro-o-o-ar. Happy eating.

PANTALONE. *(Confronts Androcles on R.)* Eat, cheat, thief! I will beat you!

(Androcles turns to L and walks into net held by Captain.)

CAPTAIN. Slide, glide, inside. I have you tied!

(Androcles is caught in the net over his head.)

PANTALONE. *(Grabs his bag of gold.)* My gold!

CAPTAIN. My captive!

ANDROCLES. Help! Help!

CAPTAIN. You stole my hat!

(Hits Androcles over the head with slapstick.)

You stole my sword!

(Hits him.)

You stole my cape!

(Hits him.)

This time you will not escape.

PANTALONE. *(Takes stick from Captain and swings it.)* Robber. Traitor. Thief! Let me hit him.

(Pantalone, in the mix-up, hits Captain several times on his head.)

CAPTAIN. Help!

(He drops the rope of the net.)

ANDROCLES. *(Runs to R.)* Help!

PANTALONE. Help! He is running away!

CAPTAIN. *(Quickly catches Androcles and holds the rope.)* Back to Rome. To the Emperor you will be delivered!

PANTALONE. Into the pit you will be thrown.

CAPTAIN. Where the wild beasts will claw, gnaw, and chew you!

(They start to lead him off, marching—Captain, Androcles, and last Pantalone.)

Munch!

PANTALONE. Crunch!

ANDROCLES. I will be eaten for lunch! Help! Lion! Signor Lion, set me free. Come and rescue me! Oh, woods, echo my cry for help. Echo so the Lion will know I am in trouble. Roar—roar with me. Echo from tree to tree!

(He roars, and the Ushers—and the children—help him roar, as he is led off L.)

Roar! Roar!

LION. *(He leaps in at R and roars.)* Someone roars for help? Androcles!

(Off, Androcles cries "Help!")

He calls for help.

(Sings.)

Oh, roar and say
Shout out without delay,
Which way, which way, which way?
Oh, roar me a clue,
Roar me two.
I have to know
Which way to go before I start.
Oh, roar, please,
An-dro-cles.
Give a sigh,
Give a cry,
Signify!
I'll sniff—I'll whiff—
Smell *(Sniffs.)*—Tell *(Sniffs.)*
Fe, fi, fo, fum.
Here—

(Shouts.)

I come!

(He exits L.)

ISABELLA. *(She and Lelio run in from R.)* Oh, Androcles, what has happened to you?

LELIO. *(To audience.)* That you will see in Act Two. Now—we must bow and say, "Our play is half done." This is the end of Act One.

(They bow.

The curtains close.)

A Short Intermission

(Or, if played without an intermission, omit the last speech of Lelio's and continue with his first speech in Act Two.)

ACT TWO

(Music: Reprise of "Oh, Roar and Say." The curtains open. The scene is the same. Isabella and Lelio stand in C. Music dims out.)

ISABELLA. Androcles. What has happened to you?

LELIO. I heard his voice, calling in the woods.

ISABELLA. He has followed us to bring the gold—my dowry, which I left behind.

(Calls.)

Androcles?

LELIO. Androcles!

(Lion roars as he enters UR. He sees the lovers and watches.)

ISABELLA. It is a lion!

LELIO. Do not fear.

ISABELLA. Androcles is alone—unarmed. What if he should meet a lion? Androcles! Androcles!

LELIO. Androcles!

LION. Someone else roars "Androcles." I will stay and hear who is here.

(Lion hides his head behind the small rock.)

ISABELLA. Androcles! Androcles!

LELIO. We are alone.

(Lion's head pops up behind rock.)

Together. It is time to speak—to sing of love!

(He turns aside, takes scroll from belt.)

ISABELLA. *(Not looking at him.)* Please, speak no prepared speech, but sing true words that spring freely from your heart.

LELIO. *(Looks surprised, glances again at scroll, then sings.)*

Oh, lovely, lovely flower,
Growing lovelier every hour,
Shower on me petals of love, Isabella—

(Lion, enjoying the music, nods his head in rhythm.)

ISABELLA. So unrehearsed—so sincere.

LELIO. *(Sings.)*

My life, my heart revolve about you.

Say yes, I cannot live without you.

(Lion, unable to refrain, lifts his head and roars musically on Lelio's last note—unnoticed by the lovers—then hides his head behind the rock.)

ISABELLA. Oh, Lelio—

(Turns to him and speaks or sings.)

My answer is—can't you guess?
Yes, yes, yes, yes, yes!

LELIO. *(In ecstacy.)* Oh, woods abound with joyous sound! Melodies sing in the trees—

(Music sound. Lion rises up and listens to R.)

Bells ring in the breeze—

(Music sound. Lion stands up and listens to L.)

Let the lute of the lily lying in the pond—

(Music sound. Lion stands and begins to move his arms like an orchestra conductor.)

Let the flute of the firefly's fluttering wand—

(Music sound. Lion motions to R.)

And let the flight of the nightingale—

(Music sound. Lion motions L.)

Harmonize!

(Music sounds blend together. Lion holds up paw, ready to begin directing an orchestra.)

The moment we will immortalize!

(Music of all sounds plays a folk dance. Lion leads, dramatically, the unseen musicians. Isabella and Lelio do a short dance. At the conclusion, they hold their pose, and Lion bows to audience.)

ISABELLA. *(Points to ground.)* Look! Footprints—boots and sandals.

LELIO. *(Examines them.)* The Captain's boots—Pantalone's sandals. The Captain and Pantalone were here—following us—following Androcles.

ISABELLA. His cry was for help. He ran away. He is—a runaway slave! And they have found him—

LELIO. Bound him—

ISABELLA. Taken him back to Rome.

LELIO. To the pit!

ISABELLA. We must stop them.

LELIO. If we can.

ISABELLA. We must help him.

LELIO. All we can.

LION. *(Jumps on rock heroically.)* And—we can!

(Roars.)

ISABELLA. Help!

LELIO. Run!

(Lovers run off DR.)

LION. Lead the way. I will follow you. To Androcles! To—the rescue!

(Lion roars, picks up rock, and runs off DR. Chase music begins —repeated. But the running is reversed, going around in the opposite direction. Lovers enter from UR and run across. At C, they look back, "Oh!" and exit UL behind backdrop. Lion runs in UR. At C, roars, and exits UL behind backdrop. Lovers enter UR from behind backdrop, running faster. At C, they look back in great fright, "OH!" and exit UL behind backdrop. Lion follows. At C, roars majestically, and shouts: "Andr-roar-cles! Here we come!" Lion exits after lovers. Lovers enter UR from around backdrop. Lelio pulls the curtain of the woods scene back to L, showing the street scene again. Chase music dims out.)

LELIO. *(Breathless.)* Safe at home—I hope. What does the scroll say?

ISABELLA. *(Reads scroll on proscenium arch.)* The next scene is—a street in Rome.

LELIO. Ah, we can stay.

ISABELLA. *(Reads, announcing.)* "The Captain enters."

(Clashing of slapstick is heard off L; Isabella runs to C.)

He will find us here.

LELIO. Do not fear. We will hide—behind a mask. Quick! We will hide behind another face, and reappear in the Market Place.

(They exit R.)

CAPTAIN. *(Enters at L.)* Make way, make way for the hero of the day! Bow, salute, kneel, and gaze upon the hero. Raise your voice with praise for the hero. The hero passes by. The hero is—I!

(Lelio and Isabella enter R. Each holds a long, sad beggarman's mask on a stick in front of his or her face. They walk and act and speak like beggars.)

LELIO. Help the poor. Help the blind.

ISABELLA. Alms for the cripple. Alms for the old.

CAPTAIN. Away, beggars! The Emperor comes this way. It is a holiday!

LELIO. What senator has died? What battle have we won?

CAPTAIN. None! We celebrate today the capture of a runaway.

ISABELLA. A slave?

(They look at each other and speak without their masks; and at the same time, the Captain speaks. They all say together, "Androcles!")

CAPTAIN. Today all Rome will celebrate! A wild beast was caught outside the wall, clawing the gate as if he could not wait to come into the city. Now in the pit the beast is locked and barred, waiting to be released—waiting to eat a juicy feast.

LELIO AND ISABELLA. *(They nod to each other and say:)* Androcles!

CAPTAIN. Ah, what a sporting sight to see—a fight—man eaten by a beast. Then I, who caught the slave, will appear. Women will swoon, men will cheer, and I will be crowned the hero of the year!

(Shouts rapidly and marches quickly.)

Hep, hep, ho! Step, step, high. Hail the hero. I, I, I!

(Exits R.)

ISABELLA. *(They take their masks away.)* Poor, poor Androcles.

LELIO. We must try and save him. Quick, before it is too late. We will go to the Arena—

ISABELLA. Yes!

LELIO. We will go to the Royal Box! Implore the Emperor with our plea!

ISABELLA. Yes!

LELIO. For only he by royal decree can save—our Androcles.

(Lelio and Isabella run off L. There is music. Captain, leading Androcles by the rope, and Pantalone, following, march in from R. As they march, they sing.)

PANTALONE AND CAPTAIN. Off to the pit we three. Who will be left?

ANDROCLES. Just me.

PANTALONE AND CAPTAIN. Who will be left alone, shaking in every bone?

PANTALONE. Just—

CAPTAIN. Just—

ANDROCLES. Me!

CAPTAIN AND PANTALONE. Off to the pit we three. Who will be left?

ANDROCLES. Just me.

CAPTAIN AND PANTALONE. Who will the animal meet? Who will the animal eat?

PANTALONE. Just—

CAPTAIN. Just—

ANDROCLES. *(Shouts.)* Just a minute. I want to be an absentee!

(Music ends as he speaks.)

I want to be free—to be—just me!

CAPTAIN. To the Arena! Forward march!

(Music: Reprise of Introductory Music of Act One. Captain, Androcles, and Pantalone march across the front of the stage or across down in the orchestra pit. At the same time, Lelio and Isabella, disguised with masks, dance in UL carrying colorful banners, one in each hand, and on stands. They set the banners

*down in a semicircle in front of the backdrop to indicate the
Arena. They dance off as music stops, and the three marchers
arrive in the middle of the scene.)*

CAPTAIN. Halt! We are at the Arena! The slave will step forward.

PANTALONE. Step forward.

ANDROCLES. Step forward.

(Frightened, he steps forward.)

CAPTAIN. The slave's head will be covered.

*(He holds out left hand to Androcles, who holds out left hand
to Pantalone.)*

PANTALONE. Covered.

*(He gives a cloth sack to Androcles, who gives it to Captain,
who puts it over Androcles' head.)*

CAPTAIN. *(Trumpets sound.)* The Emperor's chariot draws near.

(Trumpets.)

The Emperor will soon appear.

(Trumpets.)

The Emperor is here!

*(A royal banner is extended from the side DL, indicating the
Royal Box.)*

Bow!

PANTALONE. Now!

*(Captain and Pantalone bow low toward Royal Box, facing
DL. Androcles, groping with his head covered, turns and bows
facing R.)*

Turn around!

(Androcles turns around.)

To the ground!

(Androcles bows to ground.)

CAPTAIN. Most noble Emperor—

(Pushes Androcles' head down, making him bow.)

Most honored Emperor—

(Pushes Androcles, who keeps bobbing up, down again.)

Most imperial Emperor—

(Pushes Androcles down again. He stays down.)

The guilty slave stands before you. Stand!

(Androcles quickly straightens up.)

As punishment for a slave who runs away, he will today fight a wild beast in the Arena for all Rome to see.

(Androcles shakes his head under the sack.)

He will battle for his life—to survive. There will be but one winner—the one who is left alive.

(Androcles, courageously, draws his fists and is ready to strike. Captain, growing more eloquent, begins to strut.)

I have fought and slain a hundred wild beasts.

(Androcles, visualizing the animals, starts hitting the air.)

With fiery eyes, with gnashing teeth, they charged at me. Fight! The crowd cried, fight!

(Androcles, ready, starts to fight, hitting wildly for his life, hitting the Captain, who is near and whom he cannot see.)

Help! Stop! I am not the wild beast.

(At a safe distance, he regains his bravery.)

I—I am the Captain, the boldest, bravest fighter in Rome—in all Italy! Go—stand at the side. Appear when you hear the trumpets blow.

(Captain points to L. Androcles starts to R.)

No. The other way!

ANDROCLES. *(He turns and starts to L. Loud trumpets blow. He stops, faces R, ready to fight.)* The trumpets! Now?

PANTALONE. No!

(Androcles, groping, exits UL. Pantalone bows to Royal Box.)

Most Imperial Emperor, I am Pantalone, master of the slave.

From me he ran away. From me he stole. I am told you plan to reward me for this holiday with a bag of gold.

CAPTAIN. I tracked and captured him. I am sure you will confer a title of bravery on me.

(Trumpets blow.)

ANDROCLES. *(Enters UL, ready to fight.)* The trumpets! Now?

CAPTAIN. No!

(Androcles turns and exits.)

Ah, the Emperor waves. It is the signal. Open the gates. Let the wild beast in!

PANTALONE. Let the entertainment begin!

(Captain and Pantalone quickly go DR, where they stand. Drum rolls are heard. Then loud roars are heard off UR. Lion, roaring, angrily stalks in from UR.)

LION. Barred—locked—caged! I am—outraged!

(Roars and paces menacingly.)

PANTALONE. What a big lion! I am glad he is below.

CAPTAIN. I could conquer him with one blow.

LION. Captured! Held in captivity! Robbed of my liberty! Only man would think of it. Only man would sink to it. Man—man—little—two-legged—tailless thing. Beware man, I am a King!

(Roars.)

The first man I meet I—will eat!

(Trumpets blow.)

ANDROCLES. *(Enters, head still covered.)* The trumpets! Now?

LION. *(Sees him.)* Ah, a man! A chew or two and a bone to pick.

(Roars.)

ANDROCLES. *(Frightened and groping.)* Oh! I am not alone. I must get out quick.

(Drum starts beating in rhythm to the fight. Androcles starts walking, then running, the Lion after him. The chase is a dance-mime, fast, comic, with surprises and suspense. It ends

with Lion holding Androcles in his clutches.)

LION. Caught! Held!

(Shakes Androcles like a rag doll.)

Flip—flop. I will start eating at the top!

(Takes off Androcles' headcovering.)

ANDROCLES. No hope ever to be free. This is the end of me!

(Lion looks at Androcles, is surprised, and roars questioningly. Androcles, frightened, freezes, then slowly feels his neck, his face and nose. He looks at Lion and he is surprised. Lion tries to "talk.")

You?

(Lion nods and roars, pantomimes pulling out a thorn from his paw, and points to Androcles, who nods.)

Me.

(Lion "talks" and points to himself.)

You!

(Lion nods and roars happily.)

Signor Lion!

(Lion "talks" and roars, and they embrace each other joyfully.)

PANTALONE. Let the fight begin! Beat him!

(Lion stops and looks at Pantalone.)

CAPTAIN. The Emperor waits to see who wins. Eat him!

ANDROCLES. He is my master—who bought me. He is the Captain—who caught me.

LION. Slave-makers! Taker of men! I will beat you! I will eat you!

(Roars and starts to C.)

PANTALONE. Help! The lion is looking at me. Draw your sword!

(Hides behind the Captain.)

CAPTAIN. *(Shaking.)* I am afraid his blood will rust the blade.

PANTALONE. Show you can do what you say—slay him with one blow!

CAPTAIN. I suddenly remember—I have to go!

(Starts off R. At the same time, Lion leaps with a roar and attacks the two.)

PANTALONE. Help! Guards! Save, attend me!

CAPTAIN. Help! Someone defend me!

(There is an exciting and comic scramble, with Lion finally grabbing each by the collar and hitting their heads together. Then he holds each out at arm's length.)

LION. Listen and learn a lesson: only a coward steals and holds a man.

(Roars. Shakes Pantalone.)

Only a thief buys and sells a man. And no one—can—own another man!

(Roars.)

The world was made for all—equally. Nod your heads if you agree.

(Lion shakes them and makes their heads nod violently. Then he releases them, and the two drop to the ground.)

The vote is "Yes"—unanimously!

(Trumpets sound. Offstage voices shout, from R and L and from the back of the auditorium: "Kill the lion. The lion is loose. Club him. Stone him. Kill the lion. Kill! Kill!" etc. Captain and Pantalone crawl to R. Hands appear off R and L shaking clubs and spears. This is a tense moment. The Arena has turned against the Lion. Lion is frightened. He crouches by Androcles, who stands heroically by him.)

ANDROCLES. Stop! Stop! Hold your spears and stones and clubs. Do not kill the lion. You see—he is not an enemy. He remembers me and a kindness which I did for him. Today that kindness he has returned. He did not eat my head, which would have been the end. Instead—he is—my friend.

(He offers his hand to Lion. Lion takes it. Music begins, and the two start to waltz together. Pantalone and Captain crouch and watch in amazement. Hands and weapons disappear from the sides at R and L. Androcles and Lion's waltz becomes big-

ger, funnier, and happier. Trumpets sound. Music and dancing stop. Lelio enters DL by royal banner.)

LELIO. The Emperor has spoken. His words will be heard.

(All bow low toward the Box as Lelio holds up a royal scroll.)

The Emperor is amazed, astounded, and astonished—with delight—at this sudden sight. A fight unlike any in history. Indeed it is a mystery. Two enemies—man and lion—dancing hand in hand! To honor this unique occasion, the Emperor has issued this command: today shall be, not one of fighting, but of dance and revelry!

(Trumpets play and people cheer.)

The Emperor gives to the master of the slave—

PANTALONE. That is I, Pantalone. How much gold does he give?

LELIO. The Emperor gives this order; *you* will give twenty pieces of gold to Androcles.

ANDROCLES. To me!

LELIO. A sum he has well earned.

PANTALONE. Give twenty pieces of gold! Oh, I shall die a poor man. No. No!

(Lion starts toward him and growls loudly.)

Yes—yes, I will pay.

(Quickly takes bag from pocket and begins counting.)

One—two—three—

LELIO. Furthermore: the Emperor decrees to the Captain who caught the slave—

CAPTAIN. Ah, what honor does the Emperor give to me?

LELIO. You will command a Roman Legion in a distant land. You will sail to the Isle of Britain, where even the boldest man must fight to keep alive, where it is so dangerous only the bravest survive.

CAPTAIN. *(Shaking violently.)* Danger? Fight? Me?

LELIO. Because of your boasted bravery.

CAPTAIN. I would prefer to stay, please. A cold climate makes me sneeze.

(Lion starts and roars loudly.)

I will go.

(Lion follows him roaring.)

I am going! I am gone!

LELIO. And to me—the Emperor has given me the lovely, lovely Isabella—

(Isabella enters DL.)

and has blessed our marriage which soon will be.

ISABELLA. For me, the Emperor decreed, Pantalone shall pay without delay my dowry which he holds for me.

PANTALONE. Pay more gold! Oh, no—no!

(Lion roars at him loudly.)

Yes—yes. I will pay. It is here, my dear.

LELIO. And finally:

(Trumpets blow.)

The Emperor has ruled that both lion and slave today have won a victory unequaled in history. So—both lion and slave are hereby—set free!

ANDROCLES. Free? I am free.

LION. The way the world should be!

ANDROCLES. Free—to find my family—to work the best I can—to raise my head—to be a man. To find out—who I am!

(Music. They all sing.)

Let us roar today,
Let us say today
We feel great.
Celebrate!
Exhilarate!
Congratulate!

PANTALONE AND CAPTAIN. *(Dejected.)* We don't feel great.

ALL. It's a great way
   To show the world how you feel.
   When in need—find a friend.
   Laws will read—have a friend.
   We feel great.
   Don't eat, but meet.
   Why wait, make a friend.
   Extend!
   Do your part, make a start.
   Roar today. Show the world today.
   It's a great way
   To show the world how you feel.

(All the actors bow; then Androcles comes forward.)

ANDROCLES. Our story is told. The lovers are joined in happiness. The bragger and the miser are undone. And a friend was won by kindness. Our masks and bells and curtains we put away for another day. And we go our way—a group of strolling players. We say—

LION. *(Points at audience.)* Be sure you roar today!

ALL. Arrivederci!

(They all bow low and the music swells.

The curtains close.)

Rags to Riches

Rags to Riches is a melodrama based on the combination of events and characters from two "dime novels" by Horatio Alger, *Ragged Dick* and *Mark the Match Boy*. The dramatic form of the play, which takes place in New York City during the 1880's, is that of the well-made melodrama with a coincidental plot in which the upright hero triumphs over the evil villain and saves the innocent victim. There are frequent asides, familiar songs of the period, and musical accompaniment to certain speeches. The two acts of the play consist of many short scenes which are alternately located among a city street, the drawing room of a Fifth Avenue mansion, and a room in a tenement.

The boldly presented theme of the play is "If one is honest, industrious, kind-hearted, and slightly lucky, one will surely go from 'rags to riches.'" The theme and the melodramatic form of the play authentically reflect the time and place of the setting: an optimistic, late-nineteenth-century America where it seemed that fortunes could be made by even the poorest boy. The message is stated directly by several of the upright characters, who most firmly believe in its veracity, and all except the villains repeat the theme in song at the conclusion of each act.

From the theme springs the underlying dramatic question which propels the plot: will Ragged Dick rise from poverty to wealth? Even the earliest minor events indicate his ascent has surely begun. As Dick rises in status from a poor shoeshine boy of the streets to a position in a bank, coincidences multiply; the characters repeatedly appear at exactly the right time and place to advance the plot. In the first half of the play alone, there are seven important coincidental meetings, from the banker who happens to meet Dick and asks to have his shoes shined to Dick's first hostile encounter with the villainous Mother Watson.

The carefully constructed plot combines two divergent groups of society, the rich and the poor, necessarily woven together by the hero Dick's appearance and acceptance in both. Scenes of suspense, vigorous physical action, pathos, and bright gaiety vary the pace of the script and maintain audience interest as the story unfolds.

As the plot is Dick's story, his characterization is the most fully drawn of all. The other characters' depth of development is determined by their various relationships to Dick. All of the characters are taken from traditional melodramatic plots and revealed through action, dialogue, and song.

Ragged Dick is the epitome of all the virtues endorsed by the play: honesty, industry, confidence, cleanliness, kindness, and courage. He is saved from being unbearably self-righteous, however, because throughout his rise to "respectability" he remains a boy of the streets who enjoys his life there enormously. He speaks with grammar which the audience recognizes as less than perfect, and his lack of proper manners provides an opportunity for comic scenes at the Greyson's mansion, particularly in his contact with the butler.

Second in importance to Dick are the characters of the victim and the villain. Both are sufficiently drawn to fulfill their essential parts in the play. Mark, the victim, serves as Dick's virtuous counterpart, whose lack of strength makes Dick's ingenuity all the more admirable. The villain, Mother Watson, is the embodiment of human evil, whom Dick must inevitably overpower.

In contrast to Dick, the aggressive, confident hero, Mark is the pathetic victim who is crushed and helpless in the face of the forces acting upon him, whether it is the tyranny of Mother Watson, the threats of Mickey Maguire, poverty, ill health, or the fact that he is alone in the world. Mark's inability to shift for himself on the streets, his reluctance to beg because his dying mother has insisted he must never do so, and his faultless grammar imply a sheltered childhood and foreshadow the final revelation that he is Greyson's lost nephew and the rightful inheritor of his family's fortune.

Mother Watson, a contemptible, drunken hag, is the traditional villain who schemes for wealth, ruthlessly wielding her power over the weak. Her villainy is mitigated for the young audience, however, because she is also portrayed as vulnerable. Not only is she always a bit tipsy and, therefore, comic, but she is made to appear foolish in her confrontations with Dick.

Other characters enrich the picture of the era as they also serve the needs of plot. There are, for example, a tough and slow-witted bully, who, lacking Dick's scruples, has allied himself with Mother Watson; a kindly Irish apple seller and mother figure; a policeman on his beat; a wealthy banker and his daughter, who become Dick's benefactors; and a pompous, supercilious butler. Each is an individual, consistently characterized.

In brief lines, the dialogue reveals not only characterization but exposition as well. The necessary background information is at times quickly presented in an exchange of direct, succinct questions and answers between two characters, as in Dick's first scene with Ida Greyson. Exposition is even presented within scenes of physical and verbal conflict between Dick and Mother Watson.

The structure of very short, rapid lines may also build suspense, as preceding and during the rescue scene, which occurs offstage and is described by the excited onlookers. The longest exceptions to the structure, Greyson's narration of the missing orphan's story and Dick's spontaneously worded prayer for Mark's recovery, are accompanied by plaintive music that further sets off the passages in contrast to the quick dialogue. The other speeches longer than three lines are either said in moments of intense conflict or are interrupted by necessary action.

A distinguishing feature of the dialogue, derivative of the nineteenth-century melodrama, is the use of asides in which every character repeatedly comments on developments in plot or exposition within the confines of his or her characterization and outlook. Usually the observations made in the aside are so integrally a part of the exchange that the flow of the dialogue is preserved. The asides verbalize the silent thoughts of the characters, but occasionally others in the scene react directly to these "silent" lines. When consistency in the use of the asides would slow the movement of the plot, the characters simply hear each other's asides and the dialogue moves on from there. In still another form of the aside, the speaker expects another character as well as the audience to have heard the line.

Song, an inherent element of melodrama, is used to accomplish five purposes in *Rags to Riches*: to establish locale, to enhance mood, to state theme, to delineate character, and to motivate plot. The tunes used are often familiar to the audience, sometimes authentic in period, and always appropriate for the scenes in which they appear. Also present is the traditional background music of melodrama, which accompanies sentimental speeches or identifies initial entrances or exits of the hero and villain.

The setting for the street, the mansion, and the tenement room are created by the lines and actions of the characters. The street is set in the lines of Mickey as he sells newspapers, Mark as he sells matches, and Dick as he offers his shoeshining services. Roswell, who places the necessary furniture in place as he sings "This Is Where the Rich Rich Live," sets the banker's drawing room. To establish the tenement room, Dick sets up a cot with ragged covers, on which the policeman then lays the unconscious Mark, and the place is truly no more than Dick has described earlier: "a rented room with a real bed in it." Even the spectacular burning tenement that is the background for the important final action is created by the words of the townspeople's song which narrates the dramatic rescue.

Rags to Riches progresses quickly and persistently to the final resolution of the intertwined plot within a carefully crafted and balanced framework of suspense, pathos, comedy, and excitement.

Rags to Riches

A Musical Melodrama

by Aurand Harris

Suggested by two stories, *Ragged Dick* and *Mark the Match Boy*,
by Horatio Alger, Jr.

Lyrics by Aurand Harris and Eva Franklin
Music, research, and continuity by Eva Franklin
Additional music arrangements and manuscript by Glenn Mack

The première production of *Rags to Riches* was presented in
August, 1966, by the Harwich Junior Theatre, West Harwich,
Massachusetts.

SCENE

The action takes place in the City of New York in the late eighteen-hundreds—on a street, in a Fifth Avenue mansion, and in a tenement room.

An intermission is optional.

Rags to Riches

ACT ONE

(Music, Cue 1, "Sidewalks of New York." Scene, a painted street scene of New York City in the late eighteen-hundreds. Unseen, Dick, a young boy of the street, is asleep in a barrel, which is spotlighted DR. Policeman enters R, glances at barrel as he passes, stops, does a double take, steps back to barrel, and raps on it with his stick.)

POLICEMAN. Wake up there, youngster. Wake up!

(Dick's head appears above the barrel.)

You can't sleep in an alley all day.

DICK. *(Yawning.)* Huh?

POLICEMAN. Wake up!

DICK. I'm awake.

(Stretches, eyes closed, then disappears into barrel.)

POLICEMAN. You'd better be.

(Sees Dick disappearing into barrel.)

And you'd better be on your way!

DICK. *(Rising.)* Who . . . who are you?

POLICEMAN. A policeman!

DICK. *(Opens his eyes and is looking straight at the law.)* Oh! Yes, sir. Yes, sir! I'm getting right up.

(Steps out of barrel.)

What time is it?

POLICEMAN. Seven o'clock.

DICK. Seven o'clock! I've missed my early shines.

(With funny business, he quickly fixes his ragged clothes.)

Excuse me, while I fix my attire. My butler forgot to brush me vest. You could do with a shine yourself, sir. No charge for an officer of the law.

(Gives Policeman's shoes a quick wipe with a cloth.)

POLICEMAN. Thank you.

(Aside.)

I believe there must be some good in him . . . under those rags.

(To Dick.)

Have you got money to buy your breakfast?

DICK. No, sir. But I'll soon earn some.

(Aside.)

If you've got some get-up-and-go, you can always get your breakfast.

(Lights come up on full stage. Music, Cue 2, "Sidewalks of New York." People on the street walk across. Dick exits L, soliciting shoeshines. Policeman removes barrel at R and exits. On Mickey's cue, people stop, holding walking postures as if a picture.)

MICKEY. *(Ragged newsboy, tough and a bully.)*

Paper . . . morning paper . . .
Boss Tweed speaks.
Latest news! Read the news!
Building Brooklyn Bridge.
Horace Greeley states his views.
Paper . . . Paper . . .

(Music, Cue 3, resumes and people start walking. They stop again on Mark's cue, in suspended action, making a picture.)

MARK. *(Ragged match boy, small and frail.)*

Matches . . . matches . . .
Light your fires.
Try . . . try a box?
Light your lamps.
Buy . . . buy a box?
Matches . . . matches . . .

(No one buys. Music, Cue 4, resumes and people continue

walking. Again, on Dick's cue, they stop and hold their positions.)

DICK. Shine your boots, sir.
Nobody better, nobody faster.
Once shined the boots of Mr. Astor.
No waiting in line.
Start the day off . . . with a shine!

(Mr. Greyson, a kindly, rich banker, puts his foot on Dick's shine box. Music, Cue 5, builds to a climax and people exit, as Dick finishes the shine.)

GREYSON. How much for the shine?

DICK. Ten cents.

GREYSON. Isn't that a little steep?

DICK. Well, you know 'tain't all clear profit. There's the blacking and brushes.

GREYSON. *(Laughs.)* And you have a large rent to pay.

(Takes out money.)

I see I have nothing less than a two-dollar bill. Have you any change?

DICK. Not a cent. But I'll get it changed for you.

(Calls.)

Hey, Mickey. Mickey Maguire.

(Mickey enters L.)

GREYSON. All right. And I will pay you five cents for your trouble.

(Starts off R.)

Meanwhile I will try to hail a carriage.

(Exits R.)

DICK. Can you change a two-dollar bill?

MICKEY. Two dollars? Where'd you steal it?

(Takes bill.)

DICK. Stealing ain't my style.

MICKEY. It's a counterfeit one.

DICK. I didn't know it.

MICKEY. You'd better beat it, or I'll tell a policeman.

DICK. Give it back to me.

MICKEY. So you can go and cheat somebody else?

(Plainly puts bill in left pocket.)

DICK. Give it back. I say, give it back!

MICKEY. Big thieves have big mouths!

(Pushes him.)

DICK. I'm not a thief. You are! Give it back!

(They start a fist fight, ad libbing. Policeman enters and separates them.)

POLICEMAN. All right! Break it up. Break it up!

(Holds each by collar on either side of him.)

What's the row?

DICK. I asked him to change a two-dollar bill and he kept it.

MICKEY. It was a counterfeit one.

POLICEMAN. Let me see the bill.

MICKEY. The bill?

(Touches his left pocket, then smiles and takes out a bill from his right pocket and gives it to Policeman.)

Here.

POLICEMAN. It *is* a counterfeit one.

GREYSON. *(Enters quickly from R.)* Have you got the . . . What is all this?

POLICEMAN. Did you give the lad a two-dollar bill?

GREYSON. Did he try to run off with it?

DICK. No, sir. I gave it to him.

MICKEY. It was a counterfeit one!

POLICEMAN. Do you remember what bank yours was on?

GREYSON. The Merchant's Bank of Boston.

MICKEY. Then he kept it . . . and gave me the bad one!

GREYSON. Or . . . you could have pocketed my bill and substituted the counterfeit one.

DICK. That's right! He put it in his *other* pocket.

MICKEY. That's a lie!

DICK. Search him!

MICKEY. I haven't got it!

POLICEMAN. Let's have a look in your other pocket.

MICKEY. I ain't got it! He's lying!

POLICEMAN. Put your hands up!

(*Pulls bill from Mickey's pocket.*)

"Merchant's Bank of Boston."

GREYSON. That is mine.

MICKEY. (*Threatens Dick.*) I'll get you!

POLICEMAN. Move along.

MICKEY. I'll get even with you . . . wait and see! I'll pay you off!

(*Shows his fists then runs off L. Policeman follows him.*)

DICK. (*Calls after him, fists raised.*) It'll be a pleasure to meet you any time, Mickey Maguire!

(*Aside.*)

Stealing ain't my style.

GREYSON. (*Interested in the plucky lad.*) What is your name, lad?

DICK. The name is Dick, sir. Well known as Ragged Dick, Esquire!

GREYSON. Well, Dick, you get the bill changed and bring the money to my office, Greyson, number 12 Fulton Street.

DICK. Yes, sir, Mr. Greyson.

GREYSON. Keep the dime . . . and fifty cents for your trouble.

(*Starts R.*)

DICK. Yes, sir. Yes, sir! A fifty-cent tip!

GREYSON. *(Aside.)* We will soon see if Ragged Dick is as honest as he says.

(Exits R.)

DICK. Ten cents and fifty cents . . . I've made *sixty* cents before breakfast! I can go to Barnum's tonight and hear 'em sing "O Susannah," and see the bearded lady, and the eight-foot giant, the two-foot dwarf, and other curiosities too numerous to mention!

(Sings, Cue 6. Tune, "O Susannah.")

I've got money in my pocket
Where the holes once used to be.
Now I'm rich as Mr. Vanderbilt,
I'll live in lux-u-ree!
Money! Money!
It's music to my ear.
Oh, a jingle in my pocket
Is the sound I love to hear!
I can eat beefstew for breakfast now,
For lunch and dinner, too.
Then drop in to Delmonico's
And order oyster stew!
Money! Money!
It's music to my ear.
Oh, a jingle in my pocket
Is the sound I love to hear!
No more shiv'rin' in the icy rain
When it begins to pour.
I can now bunk in a five-cent bed
And snore and snore and snore!
Money! Money!
It's music to my ear.
Oh, a jingle in my pocket
Is the sound I love to hear!

(Mrs. Flanagan enters, a good-natured Irish woman who sells apples. She speaks with a musical Irish brogue. Busy with her basket, she does not see Dick. He slips near her and speaks in a deep voice as he teases her.)

Ah, Mrs. Flanagan! Have you paid your taxes for the year?

MRS. F. *(Surprised, but not turning around.)* Me taxes?

DICK. I've been sent by the mayor to collect your taxes. But I'll take it out in apples just to oblige. That big red one will be about the right size.

MRS. F. *(Turns and laughs.)* I'm thinking it will be the size of a good breakfast for you, Mr. Ragged Dick.

DICK. Oh, I can pay . . . but the smallest change I got is two dollars.

MRS. F. Two dollars!

DICK. Sixty cents of it is mine!

(Sings, Cue 7.)

I've got money in my pocket.
Where the holes once used to be . . .

MRS. F. *(Offers him apple. Music continues as they speak.)* One . . . you say?

DICK. And one . . . to keep the Doc away.

(Takes two apples and puts them into his pockets.)

MRS. F. *(Sings. Makes change with money.)*

Money! Money!
It's music to my ear.
Oh, a jingle in my pocket
Is the sound I love to hear!

DICK. I can go to see a Bow'ry show.

MRS. F. Just like a reg'lar swell.

DICK. Hiss the villain . . .

MRS. F. . . . . Cheer the hero

DICK. When he saves poor little Nell!

DICK AND MRS. F. Money! Money!
It's music to my ear.
Oh, a jingle in my pocket
Is a sound I love to hear!

(They dance. Dick exits L. Mrs. F. looks after him fondly.)

MRS. F. Git along with ye, Dick. You're a scamp . . . and a good-for-something boy.

(Villain music, Cue 8. Tune, "Kings of Bal Masqué." Mother Watson enters R. She is a ragged, evil old crone.)

MRS. F. *(Aside.)* It's Mother Watson . . . up before noon. And already she's been tipping the bottle.

MOTHER W. I'm looking for him, the lazy little imp. Have you seen him?

MRS. F. Are ye meaning Mark the match boy?

MOTHER W. He's a lazy scalawag. Don't earn his keep. And I'm out of my medicine.

(Takes bottle from pocket.)

MRS. F. Medicine, is it?

MOTHER W. It's for my cough.

MRS. F. *(Aside.)* A cough never gave nobody that red nose.

MOTHER W. He'd better sell his matches . . . and have the money, or I'll . . .

MRS. F. What will ye be doing?

MOTHER W. I'll give him a taste of this!

(Pulls out a small whip.)

MRS. F. May the Saints protect the little lamb!

(Looks off L.)

And may they indeed . . .

(Points.)

for here he comes now.

(Mark enters L.)

MOTHER W. So here you are!

(Mark is surprised and frightened at seeing Mother W.)

Where have you been hiding?

MARK. I've been trying to sell my matches.

MOTHER W. How many have you sold?

MARK. Only three boxes.

MOTHER W. Three! You don't earn your salt. Give me the money.

(Fearfully he crosses and gives her a few pennies. She counts them.)

There's a penny short! Where is it?

MARK. I . . . I was so hungry I bought a bit of bread.

MOTHER W. You little thief!

MARK. I didn't have any breakfast . . . or supper last night.

MOTHER W. You didn't earn it! But I have something for your appetite!

(Holds up whip.)

I'll give you a taste of this!

(Starts after him.)

I'll beat the laziness out of you!

MRS. F. *(Mark runs behind her.)* Shame on you, Mother Watson! Leave the poor laddie alone.

MOTHER W. Buying himself a grand breakfast!

MRS. F. Sure and he was hungry.

MOTHER W. Beggar! Little beggar. That's what you are. Ah, and *that's* what you'll be! If you can't sell matches, you can beg for money.

MARK. Beg?

MOTHER W. Hold out your hand and beg from the kind-hearted people.

MARK. I don't want to beg.

MOTHER W. Don't want to beg! Do you mind that now, Mrs. Flanagan? He's too proud to beg.

MARK. My mother told me never to beg if I could help it.

MOTHER W. Well, you can't help it! Do you see this?

(Raises whip.)

Do as I say or you'll feel it! Now . . . get on the corner! And don't come back until you have twenty-five cents!

(Villain music, Cue 9, as she exits L.)

MARK. I don't want to be a beggar.

MRS. F. Tell me, Mark darling, why are you living with her anyway? She ain't your mother, is she?

MARK. No. My mother was a good woman . . . and kind . . . and beautiful.

(Takes from pocket a small picture.)

MRS. F. Is that a picture of her?

MARK. Yes. It is all I have left.

MRS. F. *(Aside.)* Sure and he looks like her, he does. Anyone would know he was her son.

(To Mark.)

When did she die?

MARK. A year ago. Mother Watson told me to come and live with her and she'd take care of me.

MRS. F. Ha! She's making you take care of her.

MARK. *(Walks away.)* Now I have to beg or she'll beat me.

MRS. F. Poor little laddie.

(Sings, Cue 10. Tune, "After the Ball." As she sings, Rich Woman and Little Girl cross. Mark tries to beg from them, but cannot.)

Poor little orphan laddie,
Poor little hungry boy.
Poor little homeless Paddy,
No mother's pride and joy.
No father's love to guide him,
No one to take his part,
Facing the world while he's hiding
His poor, aching heart.

(Song ends. Rich Man enters. Mark with great effort approaches him. Music stops.)

MARK. Sir, will you give me a few pennies, please?

MR. RICH. Pennies?

MARK. If you please, sir.

MR. RICH. I suppose your wife and children are starving, eh?

MARK. No. I don't have a wife or any children.

MR. RICH. *(Aside.)* He hasn't learned his trade, but he will.

(To Mark.)

Soon you'll have a sick mother starving at home.

MARK. My mother is dead.

MR. RICH. You'll get no money from me. Be off! Go home . . . go home.

(Exits.)

MARK. Home . . . I haven't any home . . .

(Takes out picture.)

or mother . . . nobody . . .

MRS. F. *(Sings, Cue 11.)*

Poor little orphan laddie,
Poor little hungry boy.
Poor little homeless Paddy,
No mother's pride and joy.

(Mark exits slowly. Mrs. F. follows him, ending her solo on a dramatic note.)

No father's love to guide him,
No one to take his part,
Facing the world while he's hiding
His poor, aching heart!

(She exits.)

(Music, Cue 12, changes to Tune, "Here We Go Round the Mulberry Bush." Roswell, a very English butler, enters L, turns the street flat at L around, showing a painted elegant room. On the second chorus he stands and sings.)

ROSWELL. *(Sings.)*

This is where the rich rich live,
The rich rich live,
The rich rich live,

> This is where the rich rich live
> In all their bee-u-tee-ful houses.

(Music repeats as he brings on two small gold chairs, then a small Victorian table which he places between the chairs. He brings in a tea service which is handed to him. He stands behind the table, pours tea, and sings.)

> This is the hour the rich have tea,
>> The rich have tea,
>> The rich have tea,
> This is the hour the rich have tea
>> At four in the afternoon

(Chimes strike four, as Ida, a pretty young girl, beautifully dressed, enters L and sits properly.)

> Your tea, Miss Ida.

IDA. Thank you, Roswell.

(Sings, holding cup elegantly.)

> This is the way I drink my tea,
>> Properly,
>> Properly,
> Wishing, wishing that I could be . . .

(Speaks rapidly, with conviction.)

Shopping today, playing croquet . . . anything!

(Sings.)

> But having tea all alone with me.

(Dick enters R, pantomimes knocking at "door.")

ROSWELL. Someone is knocking at the door.

(Crosses to "door.")

DICK. Good afternoon, general.

(Walks past butler into "hall.")

I've come to see the president . . . on business.

ROSWELL. Mr. Greyson is not at home, sir.

IDA. *(Calls from L.)* Who is it, Roswell?

ROSWELL. Your name, sir?

DICK. Ragged Dick.

ROSWELL. It is Mr. Ragged Dick.

DICK. Esquire.

ROSWELL. Esquire.

DICK. Who is she?

ROSWELL. Mr. Greyson's daughter, Miss Ida.

IDA. Show him in, Roswell. And pour another cup of tea.

ROSWELL. Miss Ida requests the pleasure of your company at tea.

DICK. Tea?

ROSWELL. *(Pantomimes lifting cup, with curved little finger, and sipping.)* Follow me.

(Dick follows butler, imitating his walk.)

Miss Ida. Mr. Ragged Dick, Esquire.

IDA. *(Sweetly.)* How do you do.

(Curtseys.)

DICK. *(Suddenly shy and ill at ease.)* How d'do.

(Uncertain, he bobs an awkward curtsey. Butler pours tea.)

IDA. *(Aside.)* His clothes are ragged, but his face is honest.

(To Dick.)

How nice of you to come. I was wishing that Papa would come ... or someone ... and here you are! Like a genie out of a bottle.

DICK. Oh, no, ma'am. I'm not a drinking man!

IDA. *(Aside.)* One good virtue in his favor.

(To Dick.)

Won't you sit down?

(She sits gracefully. Dick starts to, stops, brushes the seat of his pants, then sits awkwardly.)

ROSWELL. *(At side of Dick, offers him tea.)* Your tea, sir.

(Dick starts to take saucer.)

May I take your hat?

DICK. My hat?

(Dick takes off cap, is confused, starts to put saucer on his head, then gives saucer instead of cap to butler, finally keeps saucer and gives cap to butler. Dick looks at Ida hopefully. She stirs her tea gracefully. Dick stirs his tea vigorously.)

IDA. Drink it while it's hot.

(Dick nods, wipes spoon on his pants, then puts it behind his ear, pours tea into saucer, blows on it loudly, then drinks it with a slurp, and wipes his chin on his cuff. Ida speaks aside.)

I have never had tea with a shoeshine boy before.

DICK. *(Aside.)* I've never had *tea* before.

ROSWELL. *(Offers two plates to Dick.)* Cakes or crumpets, sir?

DICK. I ain't got nothing against neither one.

(He takes a handful from each, starts eating, putting some in his pockets. He smiles.)

Bully!

IDA. I'm glad you like them.

DICK. Yes, ma'am. Better than the peanuts at the Old Bowery!

IDA. *(Rises excitedly.)* Have you been to the Old Bowery? Have you seen . . . a *play*!

DICK. Every night in the gallery when I got the price. This week I saw the "Demon of the Danube."

IDA. Oh, how exciting. Tell me all about it!

DICK. *(As he tells the story, he starts acting it out with musical accompaniment. Cue 13. Or, if preferred, the scene may be danced with two dancers as a comic ballet.)* Well . . . you see . . . there's this Demon, and he's in love with a girl.

IDA. How romantic!

DICK. *(Music. If danced, Demon enters dragging Girl, then a comic dance of protesting and conquering follows. If Dick tells the story alone, music accompanies his actions.)* He drags her by the hair up a cliff to his castle.

IDA. *(Aside.)* What a strange way to show his affection!

DICK. She is in love with another chap, and when he hears that she is carried off, he swears an oath to rescue her.

(If danced, Dick becomes the hero and joins the ballet.)

He gets to the castle . . . using an underground passage . . . he and the Demon fight it out! First one and then at the other . . . cut and slash and fight!

IDA. Who wins?

DICK. The young Baron draws a dagger and plunges it into the Demon's heart and says, "Die, thou false and perjured villain, die. The dogs of prey shall feast upon thy carcass." Then the Demon gives an awful howl and dies. The Baron seizes his body and throws it over the precipice. The girl kneels before her hero, who speaks these words: "So ends your life of captivity and begins a life of married bliss 'twixt thee and me."

IDA. How wonderful!

(She applauds. If danced, Demon and Girl exit. Dick bows. Music stops. Ida speaks aside.)

He is quite a hero himself.

(To Dick.)

Does your father let you go every night?

DICK. He ain't around to ask.

IDA. Where is he?

DICK. I don't know. They said he went off to sea. I expect he got wrecked or drowned.

IDA. And your mother?

DICK. She died when I was three. Some folks took care of me. But when I was seven I had to scratch for myself.

IDA. *(Aside.)* Out in the world at seven!

(To Dick.)

What did you do?

DICK. Sold newspapers . . . sold matches . . . one night I was so cold I burnt all my matches to keep me from freezing.

IDA. Where do you live?

DICK. Last night I slept . . . at the Box Hotel.

IDA. The Box Hotel?

DICK. Yes, ma'am. I slept in a box behind a hotel.

IDA. *(Aside.)* Many of our greatest men were poor, but they climbed the ladder to success.

(To Dick.)

I think you will, too . . . if you try.

DICK. Oh, I ain't lazy! But who'd hire Ragged Dick? I ain't had no learning.

IDA. I know a teacher . . . who will give you a free lesson every day . . . if you apply yourself.

DICK. You do? Who?

IDA. *(Goes to table, picks up book, and becomes a proper teacher.)*

Our first lesson today will be in Reading.

(Reads.)

"One befriends himself when he befriends another."

DICK. You?

IDA. I don't know too much, but I'll gladly teach you all I know.

DICK. Teach *me*? Ragged Dick?

IDA. I think you'll become a great man if you only get a little education.

DICK. Do you?

IDA. I am sure of it.

DICK. Then I've decided what I'm going to do. Starting today . . . with your help . . . I'm going to grow up respectable!

(They sing. Music, Cue 14. Tune, "Glow Worm.")

IDA. *(Chorus.)*

Each day we'll study reading.

DICK. See-the-cat.

IDA.   Each day we'll study grammar.

DICK. What is *that*?

IDA.   You will learn to write with ease . . .
To dot your i's and cross your t's, and
Each day we'll study history.

DICK. *(Poses like Napoleon.)* Na-po-le-on!

IDA.   Each day we'll study numbers.

DICK. Three-two-one.

IDA.   Study hard so you will pass!

DICK. I'll be the head of my class!

IDA. *(Verse.)*

We must work on etiquette.

DICK. I'll do my best, you bet . . .
If you will show me.

IDA.   Don't forget to be polite . . .
With table manners right . . .

DICK. My friends won't know me.

IDA.   You must get some culture, too,
And learn to parlez-vous.

DICK. *(With a flat accent, rhyming with "concentrate.")*

Like s'il vooz plate, ma'am?

IDA.   When you're in society,
Act with propriety.

DICK. I'll concentrate, ma'am.

IDA.   At a party
Or a ball,
You must know all the dances.
Should you meet
A charming girl
It always helps your chances.

(She dances to a phrase of music. Reprised chorus.)

Who was President Number One?

DICK. I know the answer. Wash-ing-ton!

IDA.   Who discovered this land for us?

DICK. That's easy, too. It was Co-lum-bus!

IDA.   If I take away a fraction . . . ?

DICK. Take away? That means Subtraction!

IDA.   Keep it up and you will pass.

DICK. I'll be head of my class!

(Mr. Greyson enters R and knocks at "door.")

ROSWELL. *(Enters L, crosses to "door.")* Someone is knocking at the door.

(Admits Greyson, takes his hat.)

IDA. It's Papa!

(Runs to him.) Papa!

(He embraces her.)

Papa, you have a caller.

ROSWELL. *(Announcing.)* Mr. Ragged Dick, Esquire.

(Greyson and Ida enter "room.")

DICK. Good afternoon, sir.

GREYSON. *(Surprised.)* Good afternoon.

DICK. I fetched your change. You wasn't at your office, so I walked up here.

GREYSON. That was a long and an honest walk. Where did you learn the virtue of honesty?

DICK. Nowhere.

(Aside.)

I just know it ain't right to cheat or steal.

GREYSON. *(Aside.)* Then he is ahead of some of our businessmen.

(To Dick.)

Do you read the Bible?

DICK. No, but I hear it's a good book.

IDA. He will be reading soon, Papa. I am going to teach him! He's promised to come every day and to study hard.

GREYSON. You want to learn to read . . . to improve yourself?

DICK. Yes, sir.

(Aside.)

I'm awful ignorant.

GREYSON. You have an open and honest face. I believe you are a good boy. I hope you will prosper and rise in the world.

IDA. Does that mean . . . I can be his teacher? Oh, Papa, thank you.

GREYSON. I think I can teach you something, too. I have a Sunday School class. Would you like to come?

DICK. Me go to church? Yes, sir!

(His spirits fall when he looks down at his ragged clothes.)

No, sir, I can't come.

GREYSON. Why not?

DICK. I'd shame you. This is my best . . . my only clothes I got.

IDA. Papa! I have an idea.

(She whispers excitedly in Mr. Greyson's ear.)

GREYSON. *(Aside.)* Fortunately she has solved the problem.

(To Dick.)

Young man, give your coat to Roswell.

DICK. Give away my coat!

GREYSON. And give him your shirt, and your shoes, and your trousers.

DICK. Me trousers!

GREYSON. And go into the next room and wash.

(Aside.)

Clean clothes and dirty skin do not go together.

(To Dick.)

Roswell will give you some of my son's clothing.

DICK. You're *giving* me . . . new clothes?

ROSWELL. This way, please.

DICK. Yes, sir! Yes, sir, general!

(Takes off coat and holds it out.)

So ends the life of Ragged Dick . . .

(Gives coat to Roswell, who holds it far away from his nose.)

. . . and begins the new life of Richard Hunter.

(Hero music, Cue 15. Tune, "American Patrol." Roswell exits L, Dick marches out after him. Music stops.)

IDA. Oh, Papa, it's a Sunday School lesson coming true!

(Embraces him. Then Greyson strikes a solemn pose.)

Papa . . . you look worried.

GREYSON. I am, my dear. I have a grave problem on my mind.

IDA. What is it?

GREYSON. *(Aside.)* Shall I tell her? Yes, I shall confide in her innocent ear.

(He motions to chair. Ida sits. He stands by her, hand on her shoulder in an old tintype pose. Music, Cue 16. Tune, "Flower Song.")

Many years ago your grandfather disowned his second daughter, your mother's sister.

IDA. How cruel.

GREYSON. She was in love with a fine young man, John Talbot, who was a clerk. But your grandfather wanted a marriage of wealth for his daughter.

(Moves.)

The two lovers eloped and were secretly wed. Two years later, Irene appeared at your grandfather's doorstep with a child in her arms. But he hardened his heart and cast her out of his life forever. A month ago he learned that both Irene and John Talbot were dead, but the child—a boy—is still living. Your grandfather has repented. I am to find the boy, so he will come into his rightful fortune.

(He stands again, hand on her shoulder in the original picture pose. Music stops.)

IDA. Where will you look?

GREYSON. *(Moves out of pose.)* His mother died in New York a year ago. Probably the boy lives in a poor section and is making his own way in the world.

IDA. Like Ragged Dick . . . like Richard.

GREYSON. Yes.

(Aside.)

She has given me an idea! Ragged Dick . . . Richard . . . can help me find the boy.

ROSWELL. *(Enters L.)* He is dressed, sir. Mr. Richard Hunter.

(Hero music, Cue 17. Dick marches in at L, dressed in new clothes. Music stops.)

IDA. Oh, how splendid you look!

DICK. I ain't sure it's me.

GREYSON. *(Crosses to him.)* You have taken the first step in becoming respectable.

DICK. Yes, sir . . . and it sure feels good.

GREYSON. Mr. Hunter?

DICK. *(Looks around.)* Mr. Hunter? Huh? *Me!* Yes, sir.

GREYSON. Would you like to become a detective?

DICK. A detective?

GREYSON. I must find a lost boy, probably living in New York and making his way even as you.

DICK. What's his name?

GREYSON. We think . . . John Talbot, after his father. Do you know such a boy?

DICK. No. 'Course some of the boys change their names. There's Fat Jack, Pickle Nose, Tickle-me-foot. Sir, if John Talbot's on the streets, I'll find him.

GREYSON. I have a man investigating, but I believe *you* will be more successful. Here is five dollars.

DICK. Oh, no, sir.

(Looks at new clothes.)

You've done enough.

GREYSON. It is your first payment as a detective.

(Dick takes money.)

IDA. *(On other side of Dick.)* You can rent a room . . . have a home!

DICK. *(To Ida.)* Yes, sir . . . ma'am!

(To Greyson.)

Thank you, ma'am . . . sir!

GREYSON. *(Shakes Dick's hand, pumping harder at the end of the speech.)* Remember, in this country you can rise as high as you choose. Your future depends upon what you do for yourself!

(He exits L.)

DICK. I'll start right now . . . detecting! Goodby.

(Nods to Ida, quickly exits at "door.")

IDA. *(Aside.)* How true is what I read: One befriends himself, when he befriends another!

(She exits L.)

DICK. *(Comes from "door" to C. During the song, Roswell unobtrusively clears the stage and changes the scenery back to Street Scene. Music, Cue 18. Tune, "O Susannah.")*

(Verse)

O-oh what a change has come to me!
A change has come to me.
From now on I am respectable
And that's the way to be.

(Reprise of verse.)

In a country that's as free as ours
A poor boy has a chance.
If he works hard to improve himself,
He always can advance!

(Chorus.)

Take Abe Lincoln . . .
As poor as he could be,
But he raised himself to President
And made great history!
O-oh what a change has come to me!
A change has come to me.
From now on I am respectable
And that's the way to be.

(Chorus.)

Work and study
Will take you off the shelf!
So I've hitched my wagon to a star
And I'll drive it there myself!
O-oh what a change has come to me!
A change has come to me.
From now on I am respectable
And that's the way to be.

(Dick exits L.)

(Music, Cue 19, changes to Tune, "Twinkle, Twinkle, Little Star." Lights dim slightly to early evening. Lamplighter enters R and lights street lamp C back. Policeman enters L.)

POLICEMAN. It's going to be a cold moon tonight.

(Lamplighter nods and exits L. Policeman looks after him. Music stops.)

A fine night to be home by the blazing fire . . .

(Mark enters R. He sees Policeman, looks for a place to hide, and quickly stands in a painted shop doorway. Policeman turns.)

Who's there? Who's there? Speak out.

MARK. *(Steps out, frightened.)* It's me.

POLICEMAN. What are you doing?

MARK. Just standing . . . in a doorway . . . for shelter.

POLICEMAN. Get along with you. Get along home.

MARK. Yes, sir.

(Starts L.)

POLICEMAN. *(Exiting R.)* Home's the place to be . . .

MARK. *(Stops, wistfully.)* Home . . .

POLICEMAN. Home with your family . . .

(Exits R.)

MARK. Home . . . home . . . I haven't got a home.

(Takes out picture. Music, Cue 20. Tune, "After the Ball."
Sings.)

O Mother, dearest Mother,
If you could only hear.
I am so cold and hungry.
How I wish you were near.
Bravely, I try my best now,
Facing life on my own . . .
But without you here beside me,
I'm so alone.

(Puts picture in pocket, takes out money and counts slowly.
Mickey enters R and sees money.)

Five, six, seven . . . seven cents. She'll beat me. I can't go back.

MICKEY. *(Aside.)* Money! And mine for the taking!

(Slips up behind Mark, who counts his pennies again. Mickey
grabs Mark's arm, pulls it behind him, and twists it.)

MARK. Let go of me!

MICKEY. Let go of the money.

MARK. It's mine!

MICKEY. *(Twists Mark's arm harder.)* Let go. Let go!

MARK. *(Cries in pain, lets money fall.)* Oh! Oh!

MICKEY. *(Quickly picks up coins.)* Finders keepers.

MARK. Give it back to me.

MICKEY. Losers weepers.

MARK. It's mine. Give it back!

MICKEY. *(Faces him, larger and tougher.)* You going to make me?

MARK. Yes. Yes!

(Starts to hit and kick him.)

MICKEY. *(Laughs.)* I'll give you something. Take this!

(Gives Mark a hard blow, which knocks him backward, and he falls.)

DICK. *(Enters L. Aside.)* What's this? Mickey Maguire and his dirty fighting.

(Poses, fists ready.)

MICKEY. *(Sneers at the fallen Mark.)* Next time pick on someone your size.

(Backs away toward Dick.)

DICK. Why don't you?

(Mickey turns and is facing Dick.)

MARK. He stole my money.

DICK. Give it back to him.

MICKEY. So *you* can steal it?

DICK. Stealing ain't *my* line.

MICKEY. You want to fight?

(Poses, fists ready.)

DICK. Not 'specially. It's bad for the complexion, around your eyes and nose. They're apt to turn red, black, and blue.

MICKEY. What's wrong? You scared?

DICK. No! Give him his money back, or . . .

(With commanding authority.)

I'll land you in the middle of next week at very short notice!

MICKEY. Like this!

(Gives Dick an uppercut, which Dick dodges.)

DICK. Like that!

(Dick hits Mickey, who stumbles.)

MICKEY. *(Down, cowardly.)* Look out who you're hitting!

DICK. Give back his money!

MICKEY. Catch me first . . . if you can!

(Chase music, Cue 21. Tune, "Midnight Fire Alarm." Mickey starts to run. Dick starts after him. It is an exciting chase, with dodging and running around the street flats, or into the auditorium and back onto the stage, ending with a scuffle on the floor, Dick on top of Mickey, the winner. Music stops.)

DICK. Give it up. Give it up!

(Twists Mickey's arm.)

MICKEY. *(In pain, releases money.)* Take the money.

(Dick quickly picks up money, as Mickey gets to his feet and, cowardly, backs away. Shouts, at a safe distance.)

I'll get you. I'll get you yet!

DICK. *(Makes a lunge at Mickey, who exits quickly. Dick goes to Mark.)* Here . . . here's your money. Seven cents.

(Gives Mark coins.)

MARK. Thank you. It's all I have.

(He shivers.)

DICK. You're cold. Come on. I'll help you home.

MARK. I don't have a home.

DICK. Ain't you got no folks? No place?

MARK. *(Shakes his head.)* She'll beat me.

DICK. Come on. I've got me a rented room . . . with a real bed! It ain't much, but it's better than a barrel. What do you say?

MARK. You want to take me . . . with you?

DICK. *(Comically imitating Roswell.)* Mr. Richard Hunter requests the pleasure of your company to share his indoor lodgings. Come on!

(Mark stands by him.)

Together we'll face the world . . . like in the play at the Old Bowery . . . we'll be the *two* Musketeers!

(Hero music, Cue 22, as they march. Suddenly Mark points off L. Music stops.)

MARK. Look!

DICK. What's wrong?

MARK. It's Mother Watson. Looking for me with her whip!

(Villain music, Cue 23, as Mother Watson enters L, with whip in hand.)

DICK. *(Aside.)* My, she's a beauty, ain't she?

MARK. What will I do?

DICK. Leave her to me.

MOTHER W. *(Sees Mark. Aside.)* Ah, there he is.

(To Mark.)

I see you! You little thief!

DICK. *(Aside.)* My, ain't she polite?

MOTHER W. Try to run away, will you? Not from me you won't!

(Advances, swaying with drink.)

DICK. Careful, madam. Your feet ain't steady.

MOTHER W. I'm not talking to you. I'm talking to him. Wait till I get my hands on you!

(Raises whip.)

DICK. Stop! You ain't never going to get your hands on him again.

MOTHER W. What?

DICK. He ain't never going back to you and your whip. He's coming with me. *I* have adopted him!

MOTHER W. *(To Mark.)* Come here, I tell you. Come here this minute!

DICK. Stay where you are.

MOTHER W. *(Shouting.)* Do you hear me. Do you hear me!

DICK. *(Shouting.)* I'm thinking they hear you in New Jersey!

MOTHER W. Don't give me your lip, you ruffian, or I'll give *you* the whip!

DICK. I ain't afraid of you! A whip is for cowards. You think because you're big you can hit little people. Lots of folks think 'cause they got a whip they can boss the world. That ain't right. And someone's got to stop them.

MOTHER W. I'll show you who's boss!

(Gives Dick a good lashing.)

DICK. You ain't never going to use that whip again!

(Angrily he grabs whip. He and she struggle.)

MOTHER W. Let go of me, you vagabond! Let go!

DICK. I'll show *you* how a whip feels!

MOTHER W. Give me back my strap! You scoundrel!

(He pushes her away. She turns and reels, bending over.)

Help!

DICK. *(Gives her exposed backside a whack.)* There!

(Mother Watson jumps and screams. Dick laughs.)

POLICEMAN. *(Enters, shouting over their yelling.)* What's going on? What's going on here?

MOTHER W. *(Aside, frightened.)* The police!

DICK. *(Aside, surprised.)* The cops!

POLICEMAN. What's all the fighting? What's all the yelling about?

MARK. *(Pause. He steps forward and speaks in a small voice.)* Me.

MOTHER W. *(To Policeman, pretending to cry comically.)* Oh, officer. I'm an old lady and . . . and my bad little boy, he's breaking my heart. Run away he did. But I'm willing to forgive him. All I want is my dear boy to come home.

POLICEMAN. Do you belong to her?

MARK. No, sir.

MOTHER W. Yes! Yes, he does!

(Remembers and becomes maudlin.)

He's my own sweet little boy.

POLICEMAN. Is he your son?

MOTHER W. No.

MARK. I'm not any of her relation. She said she'd keep me after my mother died. But she starves me and beats me when I don't bring back money for her whiskey.

POLICEMAN. Whiskey? I thought I recognized you. You were drunk last week on Mott Street.

(Mother Watson looks at audience, frightened, and gives an aside burp. To Mark.)

Go along boy. You are free to go wherever you want.

MOTHER W. *(Aside.)* Curses. Curses on them all.

POLICEMAN. Get along. Off the street with you and your bottle.

MOTHER W. Beware! Beware! I am not through with you scalawags!

(Aside.)

I'll have my revenge. I'll have my revenge on both of them.

(Villain music, Cue 24, as she exits L. Policeman follows her off L.)

DICK. Come on, Mark! We're on our way!

(Mark bravely stands by him.)

We're going to climb . . . up . . . up the ladder of success!

(Aside.)

No matter how patched your pants are, you can still rise . . . to fame and fortune!

(Music, Cue 25. Tune, "The Man Who Broke the Bank at Monte Carlo.")

DICK. *(Sings.)*

If you want to be a millionaire,
It's an easy game today.
You can always find a way
In the good old U.S.A.
You can be just what you want to be
In this land of opportunity,
For with pluck and luck
You'll go from rags to riches.

(As various people are mentioned, they enter, or some of them, and sing, making it a large chorus for a stirring finale. Dancing will also add to the scene.)

Be a soldier . . . be a sailor,
Be a railroad engineer,
Be a wealthy financier.
You may pick your own career!
You can be just what you want to be
In this land of opportunity,
For with pluck and luck
You'll go from rags to riches.
Drive a carriage . . . drive a trolley,
Ride a horse or ride a hack,
Be a mailman with a sack,
Be a sleuth who's on the track.
You may lead a lamb to slaughter . . .
You may wed the boss's daughter,
As with pluck and luck
You go from rags to riches.
Be a doctor . . . be a lawyer,
Be a jockey with a whip
Or a waiter with a tip,
Be a captain of a ship.
While Old Glory's banner is unfurled . . .

(A large American flag descends at back, to which they point.)

Any day may bring a bright new world . . .

(Straight line for curtain.)

For with pluck and luck
You'll go from rags to riches.

(Musical tag.)

Yes, for with pluck and luck
You'll go from rags to riches!

(Curtain.)

ACT TWO

(Music, Cue 26. Tune, "The First Noel." Scene: street. A group

of Christmas Carolers sing. A few shoppers with Christmas boxes and the Policeman cross during the scene. While Mickey calls the news, the Carolers hum.)

MICKEY. Paper . . . evening paper.
 Christmas Party at Mrs. Astor's.
 Mark Twain's latest story.
 New York sings Christmas glory.
 Paper . . . Paper . . .

(Carolers sing. Mrs. Flanagan enters selling apples. Mickey exits. Dick enters.)

DICK. Shine your boots, sir.
 Like I shine the rest, sir.
 Christmas time is the time, sir,
 To look your best.
 Shine . . . shoe shine . . .

(Dick exits. Carolers sing, then hum when Mark calls, entering L.)

MARK. Matches . . . matches . . .

(Puts hand to head and sways.)

Light . . . light your Christmas candles . . .

(Weakly. He is ill.)

Matches . . . mat—ches . . .

(He falls limply to ground.)

LADY CAROLER. The little boy . . . he fell!

(She and Mrs. Flanagan rush to Mark. Others group around, talking excitedly.)

MRS. F. *(Kneels by him, holding his head.)* It's Mark the match boy. Poor little laddie.

POLICEMAN. *(Enters.)* What's the trouble? What's happened?

MRS. F. Poor laddie. Fainted, he did.

POLICEMAN. Let's have a look. He has a fever.

MRS. F. Starved he is, and shivering with the cold.

POLICEMAN. Does he have a home?

MRS. F. Sure and Ragged Dick has took him in. They have a room on the top floor of the same house with me.

POLICEMAN. *(Mark moves and tries to talk.)* Are you all right?

MARK. Mother . . . mother . . . ?

MRS. F. Out of his head. Delirious, he is!

POLICEMAN. I'll take him home.

> *(Picks Mark up in his arms.)*

DICK. *(Rushes in.)* What happened! What's happened to Mark?

POLICEMAN. Toppled over . . . fainted.

DICK. *(Shakes Mark.)* Mark! Mark! What's wrong with him?

POLICEMAN. He's needing some rest. I'm taking him home. Lead the way.

DICK. Yes, sir. Yes, sir!

> *(Dick goes to R. Policeman, carrying Mark, follows. Dick turns the street flat at R around, and the scene is a poor tenement room. He places a small cot with ragged covers at R. Carolers and Mrs. Flanagan sing, Cue 27, during scene change and exit, backing slowly away at L. Policeman puts Mark on bed and helps Dick take off Mark's coat and cap, which he hangs on wall. Music stops.)*

DICK. Is he going to be all right?

POLICEMAN. He's got a fever . . . and he's delirious.

DICK. But he'll be all right, won't he?

POLICEMAN. He needs to stay in bed and be cared for.

DICK. I'll look after him.

POLICEMAN. He needs a doctor.

DICK. I'll get a doctor.

POLICEMAN. If you need me, I'll be on duty.

DICK. Thank you, sir.

> *(Fixes cover on Mark.)*

> I'll stay by him. I'll get him well.

POLICEMAN. *(Aside.)* A friend in need is a friend indeed.

(Exits R.)

DICK. *(Carolers sing softly off L, "Silent Night," Cue 28. Dick speaks tenderly to Mark.)*

Mark . . . Mark . . . are you asleep, Mark? I . . . I'll get a doctor, Mark, and he'll give you medicine . . . and get you well . . .

(Singing stops. Dick walks away, counting money from his pocket.)

Fifteen . . . twenty . . . thirty . . . forty . . . forty-five . . . fifty . . . sixty . . . sixty-five cents. It ain't enough for a doctor . . . and medicine . . .

(Dick looks back at Mark.)

But I'll make more money. I'll shine every boot in New York City. You bet I will! Only . . . only you need a doctor now . . . for the fever.

MARK. *(Sits up, delirious.)* Mother . . . mother . . .

DICK. What did you say, Mark? I'm listening.

MARK. Mother . . . mother . . .

DICK. No . . . no, your mother isn't here . . . just me.

(Mark leans back on pillows.)

But don't you be afraid. I'm not going to leave you. I'll stay right by you.

(Walks away, worried.)

and I'll help you . . . someway . . . somehow . . .

(Off L, Carolers sing, Cue 29. Dick looks off L and listens, then he smiles with an idea.)

I know a way, Mark. We'll get some help!

(He kneels and speaks earnestly.)

God . . . I hope you're listening, God. I know I never talked to you until I went to Mr. Greyson's church. But I . . . I never thought you'd listen to Ragged Dick. If . . . if you are listening and if . . . if you know even when a sparrow falls, then you know that Mark fell in the street, and he's got a fever and he's not talking straight. He hasn't anybody . . . nobody to help him . . . but me. So what I'm asking is for your help. Please . . . please help Mark get well.

(Singing stops. There is a knock off R.)

Someone is at the door.

(He rises as Ida enters R.)

IDA. Hello.

DICK. Miss Ida!

IDA. I hope you don't mind my coming . . . uninvited. But it was after four o'clock and you've never been late for your lesson before and, when you didn't come, I thought something had happened. Has it?

DICK. It's Mark.

IDA. *(Goes to bed.)* Mark?

DICK. He's got a fever. He doesn't know me.

IDA. Delirious.

(Aside.)

How fortunate I came!

(To Dick.)

He must have a doctor right away. Go tell Papa and he will send Doctor Morrison.

DICK. A doctor! And I'll earn the money to pay your Papa back!

IDA. Run!

DICK. Yes. Mark's going to get well.

(Looks up.)

Thank you.

(Carolers begin to sing off L, Cue 30. Mark sits up smiling.)

IDA. He's trying to say something.

MARK. Singing . . . singing . . .

IDA. Yes. The Christmas carolers.

MARK. Singing . . . like angels . . .

(Mark smiles and holds hand toward her.)

angels . . . angels . . .

DICK. He thinks you are an angel.

IDA. *(Aside.)* Me?

DICK. And maybe . . . you are.

(Looks up again, gratefully.)

I'll run.

(Dick exits quickly at R. Mark sleeps peacefully. Ida stands by bed, then slowly backs off at R, as Carolers end their song.
Lights dim down on the "room" area at R, and come up at L. Music, Cue 31, changes to the lively "Deck the Hall." Mother Watson enters L in a gay mood, wearing a bit of red and green for Christmas.)

MOTHER W. *(Sings comically with great joy.)*

Deck the hall with boughs of holly,
Fa, la, la, la, la, la, la, la, la.
'Tis the season to be jolly
Fa, la, la, la, la, la, la, la, la.

(Looks about, seeing no one, takes out bottle and sings wildly.)

Don we now our gay apparel,
Fa, la, la, la, la, la, la, la, la.

(Takes cork from bottle and smells bottle happily.)

Troll the ancient Yuletide carol,
Fa, la, la, la, la, la, la, la, la.

(Looks at bottle suspiciously, turns bottle upside down. Her joy changes to doubt. She shakes bottle, slowing down the song to rhythm of her shaking. Then stops. Bottle is empty. Music stops.)

Deck the hall with boughs of holly,
Fa, la, la, la, la, la, la, . . .

(Aside.)

I hate Christmas!

MICKEY. *(Enters L.)* Merry Christmas!

MOTHER W. Bah! Bah! Bah!

MICKEY. Have you heard? They're looking for a lost boy. They say there's a fortune waiting for some lost boy.

MOTHER W. Lost boy?

MICKEY. Limpy Jim told me and Pickle Nose told him and Little Runt told him that Ragged Dick told him.

MOTHER W. *(Aside.)* Ragged Dick! I have a score to settle with him!

MICKEY. They think the boy is on the streets.

MOTHER W. What's his name?

MICKEY. John Talbot.

MOTHER W. John Talbot? John Talbot!

(Aside.)

Luck is with me!

(Laughs triumphantly.)

MICKEY. Do you know him?

MOTHER W. *(Aside.)* Ha, I am the only person who knows who John Talbot is.

(To Mickey.)

There is money waiting for him, you say?

MICKEY. A fortune!

MOTHER W. *(Aside.)* They will never find him unless I tell who he is.

MICKEY. What are you mumbling?

MOTHER W. Hold your tongue! I'm thinking!

(Gives him a slap in the stomach. Aside.)

John Talbot is . . . Mark the match boy. But he doesn't know it. His mother changed her last name. She told me that before she died.

MICKEY. Are you still thinking?

MOTHER W. Shut your lip, you vagabond!

(Gives him another slap. Aside.)

Some *other* boy could get the fortune. I could prove *another* boy is John Talbot and cheat him out of the money. I must find me some stupid boy.

MICKEY. Can I help you?

MOTHER W. *(Aside.)* Ah, ha! He can and he will!

(To Mickey.)

You . . . you are going to help get the fortune.

MICKEY. Me?

MOTHER W. *(Suddenly bursts into loud singing.)*

Deck the hall with boughs of holly,
Fa, la, la, la, la, . . .

MICKEY. *(Aside.)* I think she's been tipping the bottle.

MOTHER W. You . . .

(Dramatically.)

You are John Talbot.

MICKEY. Me?

MOTHER W. *(Suddenly bursts into song again.)*

'Tis the season to be jolly,
Fa, la, la, la, la, . . .

MICKEY. *(Aside.)* I know she's been tipping the bottle.

MOTHER W. *(Lost in revery.)* Rich! Rich! We're going to be rich!

MICKEY. We are?

MOTHER W. *(Already acting elegantly rich.)* Diamonds and jewels, capes and furs, and a feather fan.

MICKEY. And shoes without no holes?

MOTHER W. Horses and carriages . . . a house on Fifth Avenue and servants whenever I call.

(Claps her hands twice. Maid and Butler . . . dancers of "Demon of the Danube" and "Cakewalk" . . . enter and place two golden chairs UL, exit.)

Every day high society. And every night a show at the Old Bowery. We'll sit on the front row.

(She and Mickey sit on chairs.)

MICKEY. And eat peanuts and watch them do . . . the Cakewalk!

(Music, Cue 32. Tune, "At a Georgia Camp Meeting." Maid and Butler become performers and dance a lively cakewalk. Mother Watson and Mickey react as if at the theatre and applaud when the dance is finished. Music starts again. Dancers dance off, taking chairs with them. Mother Watson and Mickey try to dance a comic cakewalk, but she soon collapses in Mickey's arms. Music stops.)

MICKEY. *(Back to reality.)* First . . . we got to get the money.

MOTHER W. I'll get the fortune!

(Aside.)

I must have the picture of Mark's mother which he carries in his pocket. The picture will be the proof that *my* story is true, and the boy who has it . . .

(Points to Mickey.)

is John Talbot.

(To Mickey.)

I have business to do. Be off! Steal a necktie. Look like an honest boy. Meet me here in two hours.

MICKEY. In two hours.

(He goes L. She goes R. Aside.)

How fine it feels to have a fortune.

MOTHER W. *(Aside.)* How sweet is revenge!

*(Villain music, Cue 33, as he exits L and she exits R. Music stops.
  Music, Cue 34. Tune, "Emmet's Lullaby," played brightly. Lights come up on the "room" area at R. Mark is still in bed. Mrs. Flanagan enters R, looks fondly at Mark. She tiptoes down and speaks an aside.)*

MRS. F. Sleeping peacefully as a puppy he is. The fever is gone, praise be to the good doctor, and Ida, and Ragged Dick. All little Mark is needing now is a heap of caring for.

(Goes to bed. Sings cheerfully, Cue 35. Tune, "Emmet's Lulla-by.")

Go to sleep my laddie,
Dear laddie, sweet laddie.
Go to sleep my laddie,
Hush-a-bye, my dear.

(Aside.)

Someone is on the stairs. Is it you, Dick?

Mother W. *(Off.)* No. It's Mother Watson.

Mrs. F. *(Aside.)* Mother Watson! What could she be wanting?

Mother W. *(Enters R, puffing.)* Two flights of stairs make me short of breath.

(Too sweetly.)

I heard that Mark is sick. I've come to cheer him up with a kiss.

(Faces audience and puckers lips.)

Mrs. F. He's asleep.

Mother W. Oh.

(Comically overacting.)

It's a lonely life I'm living since he left. I miss his footsteps coming home in the evening . . . his sweet voice calling in the morning . . . and his coat . . .

(Goes to coat hanging on wall.)

His coat hanging by the door.

Mrs. F. *(Aside.)* Faith, I'm believing she's had a change of heart, that she's sorry for the wickedness she's done.

Mother W. *(Feeling the coat, comically searching for the picture.)* His little ragged coat . . . too thin to keep him warm.

Mrs. F. Mother Watson, would ye be liking a cup of tea?

Mother W. Oh, it would warm a body up.

Mrs. F. I'll step into my room and fix it. I have to be careful about the blaze in the stove. We almost had a fire in the house last week. If he gets restless, just sing a bit.

(Mrs. Flanagan sings softly the Irish song. Mother Watson nods, sings with her . . . nasal and comic. Mrs. Flanagan exits R. Mother W. ends the song with her true feeling of revenge.)

MOTHER W. *(Aside.)* The picture is still in his pocket. All I have to do is take it.

(She tiptoes toward coat. Mark moves in bed. She stops. She begins singing the Lullaby urgently and comically. Stops when she is satisfied Mark is asleep.)

Drat the little brat!

(As she puts her hand into pocket, Mark turns and mumbles loudly. She stops as if caught, starts singing Lullaby loud and fast; sees that he is asleep, stops singing. Cautiously takes picture from pocket and holds it up.)

The picture is mine! You and Ragged Dick thought you could outsmart me, but Mother Watson has outwitted the two of you!

(Aside.)

The fortune is mine!

(Laughs and exits R.)

MARK. *(Sits up, frightened.)* Mother Watson. I heard her voice. I heard her laugh. She's here!

MRS. F. *(Enters R, quickly.)* What is it, Mark?

MARK. Mother Watson!

MRS. F. Sure and you mustn't excite yourself. She's not going to harm you.

MARK. *(Weakly lies down.)* I heard her . . . I heard her . . .

MRS. F. She's gone! Left in a hurry she did. But why? I'm thinking she is up to no good. Sure it was crocodile tears she was crying.

(Aside.)

Everyone knows a crocodile weeps best when it is ready to bite!

(Music, Cue 36. Tune, "Drill, Ye Tarriers, Drill." Lights dim down on "room" at R. Mark and bed exit R. Mrs. Flanagan turns the room-flat so that it is the Street Scene.

Mother Watson enters R. Mickey enters L. They both creep in sinisterly and in rhythm to music. He wears a new hat, comic

*on him, and a big bright necktie. They meet in C. The scene is
played secretly and mysteriously. Music stops.)*

MOTHER W. Are ye ready?

MICKEY. Ready. Stole the tie at Stewarts. Hooked the hat at City
Hall.

MOTHER W. Listen carefully. Your name is John Talbot.

MICKEY. John Talbot.

MOTHER W. Named after your father.

MICKEY. After me father.

MOTHER W. This is a picture of your mother.

(Gives him picture.)

MICKEY. Me mother.

MOTHER W. Her name was Irene.

MICKEY. Irene.

MOTHER W. He died first. She died last year.

MICKEY. Last year.

MOTHER W. Mother Watson has took care of you ever since.

MICKEY. Ever since.

MOTHER W. *And* I'm going to keep on taking care of you . . . and the
fortune.

MICKEY. Me fortune!

MOTHER W. If you don't know the answer to what they ask you,
think of your departed mother . . . and start crying.

(Shows him how . . . comically.)

MICKEY. Start crying.

(Cries comically.)

MOTHER W. Then call me to explain it all.

MICKEY. Explain it all.

MOTHER W. Now be off!

MICKEY. Be off.

MOTHER W. *(Starts L. Aside.)* And the fortune will soon be . . . not his . . . but mine!

MICKEY. *(Starts R. Aside.)* And the fortune will soon be . . . not hers . . . but only mine!

(Music, Cue 37, builds to climax as they exit.
   Music, Cue 38, changes to "The Mulberry Bush." Roswell enters L and turns street-flat at L to show rich-room flat. Then he stands and sings.)

ROSWELL. *(Sings.)*

In the parlor the rich rich sit,
      The rich rich sit,
      The rich rich sit,
In the parlor the rich rich sit
      When night begins to fall.

(Pantomimes turning on ceiling lights.)

The fire and the lamps are lit,
      The lamps are lit,
      The lamps are lit,
The fire and the lamps are lit
      In the parlor and the hall.

(Mickey enters R, knocks at "door." Aside.)

Someone is knocking at the door.

(Opens "door.")

MICKEY. I've come to get my fortune.

ROSWELL. Your name, sir?

MICKEY. Mickey Ma . . . John Talbot!

ROSWELL. I shall announce you, sir.

(Crosses to L, speaks off.)

Excuse me, Mr. Greyson, but there is a gentleman who says his name is John Talbot.

GREYSON. *(Enters L.)* John Talbot?

MICKEY. At your service, sir.

GREYSON. You?

MICKEY. I've come to receive my rightful fortune.

GREYSON. I assume you can prove you are the boy.

MICKEY. Yes, sir.

GREYSON. What was your mother's name?

MICKEY. *(Thinking, which is difficult.)* Me mother's name? It was . . . was . . . Irene!

GREYSON. *(Aside, amazed.)* That is true. It was Irene!

(Looks at Mickey with interest.)

When did she die?

MICKEY. Me father kick off first, and she . . . departed . . . a year ago.

GREYSON. Where?

MICKEY. Where?

(He is desperate, then he begins to cry comically.)

Excuse me, sir, but when I think of my departed mother, I . . . I . . .

(Cries louder.)

GREYSON. Come now. You are a big boy.

MICKEY. When do I get the money?

GREYSON. *How* did your mother die?

MICKEY. How?

(Wild moment of panic, then he cries very loud and comically.)

Oh, me poor mother . . .

GREYSON. I must have more proof that she was your mother.

MICKEY. Proof? Oh, I've got proof a-plenty. Here . . . here . . .

(Desperately feels pockets.)

Here's proof. Here's her picture!

GREYSON. Her picture? Surely you don't think you can fool me with some faded photograph?

(Takes picture. Gasps. Aside.)

It is . . . it is Irene!

(Looks at Mickey.)

Could it be possible? Are you . . . John Talbot?

MICKEY. Yes, sir. Waiting for me fortune!

(Aside.)

There ain't nobody that can stop me now!

(Hero music, Cue 39, as Dick enters R and knocks at "door." Music stops.)

ROSWELL. *(Crosses and opens "door.")* Someone is knocking at the door.

DICK. *(Proudly hands Roswell book.)* I have finished reading *Little Men* by Miss Louisa May Alcott, and I am returning it to Miss Ida.

GREYSON. *(Aside, elated.)* Richard! He has arrived at the right time.

MICKEY. *(Aside, frightened.)* Ragged Dick! He's come at the wrong time!

GREYSON. Come in.

(Dick enters "room.")

I believe we have found John Talbot.

DICK. Him?

MICKEY. *(Trying to bluff.)* John Talbot . . . named after me father.

DICK. His name is Mickey Maguire, and he never saw his father!

MICKEY. It's a lie!

DICK. It's the truth!

GREYSON. He has Irene's picture.

DICK. Then he stole it from somebody. Who'd you steal it from?

MICKEY. This time I'll pay you off!

(Fists ready.)

DICK. I'll give you all you want!

(They grab each other and start wrestling. Mickey quickly trips Dick. They fall . . . Mickey on top. As he pounds Dick, he shouts, "Liar . . . liar.")

GREYSON. Boys! Boys! Stop them, Roswell!

(Dick is on top and shouts, "Thief . . . thief.")

ROSWELL. Yes, sir. Gentlemen . . . please.

MICKEY. *(In a helpless hold.)* Let me go!

DICK. *(Sitting on Mickey, holding him down.)* I can prove to you, sir, he ain't . . .

(Aside.)

isn't . . .

(To Greyson.)

John Talbot. He is a forgery!

(Loud fire alarm and bells are heard.)

GREYSON. What is it?

ROSWELL. The fire bell, sir, and the fire engine.

(Roswell goes to R and exits. Ida runs in from L.)

IDA. There's a big fire, Papa. I can see flames and smoke from my window.

GREYSON. Fire!

ROSWELL. *(Enters R.)* A big fire, sir, on Mott Street!

DICK. *(Jumps up.)* Mott Street!

ROSWELL. The corner of Mott and Park Row.

DICK. The corner? It's *my* house. Mark is alone! Trapped on the top floor! I must help him. Mark must be saved!

(Dick rushes off R.)

GREYSON. To the rescue!

(Fire music begins, Cue 40. Tune, "Petite Overture." Ida, Greyson, Mickey rush off R. Roswell turns the room-flat at L, so the Street Scene is shown.

There is a cross-over of people. A stroboscopic light can help to give a fast running effect as people rush across the stage, ad libbing loudly and excitedly.

Smoke starts to pour from one of the painted building fronts. The stage is lighted with a red glow. There can be a brief fast dance with bucket brigade, etc. Policeman blows whistle and pushes people back at L.)

POLICEMAN. Stand back. Stand back! Let the firemen through!

(People shout, scream, etc. A Fireman enters from door of burning building, helping Mrs. Flanagan, who is weak and coughing. Music stops.)

Stand back. Give them room. Are you all right, Mrs. Flanagan?

MRS. F. Yes . . . yes . . .

POLICEMAN. Is there anyone left? Anyone else inside?

MRS. F. Mark! The match boy! He is alone in the top room!

(Fire music starts again, Cue 41, and Dick, Ida, Greyson, Mickey, Roswell rush in from L.)

DICK. It *is* my house!

(Music stops.)

Mark! Where is Mark?

MRS. F. Inside . . . trapped . . . save him!

FIREMAN. Too late! The house is a blazing furnace!

DICK. *(All look up as he calls.)* Mark!

POLICEMAN. No one can save him *now*!

DICK. I will.

POLICEMAN. You?

DICK. I will rescue him!!

(Hero music, Cue 42, as Dick shields his face with his arm and marches into the burning building. People call, "Come back . . . stop." Music changes to Cue 43, the rescue song, "Marguerite." All line up quickly at footlights, facing audience and sing dramatically.)

ALL. Help! Help! Help!
　　Oh, look . . . the wall is falling!
　　Help! Help! Help!
　　Poor Mark is in there calling.
　　Save him, Dick!
　　Oh, save him from his fate,

Oh, carry him to safety
Ere it is too late.

(All turn and look at burning building at back, except First Soloist, who faces audience and sings.)

Up! Up! Up!
He's made it through the first door!
Up! Up! Up!
He staggers to the next floor!
Up! He stops.
The steps are all ablaze.
He stumbles and he falls,
Into the smoky haze.

(First Soloist turns and faces building with others. Second Soloist faces front and sings. Music changes to "Rumours.")

Will he . . . won't he rescue Mark?
The situation's mighty dark.
He's getting up . . .
He moves ahead . . .
He's in the room . . .
The flames have spread.
He can't see Mark!
The room is smoking . . .
Mark is on the floor . . .
He's choking.
Find him, Dick . . . please look his way.
The Lord may help him if we pray!

(Second Soloist turns and faces building with others. Third Soloist faces front and sings.)

Thank the Lord,
At last he's found him . . .
Lifts him up
With flames around him . . .
Through the smoke and through the fire,
Will he make it or expire?

(All turn and face front and sing. Music changes back to "Marguerite.")

Down, down, down,
Be careful or you'll drop him.

Step by step . . .
Oh, will the danger stop him?
Courage, Dick . . . have courage and you'll win.
Will his strength uphold him
Or will he give in?

(All turn and look at burning building in back, except First Soloist, who faces front and sings. Music changes to "Rumours.")

Now they've reached the second landing.
Crash! The staircase isn't standing.
Jump! Oh, take a chance. Go through it.
Will he? Won't he? He must do it!

(First Soloist turns and faces burning building with others. Second Soloist faces front and sings.)

Jump! He did and caught a wire!
Help! His coat has caught on fire!
Roll before you both get toasted . . .
Over . . . over or you're roasted!

(Second Soloist turns and faces building with others. Third Soloist faces front and sings.)

Off he sheds his coat . . .
Now burning . . .
Crawling forward
Without turning.
Weak! His strength is almost gone . . .
He stops! He falls! He can't go on!

(All turn and face front and sing very softly but intently. Segue to "Marguerite" music.)

Try! Try! Try! With all your strength and power!
Try! Try! Try! Or it's the final hour.

(All turn and face back, except First Soloist, who faces front and sings.)

Look! Look! Look! A miracle's in view . . .

(Second Soloist faces front and sings.)

He moves his arms . . .

(Third Soloist faces front and sings.)

He's reached the door . . .

(All sing. The straight line breaks, forming two lines, one on either side of the door. All point to the door and hold the last note triumphantly.)

And he's come through!

(Door opens. Hero music, Cue 44, as Dick marches in, carrying Mark. Mother Watson enters at L.)

GREYSON. Who . . . who is this boy?

(Aside.)

His face has a familiar look.

MARK. *(Points to photograph Greyson holds.)* My picture! Where did you get my picture?

GREYSON. Your picture?

DICK. So . . . Mickey Maguire stole it from *Mark*!

(Mickey starts to exit R.)

Stop him!

(Policeman grabs him.)

MARK. It is the picture of my mother.

GREYSON. Your mother! Yes! It is Irene you look like. I know by your face you *are* her son!

MOTHER W. *(Aside, DL.)* Curses! Curses!

MICKEY. Let me go. I ain't to blame. Mother Watson did it.

(Mother Watson starts L.)

POLICEMAN. Mother Watson?

(Crosses and grabs her.)

Halt!

GREYSON. Arrest that woman!

MOTHER W. Let loose of me, you rogue!

POLICEMAN. The law holds you now. You will be justly punished for the wickedness you have done.

DICK. Mark! *You* are the lost boy. You are rich!

MARK. *(Aside.)* Rich?

GREYSON. My nephew.

MARK. My uncle.

GREYSON. And you, Richard, you saved his life! You shall be richly rewarded. And I offer you a position in my bank!

DICK. A big reward! Work in a bank! It's come true, Mark. We've made our fortune. We've come from . . . rags to riches!

(Entire company lines up for the finale. Music, Cue 45. Tune, "The Man Who Broke the Bank at Monte Carlo," reprise.)

ALL. *(Sing.)*
If you want to be a millionaire,
It's an easy game today.
You can always find a way
In the good old U.S.A.
You can be just what you want to be
In this land of opportunity,
For with pluck and luck
You'll go from rags to riches.
Be a doctor . . . be a lawyer,
Be a railroad engineer . . .
Be a wealthy financier.
You can pick your own career!
While Old Glory's banner is unfurled,
Any day may bring a bright new world.
For with pluck and luck
You'll go from rags to riches.

(Musical tag.)

Yes, for with pluck and luck
You'll go from rags to riches!

(Curtain.)

ACKNOWLEDGMENTS

"The Sidewalks of New York," by Charles B. Lawlor and James W. Blake, 1894.

"O Susannah," by Stephen Foster, 1848.

"Kings of Bal Masqué," by Theodore Bendix.

"After the Ball," by Charles K. Harris, 1892.

"Here We Go Round the Mulberry Bush," Traditional.

"Funeral March of a Marionette," by Charles Gounod, 1879.

"Glow-Worm," by Paul Lincke, 1902.

"American Patrol," by F. W. Meacham, 1891.

"Flower Song," by Gustav Lange.

"Twinkle, Twinkle, Little Star," by Haydn.

"Midnight Fire Alarm," by Harry Lincoln, 1900.

"The Man Who Broke the Bank at Monte Carlo," by Fred Gilbert.

"The First Noel," Traditional.

"Silent Night," by Franz Gruber, 1818.

"Deck the Hall," Traditional.

"At a Georgia Camp Meeting," by Kerry Mills, 1897.

"Emmet's Lullaby," by J. K. Emmet, 1878.

"Drill, Ye Tarriers, Drill," by Thomas Casey, 1888.

"Petite Overture," by Johann Huss.

"Marguerite," by V. Fassone, 1883, Theme A; "Rumours," by Eva Franklin, 1956, Theme B.

Punch and Judy

The dramatic form of *The Tragical Comedy or Comical Tragedy of Punch and Judy* is adapted from the traditional English Punch and Judy puppet show, from which come certain distinguishing characteristics that determine the framework for the play. The plot is not an unfolding, tightly constructed story with a beginning, middle, and end, but a succession of short confrontations involving Punch. The scenes usually have only two characters, whose movements are limited to those possible for puppets, especially beating one another with a slapstick. The characters constantly engage in direct address to the audience, commenting on events, their thoughts, or each other. The locale remains that of a puppet stage, regardless of the suggested settings of the individual scenes.

Special adaptations of the Punch and Judy form have been made for the needs of the young audience. Traditionally Punch and Judy shows are violent and are performed primarily for adults. Beating and sometimes murdering his antagonists is the most efficient method for Punch to dispose of them so that he may proceed to the next encounter. In this script for children, however, the willful, malicious violence of Punch is reduced to mischievous pranks which either do no lasting harm or are aimed at those who unquestionably deserve the consequences. Punch, who is not warm and appealing in his relationships with the other characters, is exactly that in his direct, open contact with the audience, whom he is delighted to discover. He continues to show his pleasure with their presence and occasionally takes them into his confidence, as when he tells the audience how he plans to repay the doctor for his "cures."

The violence is also tempered through careful treatment of the action. For example, when Punch tosses Little Punch out of the window because he will not stop crying, Toby is coincidentally nearby to catch him. Judy appears carrying Little Punch in a subsequent scene to underscore the fact that the baby was not harmed by the action.

To stimulate audience interest in the characters, the puppets are transformed into human actors in a brief segment of prologue and revert to their original form only at the conclusion of the play. The children are regularly reminded by Punch that they are seeing a play-within-a-play; that the action takes place in a world of make-believe in which anything may happen. That the antics are merely a show is emphasized further by the actions of Toby, who first places a placard on stage which announces the succeeding scene and then arranges the necessary set pieces.

The theme of *Punch and Judy* unites the unrelated episodes in the absence of a strong story with overlapping events. The theme, symbolized by the character and actions of Punch and explicitly stated in dialogue and song, is that within every person there is a desire to defy the traditional restraints of society, and then to prevail unpunished. The exuberance of Punch's comic victories is mollified by the sober realization that as one attains such freedom one becomes less than human.

Punch, who initially makes brief references to the long theatrical history of his characterization, is portrayed as a clever, tricking opportunist with no concern for the rights and feelings of others if they interfere with his own. His selfishness and ego know no bounds. Sometimes, in his mischief, he suffers defeat, but only temporarily. His characteristic expletives have been subdued into terms of insult that are amusing to children.

Punch's exaggerated reactions to the foibles of his fellow men and women are justified because of the absurdity of his antagonists, whose characterizations are undeveloped, and who serve as foils for Punch. He faces a nagging wife whose primary interest in him is to force him into the role of a conforming husband with a secure job, a pedantic professor who would have him fill his brain with lists of facts, an unqualified doctor who would cure his injuries with "doses from the slapstick," a stupid hangman who is unable to explain to the victim how one is hanged, and a deceptive devil who is after his soul.

In contrast to the others, Toby and Hector, the animals of the cast, are the only ones whose victories over Punch are not reversed, but as characters they, too, are not defined in depth. To differentiate them from the human characters, animal sounds and movements are their only means of communicating with Punch. Occasionally, when their sounds must be understood, Punch restates the meaning in words.

The characters of the devil and the ghosts are presented in such a way that their capacity to alarm is mitigated. The awesomeness of the ghosts is softened not only by their comic "Boo" to the audience, but by the fact that Punch is able to fool them. When the devil enters in the midst of the frightening red glow and smoke, he immediately establishes rapport with the audience by singing and speaking directly to them.

Although the play has no dominant story line with tightly interwoven events, Punch's series of confrontations create a strong forward movement, propelled by the major dramatic question, which is not, "Will Punch succeed?" but "How will he succeed this time?"

The brief rapid scenes repeat his conflicts with variety, and each builds to a climax, often with abundant use of the slapstick. Sometimes he loses temporarily, as with Judy and the Policeman. In other scenes, the characters' meanness and stupidity makes him deserving of success, as with the doctor and the professor. His victories, even over such unconquerable foes as death (as the hangman) and the devil himself, build in intensity, and the last victory provides the highest climax of the play.

Basically a series of two-character episodes, the scenes sometimes overlap, as a new adversary arrives before the former has left. In several scenes a character who will soon be his victim finds Punch waiting in defeat at the hands of another. The most important exception to the two-character format helps build the climax which closes Act One. Most of Punch's opponents up to that time appear *en masse* to accuse him in song of his wrongdoings. Characteristically, Punch has the final word.

Dialogue is intimately interwoven with song throughout the play. Speech flows into the lyrics of song and as easily becomes dialogue again. The brief, funny lines create a lively, fast-moving dialogue which never falls into predictable patterns of rhythm, rhyme, and word choice. The quality of the unexpected makes the exchanges sizzle with excitement and zaniness.

Play on words within an exchange between characters is an important source of humor because of the resulting misunderstanding. The double meaning in the language is occasionally made even funnier by action, as in the scene with the doctor.

Another source of amusement is Punch's steady stream of short riddles. Usually, his riddles are recognizable favorites with a predictable ending in which he asks and answers his own question. In some instances the riddle is part of the conversation between Punch and another character.

The amount of song is nearly equal to that of dialogue, and its use is varied greatly. Each episode of conflict includes song to highlight moments of action, and musical interludes connect most of the scenes as a unifying device. Punch accents his comic lines with a sung "Rootle-dee-tootle-dee-toot" and a quick little dance, both accompanied by music. Six of the characters have at least one musical number of their own, including Hector, who does not sing but dances. All the characters who sing, except Toby, do so to express the particular restraint they wish to impose on Punch. Eerie mood music makes the foolish ghosts more awesome, but the devil's gleeful song reduces his lurking evil. Punch and Judy close the play with "There'll Always Be a Punch and Judy" and, as they sing, return to being puppets.

The spectacle requirements of *Punch and Judy* are few, for locales are set primarily through the dialogue. The play opens on a deserted stage with only a faded puppet booth. Although the action immediately moves to the stage, the booth remains in place on stage as a reminder that the source of the play is a puppet show.

Punch and Judy is a bright, quickly paced comedy with sober overtones which is drawn together by the antics of the irrepressible Punch in conflict with the characters of his world.

The Comical Tragedy or
Tragical Comedy of

Punch and Judy

A Play with Music in Six Scenes
and Several Interludes

by Aurand Harris

An adaptation suggested by various traditional
Punch and Judy puppet plays

Original music by Glenn Mack

(Except for Punch, Judy, and Toby, all the other parts may be played by three or four actors, making it possible for the play to be performed by a cast of six or seven.)

SCENE

A deserted Punch and Judy puppet theatre.

Scenes of the Puppet Play :

1. Home, Sweet Home
2. Dog Bites Nose
   Professor Loses Head
3. Dancing Horse
   Dr. Cure-All

4. Fly Away Baby
   Off to Jail
5. Hung by a Rope
6. Out Pops the Devil

An intermission is optional.

Punch and Judy

(There is soft music. Cue 2, "There Will Always Be a Punch and Judy," and the curtains open. On a bare stage, in subdued light, stands an old Punch and Judy puppet theatre. The words "Punch and Judy" are faded, the little curtain is drawn, and a large sign reads "Closed." After a pause, the little curtain shakes. Toby, a hand-puppet dog, peeks out. He looks to R and barks sadly, then to L and gives another mournful bark. He shakes his head and gives a loud, sighing growl. He leans out, points to the sign, shakes his head, lifts his head and howls sadly, then collapses with a big sigh. He lifts his head inquiringly, looks quickly to each side, then toward audience, sees the children, barks excitedly, holds out his paws eagerly, then claps happily. He barks loudly, meaning "Stay there," and waves. He disappears behind the little curtain but immediately reappears and barks again, "Stay there," waves, and disappears. The barking continues, and Toby, an actor dressed like the dog puppet, enters from behind the puppet theatre and hurries downstage. Cue 3 optional. Lights come up gradually. Over the footlights he greets the children again with happy barks, waves, and a wagging of his tail. He runs to puppet theatre, lifts his head, and barks loudly.)

PUNCH. *(Off, inside the puppet theatre.)* What's going on? What's going on? What's up?

(Toby twists and barks and points, trying to tell Punch there are children out front. The little curtain moves violently and Punch, a hand puppet, appears.)

What's the calling? What's the brawling? What's up?

(Toby barks and motions for Punch to look at the audience.)

Quiet! Go back to sleep.

(Toby shakes his head and barks. Punch leans over the stage shelf and talks consolingly.)

I know. You want to give a puppet show. So do I. But no one comes to see Punch and Judy any more. Mister Puppet Man has gone and left us. We are faded and old and forgotten. Go—go to sleep. Our little show is over.

(Toby turns to audience, shakes his head angrily, and barks with determination. Punch, surprised, looks at Toby again. Toby runs to footlights, barks, and motions toward audience.)

What is it? Who is it? Is someone there?

(He peers. Toby barks and motions for children to answer, too.)

Who? Children! An audience! Have you come to see the puppet show?

(Sings and dances.)

Well, rootle-dee-tootle—dee-toot! We've been saved, Toby!

(Toby barks.)

Punch and Judy have been saved by the children. Don't go away. I'll be with you—I'll be with you before you can say—

(Puppet disappears behind little curtain. Punch, an actor dressed exactly like the puppet, immediately hops from behind the puppet theatre.)

—Punch and Judy!

(Dances down to footlights.)

Oh, allaca-zoop, allaca-zand! It's Mr. Punch. Give him a hand.

(He applauds himself. Toby claps and encourages children to applaud. Punch bows.)

How do you do? How *do* you do? How do *you* do?

(Dances.)

Rootle-dee-tootle-dee-toot! How many are here. I'll count.

(Points and counts audience.)

One, two, three, four—five-five!

(Stretches out the word.)

He is a big one! Six, seven, seven-and-a-half. She is a small one. Eight, nine and nine. Twins! And there's Tom. Hello, Dick. Hello, Mary. And Mrs. Bigger and her baby! Which is bigger, Mrs. Bigger *or* her baby?

(Toby barks and shakes his head.)

Why, the *baby*, because he is a *little* bigger!

(Dances.)

Rootle-dee-tootle-dee-toot! We'll give you a show. We'll always give you a show! For your enjoyment we proudly present—the Comical Tragedy—or the Tragical Comedy—of Punch and Judy.

(Aside.)

It is the wickedest play that ever was—and the one that's run the longest.

(Dances.)

Rootle-dee-tootle-dee-toot! I'll call Judy. Oh, Judy's a beauty. Wait until you see her.

(Calls.)

Oh, Judy, my dear. Judy, my love. Judy, my little dove.

(Shouts.)

Judy, stick your head through that curtain!

JUDY. *(Judy, a hand puppet, appears in front of the little curtain of the puppet stage.)* Yes, Mr. Punch?

PUNCH. Knock, knock, knock.

JUDY. Who is there?

PUNCH. Children! Children!

JUDY. *(Peers.)* Children?

PUNCH. Punch and Judy have been saved by the children.

JUDY. Saved by the children! Oh, I'm so happy I am going to cry.

PUNCH. No, Judy. Smile! Everyone laughs at Punch and Judy. Oh, rootle-dee-tootle-dee-toot! Tell me what is black and white and red all over?

JUDY. You tell me.

PUNCH. A blushing zebra! Oh, rootle-dee-tootle-dee-toot! We'll begin the show. Call the others! The doctor, the policeman, the horse, the devil.

Judy. Yes, Mr. Punch. Oh, oh! We're going to have a show!

(Puppet disappears behind curtain.)

Punch. *(To Toby.)* Start the music! Beat the drum. Ring the bell. Oh, rootle-dee-tootle-dee-toot!

(Toby runs quickly behind puppet theatre. Punch points to audience.)

One to get ready. Two for the show. Hold on to your seats. Here —we—go!

(Music begins. Cue 4. Punch runs to L back of puppet theatre. Immediately Toby comes around R of theatre, ringing a bell. Judy, an actor dressed exactly like the puppet, marches after him, hitting a tambourine. Punch follows last, beating a drum. They circle, then line up at front and sing.)

Punch and Judy are coming today,
Punch and Judy are coming this way.
Punch and Judy are near—

(Toby rings bell and barks a long—OOOOOOOOOO.)

Punch and Judy are here.

(Toby repeats bell and howl—OOOOOOOOOO.)

Punch and Judy are coming this way.
Punch and Judy are coming today.

With your kind permission—

Judy. And your polite attention—

Punch. We will begin our Punch—

(She bows to him.)

And Judy—

(He bows to her.)

Show!

(Toby barks a long "OOOOOOOOOO," rings bell, and runs off L. Punch and Judy "cakewalk" off as march music swells. She exits. Punch embraces audience and shouts.)

I love you. I love you.
I love you divine.

Save me your chewing gum,
You're sitting on mine!

(He exits R.)

(Same music continues softly. Toby enters L and puts up sign on an easel which reads, "Scene 1," and exits. The sign may also have printed on it, "Home, Sweet Home." Punch, off R, waves the main curtain. He puts his arm out and waves, then waves his hat, then waves a shoe, then peeks out and grins, pulls back, then lifts a leg out and kicks, peeks out again, pulls back, shakes curtain violently, then marches out to C. He carries a slapstick hooked to his belt. Note: it is advisable to have two extra slapsticks on each side, off stage, in the event that one breaks. Music stops.)

PUNCH. Ladies and gentlemen, how do you do?
If you are all happy, I'm happy too.
Stay and hear my merry little play—
If I make you laugh, I need not make you pay.

(Sings. Cue 5.)

Mr. Punch is a jolly good fellow.
His coat is always scarlet and yellow,
With a bump on his nose and a hump on his back
And a big stick to give you a whack!

(Slaps stick in air. Speaks.)

My fame is known from sea to sea!
My name is known, but pronounced differently.
In Italy—I am called PULCINELLA!

(Italian music. Cue 6. He dances Italian steps and shouts in Italian.)

In Russia—they cheer and I appear—PETRUSHKA!

(Russian music. Cue 7. He dances Russian steps and shouts in Russian.)

In France—they shout and I come out—POLICHINELLE!

(French music. Cue 8. He dances French steps, shouts in French. Sings.)

But—

(Speaks quickly.)

Pulcinella, Petrushka, Polichinelle—

(Sings. Cue 9.)

Anywhere and everywhere,
Whatever the name,
I am always the same,
A bump on my nose and a hump on my back
And a big stick to give you a whack!

Oh, it's so glorious to be so notorious!

(Calls.)

Judy! Judy, my beauty.

(Aside.)

Oh, her eyes twinkle and shine—like mine. Her nose is like a rose—like mine. Her mouth runs from north to south—

(Points to audience.)

like yours! JU—DY!

JUDY. *(Enters R, sweeping with broom. All the scenes can be played downstage, almost leaning over the footlights, as if leaning out from the puppet stage. The close contact with the audience is part of the effectiveness of a puppet show.)*

Mr. Punch, I am sweeping and keeping the house clean . . .

(Sweeps in short strokes, backing Punch across the stage.)

Working all day while you are away . . . Rubbing and scrubbing . . . knitting and sitting . . . like a good wife . . .

(Aside.)

My house . . . my family . . . are the joys of my life.

PUNCH. *(Romantically.)* Oh, Judy, my love.

JUDY. Mr. Punch.

PUNCH. Judy, my dove.

JUDY. Mr. Punch.

PUNCH. *(Aside.)* Oh, Judy is my beauty.

(Offers his hand. She takes it. Music. Cue 10. They dance in circle, then face audience. He sings.)

Judy is my wife,
Down the aisle I led her;
She promised to obey me,
That's why I wed her.

(She holds dance pose. He turns to audience and speaks fast.)

Now that I've got her
She'd rule the house and me;
All she ever thinks of—
Is the family.
Now that I've got her
She tries to order me,
But I can tell you who
Will win that victory.
Me!

(They dance, then bow sweetly to each other. Punch aside.)

Watch and see!

(They dance again. The music ends as the dance ends with a bow.)

Judy, my beauty, give us a kiss.

JUDY. I have other things to do—all of them for you.

PUNCH. Come, Judy. A little smack—right on the kisser.

(Puckers mouth.)

JUDY. I have to polish the brass and shine the looking glass.

PUNCH. *(With romantic abandonment.)*

Oh, love is a wiggle thing.
It wiggles like a lizard.
It wraps its tail around your heart
And crawls into your gizzard.

(Dances.)

Rootle-dee-tootle-dee-toot!

JUDY. A husband should think of money, mortgages, and security.

PUNCH. Oh, Judy, don't be an old shoe.

JUDY. An old shoe!

PUNCH. Oh, Judy is an old shoe,
And I'm a fine piece of leather.
Hammered and nailed—
And here we are together!

JUDY. *(Aside.)* He called me an old shoe! I work and work and all you do is Rootle-dee-tootle-dee-too!

PUNCH. *(Dances.)* Pickles are green,
Violets are blue,
I am the boss.
I'll show you.

JUDY. *(Angrily.)* I'll show you what a wife can do!

PUNCH. Give us a kiss.

JUDY. A kiss?

PUNCH. Give us a smack.

(Puckers lips.)

JUDY. A smack?

PUNCH. Right on the smacker.

(Shuts his eyes, ready.)

JUDY. I'll give you a smack.

(Raises broom.)

PUNCH. A big one.

JUDY. A big one! A smack for the money you don't bring home!

(Hits Punch with broom.)

A smack for the husband you should be!

(Hits again.)

PUNCH. Oh, Judy! You kiss too hard!

JUDY. And a smack for the family!

(Hits him again.)

PUNCH. Stop! Stop kissing me! No more kisses! No more kisses, please!

JUDY. Remember you are a husband, a father, a breadwinner!

PUNCH. I am Mr. Punch. I am—me!

JUDY. *(Sweetly.)* Now I will cook and bake and make your favorite dish.

(Sweeping to R.)

Mend and patch each hole, and feed the goldfish in the bowl.

(Aside.)

Oh, life is sweet. Life is complete in my home, sweet home.

(Exits R.)

PUNCH. *(Sings, comically. Cue 11.)*

Oh, Mr. Punch is a sad, sad fellow.
His coat is always scarlet and yellow,
With a lump on his nose and a bump on his back,
And on his head he got a whack!

Some men fight dragons. Some men fight windmills. Mr. Punch hereby announces—he will fight for his right—to be free!

(Sings. Cue 12.)

Nobody is going to make and shape, roll and mold me in a form,
Nobody is going to make and take and break me 'til I conform.
Each rope, each chain, each fetter that would hold and mold all men fast,
I'll fight, I'll fight, I'll fight, I'll fight, I'll fight them all to the last.
I will be—the man *every* man wants to be.

I'll be—me!

(Holds stick high. Sings fast and joyfully. Cue 12A.)

I'll give a smack, smack, smack on the chin.
I'll give a whack, whack, whack on the shin.
A whack-whack, a smack-smack, and I'll win!

Let's begin!

(Dances off R.)

Rootle-dee-tootle-dee-toot!

SCENE TWO

(Music. Cue 13. Toby appears at L, puts up second sign which reads, "Scene 2." It may also have printed on it, "Dog Bites Nose. Professor Loses Head." Toby wears a large cap and a large bow around his neck. Also around his neck hangs a hand-mirror. He admires himself in the looking-glass. At C he sings.)

TOBY. *(To audience.)*

> I've got my cap set for you,
> I've got my tie tied for you,
> I've trimmed my beard for you,
> I've got my eye on you.

> Be my friend, be my pal,
> Be my buddy, be my gal,
> Cross your heart and swear it's true,
> And I'll be a pal to you . . .

(Holds up mirror and reflects light from it onto faces in the audience.)

> To you . . . to you . . . to you . . . to you.

> I've got my cap set for you,
> I've got my tie tied for you,
> I've trimmed my beard for you,
> I've got my eye on you.

> Without a friend, without a pal,
> Without a buddy, without a gal,
> It's a life I don't recommend,
> It's a dog's life without a friend.

(Reflects light from mirror again onto faces in audience.)

> Come on—

> Be my friend, be my pal,
> Be my buddy, be my gal,
> Cross your heart and swear it's true,
> And I'll be a pal to you . . .
> To you . . . to you . . . to you . . . to you.

> I've got my cap set for you,
> I've got my tie tied for you,
> I've trimmed my beard for you,

I've got my eye—eye—eye—
I've got my eye on you.

(Toby exits L and immediately returns and bows and exits.)

PUNCH. *(Enter R.)* Toby. Toby.

(Toby enters and bows again, throwing kisses.)

Toby. Toby! Go away. Get off the stage.

(Toby keeps bowing.)

Toby! It is Scene Two. Go! Get! Skdoo!

(Toby gives him an aloof look, shakes his tail at him and continues to bow to audience.)

Tob—y!

(Raises his stick. Toby turns on him, growls, and raises fists.)

I think he woke up on the wrong side of the bed.

(Toby growls louder.)

I think he fell out of the bed!

(Toby growls.)

Nice Toby. Sweet Toby. Look at him smile.

(Toby bares his teeth and advances.)

He wants to shake hands. Here old friend, take my hand.

(Toby bites Punch's hand.)

Oh! He thinks it is a piece of baloney. I said "Shake." Not "Bite."

(Toby growls and puts up fists.)

Oh, you want to fight. All right! Round one!

(They circle, facing each other. Music optional. Cue 14. Toby hits at Punch.)

Round two!

(Punch gives him a hit with the stick.)

Round three!

(Toby bites and holds Punch's nose.)

Oh, my nose! Let go! Let go! O-o-oh! You bit my nose. My beautiful nose!

(Punch sits wailing.)

TOBY. *(Dances to side, sings. Cue 15.)*

I've got my eye—eye—eye—
I've got my eye on you.

(He takes a final bow and exits.)

PUNCH. *(Rises.)* Judy! Help! Judy, come. Judy, run! Mr. Punch has been eaten—for lunch!

JUDY. *(Enters R, sweeping.)* Shout! Shout! Shout! What is it about?

PUNCH. My nose! My beautiful nose. Oh, Judy, how will I smell without a nose?

JUDY. *(Pointedly.)* Terrible.

(Exits R, sweeping.)

PUNCH. *(Wails loudly.)* O-o-oh! When you smile the world smiles with you, but when you cry—you use your own handkerchief.

(Takes handkerchief from pocket, dabs eye, holds handkerchief away, squeezes concealed sponge, and water drips.)

O-o-o-oh!

(Wipes other eye, holds handkerchief away, squeezes tightly, and much water pours.)

O-o-o-o-oh!

PROFESSOR. *(Enters L.)* Mr. Punch. Good morning. Good afternoon. Good evening. How do you do.

PUNCH. *(Awed.)* Who are you?

PROFESSOR. I am the Professor, Ph.D, A.B.C., M.A., U.S.A.

PUNCH. A professor!

PROFESSOR. A teacher. My head is full, crowded, crawling with information, observations, and generalizations.

PUNCH. He's got a big head!

PROFESSOR. I make and shape the mass media. I am a walking, talking encyclopedia.

PUNCH. That's the trouble with teachers. All they do is talk.

PROFESSOR. Problem one. What is one thing a bird can do which you cannot do?

PUNCH. Take a bath in a saucer! Rootle-dee-tootle-dee-toot.

PROFESSOR. We will now verify, clarify, and qualify your knowledge of dogs.

PUNCH. Oh, I have a dog.

(Calls.)

Toby. Toby.

PROFESSOR. Is he a *bird* dog?

PUNCH. No. He can't sing a note. Rootle-dee-tootle-dee-toot!

PROFESSOR. Is he a *watch* dog?

PUNCH. No. When I hear a noise I bark myself. Wolf-wolf-wolf!

PROFESSOR. Mr. Punch, I must teach you your responsibilities.

PUNCH. Responsibilities?

PROFESSOR. To your wife, your home, your country. You must—reform.

PUNCH. Reform?

PROFESSOR. And conform! Throw away your stick. The days of whacking are over. Instead—use your head. Fill your head with dates and weights, historical situations and geographical locations.

PUNCH. Stop! Your head will pop!

PROFESSOR. Good or poor or mean or rich, each man must fit into a niche. Learn the rule and pass the test.

PUNCH. *(Aside.)* And be a fool like all the rest? No. I will be—Mr. Punch.

PROFESSOR. Lesson one.

PUNCH. School has begun!

PROFESSOR. I will give you something for your head.

PUNCH. No. I will give *you* something instead!

(Raises stick.)

PROFESSOR. Ready?

PUNCH. Ready!

(Swings stick.)

PROFESSOR. Fact one.

PUNCH. Whack one!

(Slaps at Professor.)

Don't try to chain, rein, or bridle me!

PROFESSOR. Help. My head is whirling.

PUNCH. Or tie, twine, or shackle me!

(Slaps.)

PROFESSOR. Help. My head is swirling.

PUNCH. Don't try to curb or bind or muzzle me!

(Slaps.)

PROFESSOR. No more facts! My head is full.

PUNCH. Don't tell me what to do! I'll paddle my own canoe!

(Slaps.)

PROFESSOR. Help! Help! I am *losing* my head!

(Runs behind puppet theatre at L.)

PUNCH. *(Aside.)* Big heads always do!

(Runs behind puppet theatre at L. There is a big crash.)

PROFESSOR. *(Off, shouts.)* HELP! I HAVE LOST MY HEAD!

(Immediately the Professor's body runs out from the R side of puppet theatre, but without a head. Professor ducks inside his robe, which covers his head. Headless, he darts this way and that, exiting at R. Punch follows his zigzag path, holding the Professor's head [papier-mâché with hat on it] on a stick, which he picked up as he ran behind the puppet theatre.)

PUNCH. *(Happily waves at audience.)* Rootle-dee-tootle-dee-toot!

(He exits R, dancing.)

SCENE THREE

(Toby enters L and changes sign, which reads, "Scene 3." It may also have printed on it, "Dancing Horse. Dr. Cure-All." He waves and exits. Off R, the head of a horse peeks around the curtain. Then Hector, a comical dancing horse—two actors under horse costume—canters to C. He pats his foot—one—two—three, and the music starts. Cue 16. Hector, with great abandonment, dances. His fast dance is suddenly stopped by Punch calling off R. Hector stops. Music stops. Hector looks off R, then runs UC to puppet theatre, hides at the L side of it, head concealed behind it, but his back legs still in view.)

PUNCH. *(Off R.)* Hector! Hector! Where are you? Hec—tor-or-or.

(Enters and crosses.)

Hector! Hector! My horse has run away. Hector! Hector! This is Scene Three. Now where the heck can Hector be!

(He exits L. Hector immediately canters downstage and taps his foot—one—two—three. Music starts. Hector dances wildly. The dance is stopped again by Punch calling off L. Hector hides at R of puppet theatre. Punch calls off.)

Hector! Hector! Hec—tor—or—or!

(Enters L.)

Hector! Where can my horse be? Hector! Hector! Oh, where in the heck is Hec-Hec-Hector!

(He exits R. Hector comes DC and taps his foot—one—two—three. Music starts and Hector dances. Punch re-enters.)

Hector!

(Dancing and music stop.)

Hector, you are dancing again.

(Hector nods his head.)

And you are dancing in public!

(Hector lowers his head.)

How many times must I tell you—a horse does not dance. A horse is a noble beast.

(Hector nods.)

He runs.

(Hector runs in one spot.)

He trots.

(Hector trots.)

He jumps.

(Hector jumps.)

He gallops.

(Hector gallops.)

But he never dances.

(Hector bows his head low, then slowly collapses to the floor.)

Come! We must do the next scene. The famous scene when Punch rides the horse!

(Dances.)

Rootle-dee-tootle-dee-toot. This is the part I like! You will see how gracefully I ride without a saddle, stirrup, spur, or dangles! Watch Punch ride in circles, squares, and rectangles!

(Straddles the collapsed horse.)

Hector! Up! Leap, lope, gallop away.

(Slaps stick in air. Hector shakes his head. Punch turns around, straddling and facing the back end of the horse.)

Hector! Getty-up, getty-up, getty-up—GO!

(Hits slapstick at Hector's rump. Hector suddenly stands up, shaking and bucking. Punch yells and falls off. Hector gallops in a circle around him, kicks a back foot at Punch on the ground and exits R.)

Help! Help! Help! I've been kicked. Oh, my head! Oh, my feet! Oh, my seat! Judy! Come! Judy! Help!

JUDY. *(Enters R, stirring with a spoon in a bowl.)* Shout, shout, shout. What is the noise about? I am making and baking and spicing and icing a cake.

PUNCH. Get the doctor. Run! Run! Run! Oh, doctor, come, come, come—before—I die.

(Falls back stiffly.)

JUDY. *(Alarmed.)* He is hurt! He is in pain. He has been slain! What will become of me? Of my home? Of my family? Oh, Mr. Punch, remain. Oh, doctor come. Oh, St. Pa-nat-o-my! Mr. Punch has had a punch in his a-nat-o-my!

(Judy exits L. Music starts for a series of fast crosses. Cue 17. First Toby skips across jumping a rope. He exits R.)

PUNCH. *(Sits up.)* Oh, doctor. No!

(He falls backward. As Toby exits, Professor's body, long robe without a head, but carrying a head on a stick, runs across from R to L and exits. Punch sits up.)

Oh, doctor. No!

(He falls backward. Hector gallops across from R to C, does a dance step, kicks his back leg toward Punch, and runs off. Punch sits up.)

Oh, doctor. No!

(Punch falls back again.)

DOCTOR. *(Enters R. He is wild and comical.)* The doctor is here. The doctor is here!

(Music stops.)

PUNCH. *(Sits up.)* Oh, doctor.

DOCTOR. *(Points at Punch.)* Someone is ill! Someone wants a pill!

(Sings with fervor. Cue 18.)

Oh, I examine every part,
Lungs and your liver and your heart.
Oh, oh, oh,
I can't wait *(Shivers.)* until I start!
Oh, stethoscope and microscope—
With a knife and doctor there is hope.
Oh, oh, oh,
I can't wait *(Shivers.)* until I start.
If you have a break, a bruise, an itch,

I will cut and sew a fancy stitch.
Oh, palpitation, vaccination,
Circulation, hallucination—
Oh, oh, oh,
I can't wait. *(Shivers.)* I have to start!

PUNCH. Oh, doctor!

DOCTOR. *(Jumps with joy.)* A patient!

(Runs to Punch.)

PUNCH. I am dying—dying—

(Falls back stiffly.)

—dead.

DOCTOR. Tell me, Mr. Punch, how long have you been dead?

PUNCH. *(Rises.)* Three years.

(Falls back.)

DOCTOR. When did you die?

PUNCH. *(Sits up.)*

Yesterday.

DOCTOR. Oh, blood and bones and kidney stones! I must examine you. Let me see your pulse.

(Holds Punch's wrist. Nods head and taps foot in rhythm.)

A-one, a-two, a-three. A waltz! Let me hear your tongue.

(Punch puts out tongue and says a prolonged "Ah.")

Say "Three" four times.

PUNCH. Twelve.

DOCTOR. Twelve?

PUNCH. I am in a hurry!

(Puts tongue out and shouts, "Ah, ha-ha-ha-ha.")

DOCTOR. *(Happy and excited.)* Smelling salts and turpentine, rubbing alcohol and iodine—stand up.

PUNCH. *(Getting up.)* Oh, doctor. I will never be able to stand up— see.

(Stands.)

DOCTOR. What is the time?

(Takes out a 12-inch watch.) Ah, it is time—to time the beat of your heart. I will time. You will beat.

PUNCH. Beat?

DOCTOR. Beat.

PUNCH. *(Nods, smiles, and raises stick.)* Beat!

DOCTOR. Ready?

PUNCH. Ready!

DOCTOR. *(Puts one hand on Punch's chest, holds watch with other.)*

Time!

(Doctor nods.)

Beat!

(Punch nods.)

One . . . two . . . three . . .

PUNCH. Out goes he!

(Slaps at doctor.)

DOCTOR. Stop! Stop! Your heart is beating too fast!

(Shakes watch.)

Oh, time is running out. It is half past time—to take your medicine.

(Hands watch to Punch.)

PUNCH. Ah, see—time flies.

(Tosses watch off R.)

DOCTOR. *(Gleefully.)* Oh, medicine, lotions, herbs, and potions—I love you all!

(Hands doctor's bag to Punch, who holds it. Sings. Cue 19.)

A pinch of sulphur, whiff of slate,
Mix and grind and add some fishing bait.

(Pulls wiggling worm from bag.)

Oh, oh, oh,
I can't—I can't—I can't wait.
Cherry root, an onion shoot,
Apple cider, and a spider,

(Pulls wiggly spider from bag.)

Oh, oh, oh,
I can't wait—*(Pause.)*—until I start.
With a dew dewberry duplicate,
With a lizard's gizzard medicate!
Oh, vaccinate, fumigate,
Oh, lubricate, intoxicate.
Oh, oh, oh,
I can't—I can't—I can't wait!

Get ready. Open your eyes. Shut your mouth and take your medicine.

(Grabs Punch and shakes him.)

PUNCH. What are you doing?

DOCTOR. *(Aside.)* Shake well before taking!

(Takes slapstick from Punch.)

First a dose for fever—

(Slaps at Punch.)

For chills up your back—

(Slaps at Punch.)

For whooping cough and sacroiliac!

(Slaps.)

PUNCH. I don't like your medicine.

DOCTOR. For influenza, extra doses—for sniffles and tuberculosis—

(Slaps.)

For lumps and bumps—

PUNCH. Stop! No more medicine!

DOCTOR. For humps and mumps and halitosis!

(Slaps.)

PUNCH. Stop! No more medicine! I am well!

DOCTOR. Well?

(Sings, elated. Cue 20.)

Wonder—wonder—wonder—wonder, wonderful is medicine.
I'm certain you'll agree.
Oh, wonder—wonder—wonder—wonder, wonderful is medi-
cine.
I'm certain you'll agree.

PUNCH. *(Sings, aside.)*

Not the medicine he gives to me.
Not the medicine he gives to me.

DOCTOR. Oh, take a dose—

(Holds up stick.)

PUNCH. Oh, no, no, no.

DOCTOR. Oh, take another—

PUNCH. No, no, no, no, no!

DOCTOR. Oh, one more. Oh—

PUNCH. No, no.

DOCTOR. Oh, wonderful is medicine!
And you are out of bed!

PUNCH. Or dead!

DOCTOR. Now you must pay me. Pay the doctor's fee.

(Holds out hand.)

PUNCH. Pay you?

DOCTOR. I cured you. You pay me.

PUNCH. Oh.

(Smiles with an idea, takes stick.)

Certainly.

(Aside.)

I'll pay him back. I'll give him back every whack he gave me!

Are you ready? Shut your eyes. Open your mouth and take *your* medicine.

(Slaps.)

DOCTOR. Stop! A doctor never takes his own medicine.

PUNCH. *(Sings without music.)*

Wonder—wonder—wonderful is medicine—
For shivers and shakes and twisters—measles, warts, and blisters!

(Slaps.)

DOCTOR. Help! Help!

(Runs. Aside.)

Is there a doctor in the house?

PUNCH. For heat and fever parches; feet and fallen arches!

(Slaps.)

DOCTOR. Help! Help! A nurse! A bed! Before the doctor—is dead!

(Exits L.)

PUNCH. *(Sings loudly and joyfully. Cue 21.)*

Wonder—wonder—wonder—wonder, wonderful is medicine.
I'm certain I agree.
Oh, wonder—wonder—wonder—wonder, wonderful is medicine
When it's not given to me!

(He exits dancing at R.)

SCENE FOUR

(Toby enters from L and starts to change the sign. Hector peeks in at R and enters. Toby quickly looks to R and to L, then nods his head and motions horse to C. Cue 22.)

TOBY. Presenting Hector the Dancing Horse—in—a Dance of the Nations.

(Hector bows.)

From Ireland—the Irish jig.

(Hector does a fast jig. Music. Cue 23.)

From Austria—the Vienna waltz.

(Hector waltzes to waltz music. Cue 24.)

From Scotland—the Highland Fling.

(Hector does a funny Highland Fling. Cue 25.)

From Hawaii—the hula hula.

(Hector circles, twisting his hips. Cue 26.)

And last a march from the U.S.A.!

(March music. Cue 27. Hector marches with high steps. Toby puts small American flag in horse's mouth, which Hector waves as he exits. Toby applauds. Hector runs back in, bows, starts dancing again, and dances off R. Toby goes to sign, puts up new one, which reads, "Scene 4." It may also have printed on it, "Fly Away Baby. Off to Jail." Toby exits.

Judy enters R with a rag-doll baby in her arms. She hums and comes to C and sings. Cue 28.)

JUDY. Sleep, sleep, sleep, little baby,
   You've had a busy day.
   Sleep, sleep, sleep, little baby,
   Dream the night away.
   Rock-a-by, rock-a-by, rock-a-by, rock-a-rock-a-a-by.

PUNCH. *(Calls, off R.)* Oh, Judy! Judy, my beauty!

JUDY. Sh, Mr. Punch. You will wake the baby.

PUNCH. *(Off.)* Judy, I am hun—gry.

JUDY. I cooked you an egg omelet.

PUNCH. *(Enters R.)* I ate it, but next time—break the eggs.

(Dances.)

Rootle-dee-tootle-dee-toot.

JUDY. Sh! The baby is asleep.

PUNCH. *(Tiptoes to Judy, baby-talk, punches baby harder and harder in the stomach.)* Oh, little Punchie-Punchie joy. You are Mr. Punch's Punchie-boy.

(Aside.)

Isn't that a picture! Oh, Judy is my beauty. Did you know we were married in a bathtub? It was a double-ring ceremony. Rootle-dee-tootle-dee-toot.

JUDY. Sh!

PUNCH. Sh!

JUDY. Take the baby, Mr. Punch. I am going around the corner.

PUNCH. Me rock the baby? That's a mother's duty.

JUDY. I forgot the bread, the cabbage head, and the jelly spread.

PUNCH. *(Aside.)* She is so forgetful she powders her shoes and shines her nose.

JUDY. Take the baby.

PUNCH. *(Screws up his face.)* I can't. I have a cold in my head.

JUDY. Oh, how can you say so many stupid things in one day?

PUNCH. I get up early! Oh, rootle-dee-tootle-dee-toot.

JUDY. It is a father's duty to help care for the baby.

PUNCH. Duties, duties, duties.

JUDY. Are you big enough, brave enough to look after a baby? Are you a man or a mouse? Well, squeak up!

PUNCH. *(Grabs baby.)* Give him to me. I'll rock him. I'll knock him. I'll sock him!

JUDY. Be careful!

PUNCH. *(Sings, comically. Cue 29.)*
Sleep, sleep, sleep, little baby,
You've had a busy day.
Sleep, sleep, sleep, little baby,
Dream the night away . . .

JUDY. I will be right back. You can wave from the window as I pass.

(She points to L. Toby enters L, carrying a window, which is a self-standing unit. He places it at L and exits.)

JUDY. Goodby, little Punch.

(Punch starts to sing loudly.)

Sh!

(Going off R.)

Let me think. Bread . . . cabbage head . . . jelly spread. No, no, instead . . . salt . . . malt . . . custard and mustard!

(Exits R.)

PUNCH. Confused . . . confused. Judy is so confused she is knitting a sweater with spaghetti! Rootle-dee-tootle-dee-toot.

(Tosses baby around. To audience.)

Sh! you will wake the baby. That's a good idea. It's no fun sleeping the day away.

(Shakes baby violently.)

Oh, little Punch! What would your nose be if it were twelve inches long? A foot!

(Tosses baby high in air.)

Rootle-dee-tootle-dee-toot. Wake up! We'll have fun! We'll put bugs in jars and smoke cigars!

(Whirls baby around by feet.)

Wake up! Wake up!

(Baby cries loudly.)

Quiet! Quiet!

(To audience.)

Now see what you did! You made him cry! Quiet! Quiet!

(Shouts.)

Stop! Shut up! Stop. Don't cry. Stop or you'll get a black eye!

(Baby cries louder.)

Oh, stop the waterworks. Turn off the waterfall!

(Runs to R.)

Judy! Judy! What will I do? Judy, he's calling for you!

(Shakes and tosses baby high.)

Stop the yelling. Stop the bellowing!

(Holds baby out to audience.)

Here, you take him. Take him . . . take him . . . shake him . . . shame him. Oh, flood! Get a boat. Get a float. Swim for your life!

(By window, calls.)

Judy, are you there? I'm drowning. Give me air! Judy, please pass by.

(Swings baby as if going to throw it through the window as he sings. Cue 30. Toby enters, and moves about to catch the baby.)

Fly, fly, fly, little baby,
Fly, fly away.
Fly, fly, fly, little baby,
I've had enough today.

One . . . two . . . three . . . goodby!

(Throws baby through the window. Toby catches it and exits.)

JUDY. *(Enters R.)* I heard a cry like a baby. Then it stopped—like it was dropped. Mr. Punch, where is the baby?

PUNCH. The baby?

JUDY. The baby.

PUNCH. The little angel?

JUDY. The little angel!

PUNCH. The little angel—flew away.

(Motions to window.)

JUDY. *(Runs to window.)* Flew away!

PUNCH. Out the window.

JUDY. Mr. Punch, you threw the baby out the window!

PUNCH. I gave him a little help.

JUDY. You big nose, red nose, lobster nose, know-nothing! I'll make you cry for help!

(Takes his stick.)

PUNCH. *(Aside, innocently.)* Every father wants to throw a crying baby out the window. I did it!

JUDY. You selfish, selfish tootle-dee-toot.

(Slaps at him.)

You mean-minded, hard-hearted galoot!

(Slaps at him.)

PUNCH. Help! No, Judy. No more kisses.

(Runs.)

JUDY. You double-dyed, cross-eyed, tongue-tied goof!

(Slaps.)

You half-wit, dim-wit, nitwit nincompoop!

(Slaps.)

PUNCH. I know you love me, Judy, but no more kisses. No more kisses.

JUDY. *(He runs. She chases, hitting when she can.)* Muddlehead, addlehead, dope head, empty head, bonehead, pinhead, blockhead, wooden head!

PUNCH. Stop!

(Grabs stick.)

I am Mr. Punch! No one punches me! I'll show you how and what a husband should be. Here are a few kisses from me! A smack and a whack!

(Slaps at her.)

JUDY. *(Running.)* Help! Help!

PUNCH. A kiss and a hug and a squeeze!

(Slaps.)

JUDY. Help! Help! Save me!

PUNCH. A little cuddling and wooing! A little billing and cooing!

(Slaps.)

JUDY. Save me! Doctor, lawyer, merchant—POLICE! POLICE!

(Exits R.)

PUNCH. *(Gives a triumphal slap and sings. Cue 31.)*

Oh Mr. Punch is a jolly good fellow,
His coat is always scarlet and yellow.
His wife and his baby he gave a toss,
And now he is—his very own boss!

Rootle-dee-tootle-dee-toot. I've done it! No family ties for me. Mr. Punch is free!

(There are three loud, slow knocks off R.)

Knock—knock—knock.

(Three knocks are repeated.)

Someone is coming after me! Oh, what have I done? What have I done? *Whatever* I've done was done in fun!

POLICEMAN. *(Off.)* Open the door! Open the door in the name of the law!

PUNCH. The police!

POLICEMAN. *(Enters R.)* Mr. Punch.

PUNCH. He knows my name!

POLICEMAN. I am a policeman.

PUNCH. But I don't want the police.

POLICEMAN. But the police wants you!

PUNCH. Oh.

POLICEMAN. I have a notation in my pocket to lock you up.

(Turns and reaches into pocket.)

PUNCH. I have a notion to knock you down.

(Raises stick. Policeman turns. Punch smiles and puts stick down.)

POLICEMAN. Here is a list of your offences. Do you know your rights?

PUNCH. Yes, this is my rights and this is my lefts.

(Holds out right and left hands.)

POLICEMAN. *(Holds up narrow scroll.)* You hit a dog.

PUNCH. He bit me first.

POLICEMAN. You smacked your wife.

PUNCH. It was a kiss.

POLICEMAN. You cracked a professor.

PUNCH. His head was too full.

POLICEMAN. You whacked a doctor.

PUNCH. I gave him back his own medicine.

POLICEMAN. You threw a baby out the window.

PUNCH. What else can you do with a crying baby?

POLICEMAN. You will be in jail a *long* time.

PUNCH. But it was a *short* baby.

POLICEMAN. When you break the law, there are other laws to punish you. You are under suspicion.

PUNCH. *(Looks up.)* I am?

POLICEMAN. You are under arrest.

PUNCH. Oh, no—no! Mr. Punch is free. I won't go. You will have to catch me!

(Runs.)

POLICEMAN. You cannot escape the arm of the law.

(Extends his arm and runs after him.)

PUNCH. Help! Judy! Judy, my beauty! Help! Save me!

(Runs into audience.)

POLICEMAN. The law will catch you!

(Blows whistle and runs after him into audience.)

PUNCH. Oh, Tom! Dick! And Mary! Save me. It was all in fun.

(Looks over shoulder.)

O-o-oh, Mr. Punch, run, run, run!

POLICEMAN. Desperate criminal loose in town! Dangerous man turning law upside down!

PUNCH. Call the police! Oh, police, save me from the police!

POLICEMAN. Search and find every clue and trick. Find the man with the stick.

(Blows whistle.)

PUNCH. Someone guide me! Someone hide me!

(Grabs scarf and lady's purse from first row.)

Thank you.

(Puts scarf over his head and runs back onstage.)

POLICEMAN. Stop!

(Blows whistle and points.)

Mr. Punch, the law has caught you and brought you to justice.

PUNCH. *(Speaks in woman's voice.)* I am an old lady, sir. Are you talking to me?

POLICEMAN. Oh, I am sorry, madam. I beg your pardon, lady.

PUNCH. I should think so! Stand aside, young man, and let a lady pass.

(Swings pocketbook at Policeman and walks away.)

POLICEMAN. Mr. Punch! Mr. Punch has escaped!

(Blows whistle.)

PUNCH. *(Throws scarf and pocketbook away.)* Rootle-dee-tootle-dee-dee. No one gets the best of me.

POLICEMAN. There he is! Surround, attack, throw a net. We'll catch him yet!

(Blows whistle and starts chase.)

PUNCH. I must leave you—fly! Rootle-dee-tootle and goodby!

(Runs to R.)

DOCTOR. *(Enters R, stopping Punch.)*

Mr. Punch.

PUNCH. The doctor.

JUDY. *(Enters R with baby.)* Mr. Punch!

PUNCH. Judy—and the baby!

POLICEMAN. *(At his L.)* Mr. Punch.

PUNCH. *(Toby enters L, barks angrily.)* What—you, too, Toby!

(Punch is in center. Others close in on him and sing. Cue 32.)

OTHERS. We're looking at you, you, you, you, you, Mr. Punch.

PUNCH. Me?

OTHERS. Yes, at you.

> Nobody else would do, do, do
> Such awful, terrible things as you.
> Nobody else would do, do, do
> Such awful, terrible things as you.
> Oh, we've added your crimes, one by one,
> All the wicked, wicked things you have done!
> But there comes an accounting day, day, day,
> When for all your crimes you must pay, pay, pay.

JUDY. He's a menace to the family . . .

POLICEMAN. Security . . .

DOCTOR. Community . . .

(Toby gives a loud "Rauff!" on beat.)

OTHERS. Behind prison bars he shall be!

(Policeman ties rope around Punch.)

PUNCH. I'm being bound by propriety—

OTHERS. He's a menace to the family.

PUNCH. Tied by rules of society—

OTHERS. He's a menace to security.

PUNCH. This must not happen , not to me—

OTHERS. He's a menace to community

PUNCH. I'm Mr. Punch. I'm always free!

OTHERS. Oh, Mr. Punch, you are in a fix,
No more smacks or whacks or selfish tricks.

PUNCH. I'll fight for my right to be me.
I'll fight for my right of liberty!

OTHERS. Oh, Mr. Punch, you are in sad shape,
　　　And this time—there is no escape!
　　　We must keep, keep, keep the social order,
　　　The state and family group;
　　　To keep the status quo, he must go—

PUNCH. No, no.

OTHERS. *(March off R with Punch.)*

　　　So—throw him in the—
　　　Throw him in the—
　　　Throw him in the coop!

(All exit R. Punch immediately returns, end of rope being held behind him offstage.)

PUNCH. Don't give up hope. What's a twist of rope? I'll be back and you'll see who gives who a whack! Rootle-dee-too—

(He is pulled backward by rope, offstage.)

oo-oo-oo-oo-oo-oot!

(Music swells to climax. Cue 33. Toby enters and puts up new sign which reads, "Short Intermission." Toby waves and exits. If no intermission, then he will put up the sign which reads, "Scene 5," and the play continues with entrance of two guards.)

Intermission

ACT TWO

(Overture. Cue 33. Scene is the same. March music. Cue 34. Two brightly dressed guards march in from R. They do a short comic military dance. They change the sign, which reads, "Scene 5." It may also have printed on it, "Hung by a Rope.")

SCENE FIVE

(The guards carry in from L a barred prison cell-front, which is a self-standing unit, and put it DL. This can be the same

frame as the window, which was removed during intermission, but now has bars on the front. Policeman pushes Punch in from L and leaves him behind the bars. Policeman and Guards exit.)

PUNCH. *(Puts head out between bars. Sings. Cue 35.)*

Oh, oh, oh, oh, oh,
Here my cry, hear my sigh, here stand I
Behind prison bars, locked with a key.
Help! Help! Help! Someone rescue me!

Oh, oh, oh, oh, oh,
If I were a butterfly, I'd fly, I'd flee.
But I'm not a butterfly, as you can see.
Help! Help! Help! Someone rescue me!

(Shouts.)

Let me out! Let me out! Let me ou-ou-out!

(Two Guards march in from R. They carry a gallows and stand it DR.)

What is that? It has one branch on the top. It's a tree! If I could reach—I'd eat a peach.

(Calls.)

Yoo-hoo, you and you. Who is the tree for?

(They point at him.)

Me!

(Guards fix rope.)

What are they doing? They are stealing my fruit! Help! Thieves! They are fixing a rope—with a loop. Yoo-hoo. The rope—with the loop—who is it for?

(Guards point at him.)

ME!

(Guards march off R. Punch sings. Cue 36.)

Oh, oh, oh, oh, oh,
A rope swings high with a noose that's crooked.
If I swing high, my goose is cooked.
Help! Help! Help! Someone let me loose!

Oh, oh, oh, oh, oh,
There is no doubt, I must get out.
Quick as quick as quick as quick can be.
Help! Help! Help! They're going to hang me!

(Yells and shakes bars.)

Let me out! Let me out! Let me ou-ou-ou-out!

(Off L, heavy drum-beat footsteps are heard.)

Someone is coming.

(Hangman strides in and takes a stance. He wears a masking hood, but he should not be all in black. There should be some colorful accents. He is a comical hangman. Punch shakes and speaks in frightened voice.)

Who is there?

HANGMAN. I am the Hangman.

PUNCH. Oh!

HANGMAN. I have come to hang you.

PUNCH. No!

HANGMAN. *(Takes out little book.)* The book says: I will fling the rope over your head. You will swing until you are dead, dead, dead.

PUNCH. I am going to die *three* times.

HANGMAN. You have broken the laws of the land.

PUNCH. No! I didn't touch them!

HANGMAN. The book says it is the hour to hang you. Come out.

PUNCH. I like it here.

HANGMAN. Come out! Before my temper goes. I am in a hurry.

PUNCH. I am in no hurry at all.

HANGMAN. Come out! Or I'll hang you by the nose!

PUNCH. *(Comes around cell-front to C.)* Oh, no. No. Not my beautiful, beautiful nose.

HANGMAN. Have you made your will?

PUNCH. My will?

HANGMAN. Your last will and testimony. You have to make a will before I can hang you.

PUNCH. Then I never will—make a will. Rootle-dee-tootle-dee-toot!

HANGMAN. The book says—hang you! And hang you I will, will or no will! Stand there.

(Points to noose.)

PUNCH. Why?

HANGMAN. The book doesn't say why. It says stand there!

PUNCH. Where?

HANGMAN. There!

(Punch stands behind noose.)

And stay! Now listen well while I tell you the words to say: goodby, goodby—farewell.

PUNCH. I'd rather say: goodby, goodby—

(Waves.)

and go away.

(Starts.)

HANGMAN. Stop! You are doing it all wrong! You must do it right!

PUNCH. *(Nods.)* Right—

(Marches.)

Right, left, right, left, right, left—

HANGMAN. Halt! Stand there.

(Punch does.)

And stay.

PUNCH. And pray.

(Clasps hands together.)

HANGMAN. Attend! The hanging will begin. First the rope I bend—

PUNCH. It is the end of Mr. Punch.

HANGMAN. What are you doing?

PUNCH. Saying my prayers.

HANGMAN. What prayers!

(In a tantrum.)

Oh, nothing, nothing is going right!

PUNCH. *(Marches.)* Right, right, left, right, left, right, left—

HANGMAN. Halt! Come back!

(Punch does.)

Say your prayers. And be quick!

PUNCH. *(Kneeling, opens mouth, then starts to stammer.)* I-I-I-I-I-I can't remember.

HANGMAN. Say something. So I can hang you!

PUNCH. Humpty Dumpty sat on a wall.
    Humpty Dumpty had a great fall.
    All the king's horses and all the king's men
    Had scrambled eggs for breakfast again.

HANGMAN. Amen. We will begin.

PUNCH. I had a little dog, his name was Tim.
    I put him in a bathtub to see if he could swim;
    He drank all the water and ate all the soap,
    And almost died with a bubble in his throat.

HANGMAN. Amen. We will begin.

PUNCH. Fuzzy-wuzzy was a bear.
    Fuzzy-wuzzy cut his hair.
    Then Fuzzy-wuzzy wasn't fuzzy, was he?

HANGMAN. Amen! We will begin—NOW!

(Picks Punch up by the collar.)

Put your head through there.

PUNCH. Where?

HANGMAN. There.

PUNCH. How?

HANGMAN. Now!

(Punch puts head below noose.)

No, not below!

(Punch puts head above noose.)

No, not above!

(Punch puts head at side.)

No, not to the side! Oh, idiot numbskull! Dumbskull!

(Punch puts arm in noose.)

No! Not your hand, not your arm! Put in your head!

PUNCH. Where?

HANGMAN. There! In the noose, you silly goose!

PUNCH. How should I know? I've never been hung before.

HANGMAN. I will hang you according to the book.

PUNCH. The book?

HANGMAN. I will quote what it says: Page one. Give your head—

PUNCH. *(Points to Hangman.)* Your head?

HANGMAN. No, your head.

PUNCH. My head?

HANGMAN. Yes, *your* head.

PUNCH. Oh, *your* head.

HANGMAN. No, no, not my head. Your head.

PUNCH. *Your* head.

HANGMAN. No, no, you blockhead. *Your* head!

PUNCH. That's what I said you said, your head.

HANGMAN. No, no, no! Listen to what I say!

PUNCH. You say?

HANGMAN. I say.

PUNCH. I say.

HANGMAN. No, no, not you—me!

(Punch opens his mouth to speak.)

Don't say anything! Watch me!

PUNCH. You?

HANGMAN. Me!

PUNCH. Me?

HANGMAN. No. Me!

PUNCH. Me!

HANGMAN. No, Me! Me! Me!

PUNCH. *(Sings up the scale.)* Do-re-ME-fa-so—

HANGMAN. Quiet! I will *show* you what to do.

PUNCH. Show me?

HANGMAN. You are so stupid you don't know your head from my head. So I will use *my* head to show you where *your* head should be. Now watch. I am going to put my head in the loop.

PUNCH. You are going to put your head into the noose?

HANGMAN. Yes!

PUNCH. *(Aside.)* I know what to do with *his* head, don't you?

HANGMAN. *(Puts head through noose.)* Page one: you give your head a thrust—clearing the rope is a must. Page two: as it tightens tightly around, you speak your last words and sound. Three! Goodby, goodby, farewell.

PUNCH. It is as easy as ABC. One: pull the rope!

(Pulls rope.)

HANGMAN. No!

PUNCH. Two: do it fast—

HANGMAN. NO!

PUNCH. And it is the last—

HANGMAN. OH!

(Drops his head forward and turns around, back to audience.)

PUNCH. Goodby, goodby, farewell. There is no more to tell!

(Tosses book over his shoulder. Sings. Cue 37.)

Mr. Punch is a jolly good fellow,
His coat is always scarlet and yellow.
They could not hang him from a shelf

Because the hangman hung himself!

Rootle-dee-tootle-dee-toot! I'm free! I have escaped death! There is nothing now that can get me!

(Ghost music is heard. Cue 38. Two Ghosts "float" in from L.)

Brr-r-r-r. I feel a cold—wind—blowing. I feel—an icy hand—on each shoulder. Whoo-oo-oo can it be?

FIRST GHOST. Whoo-oo-oo.

PUNCH. It sounds like a ghost!

SECOND GHOST. Whoo-oo-oo.

PUNCH. Like two ghosts!

FIRST GHOST. We have come for Mr. Punch.

PUNCH. Mr. Punch!

SECOND GHOST. Do you know him?

PUNCH. Yes. Oh, yes. Do you know him?

GHOSTS. No.

PUNCH. Oh! So—you don't know him, do you? Then I'll show him— to you.

(Points to gallows.)

There he hangs!

(Aside.)

He was wet so I hung him up to dry. Rootle-dee-tootle-dee-toot.

GHOSTS. *(Float to noose.)* We have come to take him away.

PUNCH. Such fast service. Take him. Take him. He's yours.

GHOSTS. Thank you . . . thank you.

PUNCH. You're welcome . . . you're welcome.

(Ghosts remove noose and put a ghost cover over Hangman. Punch speaks to audience.)

Rootle-dee-tootle-dee-toot. Spooks and ghosts dance in a ring and sing. Tell me, what sings better than *two* ghosts?

(Points to three ghosts.)

Three!

GHOSTS. *(Ghost music. The two ghosts with the Hangman, now a ghost, float to footlights.)* As we fade away from your view . . . this is what we say . . .

(Each points to a child as he speaks.)

to you . . . and you . . . and you . . .

(They shout.)

Boo!

(They float quickly off L.)

PUNCH. *(Sings. Cue 39.)*

Mr. Punch is a jolly good fellow,
His coat is always scarlet and yellow.
There are no laws that can mold him.
There are no bars that can hold him.

(Two Guards enter R and carry off cell-front. Return and carry off gallows.)

Take away! I've fought them all. Mr. Punch and his individual—ity are free! Rootle-dee-tootle-dee-toot!

(Remembers.)

There is one more. The last fight of every man. He must fight— win or lose—with—the Devil. Oh, Rootle-dee-tootle-dee-toot! I'll fight—I'll fight the Devil himself, if he comes after me!

(Aside.)

And he will in the next scene. What a fight you'll see! And there will be one winner.

(Aside.)

Guess who that will be? ME! Rootle-dee-tootle-dee-toot!

(Dances off R.)

(Toby enters and changes sign, which reads, "Scene 6." It may also have printed on it "Out Pops the Devil." The sign is on a red background. Toby waves his paw as if the sign is hot, blows on his paws, looks back at the sign, jumps, barks, and exits quickly.)

SCENE SIX

(The stage begins to glow with red light. Smoke effects may be used. Cue 40. The Devil, with horns and tail and dressed in bright red, dances in from R. He is gleeful in his wickedness. Sings.)

DEVIL. Fiery furnace, horns and hoops,
He skips and steps and steps and hops,
Anywhere, everywhere,
He'll be there. Out pops—the Devil.

He's an imp, a scoundrel, a rascal, a rogue,
A fallen angel, with a tail,
A robber, a thief, a pirate, a cheat,
A crook who ought to be in jail.
But, oh, the fun, the fun, fun, fun, when one
    is a little devilish.

(He looks and points at audience.)

Hello . . . hello. So many people I know. So many friends of mine. Ah, I see you. You are one of my little devils!

(Points to second child.)

And you! Ah, you're a devilish little devil!

(Points to third.)

Ah ha! You over there! You are going to be one of my best big devils!

(Opens his arms to all.)

Oh, come—everyone! We'll have fun—fun—fun!

(Sings. Cue 41.)

Get in line, the fire is fine.
We'll skip and step with steps and hops,
Anywhere, everywhere,
I'll be there. Out pops—the Devil.

He's a traitor, a squealer, a heel, a rat,
He's a villain with mischief to sell:
He lures, he tempts, he slanders, and hates,
He's a sneak, a stinker, a *skunk* with a smell.
And oh the fun, the fun, fun, fun, when one is a little devilish.

Suit of red, flame and smoke,
We'll skip and step with steps and hops.
Call my name. Play my game.
I'll be there. Out pops—the Devil.

Someone is coming. Ah, it is Mr. Punch. I have my tail—pointed at him! And today I will get him. Today Mr. Punch is going to go to hel—to where I dwell. First, I must disguise myself because—*you* know the Devil never *looks* like the Devil when he is with you.

(Devil exits L. Punch enters R.)

PUNCH. *(Walks to C, talking to audience.)* Walking along the street today . . . walking in my leisurely way . . . thinking of a joke to say . . . Why does a hummingbird always hum? He hums because he doesn't know the words. Oh, rootle-dee-tootle-dee-toot.

DEVIL. *(Enters L, disguised as Blind Man.)* Mr. Punch.

PUNCH. I smell smoke.

DEVIL. Mr. Punch, I am old and wise. I will give you a great future.

PUNCH. I feel hot air.

DEVIL. I can make you famous. I can write your name in the history book, if—

PUNCH. If?

DEVIL. If you shake my hand.

(Offers red-gloved hand.)

PUNCH. It's red! It's red hot!

(Aside.)

There's something devilish here! It is—it is the Devil in disguise! This is the way I shake hands with the Devil! Shake.

DEVIL. *(Laughs cunningly.)* Shake.

PUNCH. *(Slaps stick at Devil, who runs off, calling "Help . . . help.")*

And may the Devil take you.

(Walking to C.)

Walking along the street today . . . walking in a leisurely way

. . . thinking of a joke to say . . . If a cow married a zebra, what would she give? Striped milk! Oh, rootle-dee-tootle-dee-toot.

DEVIL. *(Enters, disguised as a Rich Woman.)* Mr. Punch.

PUNCH. I smell smoke again.

DEVIL. I am rich, rich, rich. I can give you wealth—money, jewels, lands, checkbooks.

PUNCH. I feel hot air again.

DEVIL. All the riches in the world can be yours.

PUNCH. Mine?

DEVIL. If—

PUNCH. If?

DEVIL. If you will sign on the dotted line.

(Opens book.)

PUNCH. Red ink! There is something devilish here! You are no lady. You are a shady Devil. This is the way I sign up with the Devil!

(Slaps stick at Devil, who runs off R, crying "Help . . . help.")

And the Devil keep you!

(Walking to C.)

Walking along the street today . . . thinking of a joke to say. One morning a mother hen laid an orange. What did her little chick say? "Oh, see the orange mar-ma-lade!" Rootle-dee-tootle-dee-toot.

DEVIL. *(Enters, disguised as an Old Man.)* Mr. Punch.

PUNCH. *(Aside.)* Can't you smell it? Fire and brimstone!

DEVIL. Mr. Punch, I have great power. I can give you power, too.

PUNCH. And I can give you a whack!

DEVIL. You can rule the world if—

PUNCH. If?

DEVIL. If you give your soul to me.

PUNCH. Never! Mr. Punch is free!

DEVIL. No man is free from me.

(Tosses off disguise.)

I am the Devil.

PUNCH. The Devil you are?

DEVIL. The Devil I am and I have come to take you.

PUNCH. *(Aside.)* Fires in Hades! It is Old Nick himself!

DEVIL. You have escaped from the others, but you will not escape from me. The Devil is the last fear of man.

PUNCH. Escape? Oh, yes, I can! I've fought the fetters of the family, the shames of society. I've cheated death himself. Now I'll fight for my life hereafter. Prepare!

(Holds up stick.)

DEVIL. *(Holds up bright red slapstick or red pitchfork.)* Beware! This is the end of your story, Mr. Punch. There will be no more to tell. I will win. And you will go to—

(Suddenly there are loud claps of thunder. The stage glows with red light. Smoke and lightning effects may be used. Fight music begins. Cue 42. Punch and the Devil start their famous fight, which is fast, frantic, and comic. The Devil laughs when he is winning. Punch "Rootle-dee-tootle-dee-toots" when he is winning. They may run through the audience. Finally Punch slaps the Devil down and stands heroically, the winner. All effects and music stop. Lights become bright.)

PUNCH. Hooray! The Devil is dead! Take him away!

(Two Ghosts float in L, pick up Devil under the arms and pull him, feet dragging, off L, as Punch speaks.)

Mr. Punch has won the fights, the strife, that every man meets in his life!

(Sings. Cue 43.)

Mr. Punch is a jolly good fellow,
His coat is always scarlet and yellow.
Mr. Punch is the man, certainly,
That every man wants to be.

(Toby runs in and barks.)

This is the end of our merry little play. We'll see you again when we come this way.

(Music. Cue 44. He holds out his hand for Judy, who enters R. They sing.)

PUNCH AND JUDY. There will always be a Punch and Judy,
    Always be . . . It's true.

PUNCH. 'Cause there's a little bit of Punch,
    A little of me, in every one of you.

PUNCH AND JUDY. There will always be a Punch and Judy,
    Always be . . . it's true,

JUDY. 'Cause there's a little Judy,
    A little of me, in every one of you.

PUNCH AND JUDY. Oh, fight for what you really do believe in,
    If it's true . . . always do,

PUNCH. 'Cause there's a little bit of Punch—

JUDY. And Judy—

(Toby barks, "And me!" Music and singing suddenly stop. Pause. Then music starts again. The three back up to puppet theatre, singing softly.)

There will always be a Punch and Judy,
Always be . . . it's true.
'Cause there's a little bit of us
A little of us, in every one of you.

(Punch exits behind puppet theatre, then Judy. Toby barks and waves to audience, then exits behind puppet theatre. Lights dim slowly. Immediately the hand puppet of Punch pops up in front of the little curtain of the puppet stage.)

PUNCH. *(Sings.)*
Oh, there will always be a Punch and Judy,
Always be . . . I hope . . . I hope . . .

Judy says—

JUDY. *(Hand puppet of Judy pops up.)* Goodby.

(Throws kisses and disappears.)

PUNCH. Toby says—

(Hand puppet of Toby pops up and waves while Toby barks loudly. Puppet disappears.)

And Mr. Punch says—goodby, goodby, goodby.

(He waves. Music continues. He disappears, but immediately reappears.)

Rootle-dee-tootle-dee-toot!

(Puppet waves and disappears. The puppet theatre stands as it was at the beginning of the play, deserted in a pool of soft light, and the music lingers, as the main curtain closes.)

Steal Away Home

Steal Away Home is a dramatic chronicle of two boys' escape from slavery on the Underground Railroad in 1854. Based on Jane Kristof's novel for children of the same title, the play retains the quality of a literary narrative. Each episode is an encounter along the brothers' travel northward, and together the scenes define an exact period of time, from their decision to leave home in South Carolina to their arrival in Philadelphia, their destination. The play is thus created from a stream of succeeding events as the boys run to their freedom.

The theme, that every human being has the right to be free, motivates the plot of Amos and Obie's journey. It is stated outright repeatedly by several of the characters who support the boys' action.

Plot is above all the key element of *Steal Away Home*. Overlapping scenes of action contain the serious and the comic, calmness and tension, danger and narrow escape to stimulate and sustain audience interest in the enslaved boys' courageous quest for freedom. Three passages of narration spoken directly to the audience by Amos, the older brother, frame the action-filled plot and create the feeling that the play is primarily a narrative brought to life. Because the boys constantly meet new people who hide and help them on their way, the plot has a linear, episodic quality in which the two boys are the only unifying characters.

Conflict with those who would prevent their escape is inherent throughout the work. The fear that at any time their pursuers may confront them creates a constant atmosphere of suspense, relieved occasionally by comedy, increased at other times by antagonists' sudden appearances and near discovery of the runaways.

Because Obie and Amos are present in each scene, much more is revealed about their characterizations than the others'. Certainly they both exhibit similar virtues and personality traits, such as optimism, trust in others, devotion to parents, courage, sense of humor, and ability to think clearly in the face of danger. The boys, however, are made separate characters particularly by their difference in age. That Amos is older than Obie is made obvious in their relationships with their mother, their attitudes toward religious faith, what each finds amusing, and Obie's reliance on Amos to lead. The omnipresent apprehension for their safety sustains interest in the fate of the two brothers, even though their characterizations do not include the usual tendency for mischief that makes the playwright's other young heroes so appealing to the young audience.

The boys are directly contrasted with Joe, another runaway who joins them for a few scenes during their escape. Hatred, fear, and distrust, which make Joe hostile and impulsive, allow minimal sympathetic identification with his plight. When he is suddenly shot as he runs from the slave-catchers, the audience's realization of the shocking turn of events results in their intensified awareness of the perilous situation of Amos and Obie.

Generally, the remainder of the characters are brief sketches of people who are representative of groups important in the history of the Underground Railroad, such as Quakers, abolitionists, freedmen, itinerant preachers who ministered to the slaves, sympathetic European immigrants, and plantation slaves who supported the escape of others. Even though each of these characters appears only briefly, characterizations of real people emerge to create a credible historical framework for the boys' journey.

To complete the picture, the antagonists are drawn to represent two groups who opposed the purpose and activities of the Underground Railroad. First is Edgar, a young attorney, who stands firmly for the principles of law. A heated exchange with his fiancée, whom he has discovered defying the law by hiding runaway slaves, presents both sides of the issue. Unconvinced of the morality of violation, he leaves to inform the authorities, and the pace of the boys' flight noticeably accelerates thereafter, as if in response to realization of the existence of such a formidable enemy. The other antagonists, armed, unfeeling men who recapture and return slaves, reveal that their only motive for chasing the boys is to collect the monetary reward awaiting the captors.

Characterizations shape the form of the brief lines so that each character speaks in a language appropriate to his or her status, education, and societal group. The differences in speech add variety and authenticity without sacrificing communication between the characters or obscuring the meaning for the audience. The uneducated speak in faulty syntax which suggests Southern dialectical patterns. Slang and emotionally laden terms in the speech of the slave hunters underscore their brutality. The lines of Melissa and Edgar, by contrast, are written in proper and occasionally formal-sounding English. The speech of the Quakers has been given a ring of authenticity by the inclusion of the single word *thee*. The absence of related pronouns, such as *thy* and *thine*, prevents the meaning of the lines from becoming obscured.

The play is completed by the element of song. Familiar Negro spirituals, to be sung by a chorus, form the bridges between the scenes and surround the action with the expression of the slaves' source of strength, their religious faith. The songs also offer a continuing comment on the action, adding appropriate emotional richness. The words and music of the selected songs have been carefully considered to insure that their combined effect reinforces the preceding scene or foreshadows the one to follow.

Actual spectacle requirements are few. The locale is always set by dialogue, and often the location of the next scene is revealed as the boys learn of their destination. Since every scene takes place in a new locale, each may only be suggested by lighting, a few props and scenic pieces, and pantomime, to preserve the rapid flow of events in the progression of the plot.

A play of social justice and an example of its realization, *Steal Away Home* presents a poignant, uplifting story from a shameful period of American history. Even as the boys' triumph over an evil system provides the reason for rejoicing with them in the final declaration of their freedom, the play probes the conscience and stimulates ideas which remain to be pondered.

Steal Away Home

by Aurand Harris

A dramatization of the book *Steal Away Home* by Jane Kristof

Musical research and accompaniments by Carolyn Geer

Preacher Prentice	*First Neighbor
Amos, twelve years old	*Second Neighbor
Obie, ten years old	*Old Man
*Man with Gun	*Young Man
Mama	Jack
*Mrs. Strauss	*Patrol
Miss Melissa	*Will
*Edgar	*Mother
Joe	*Conductor
*First Man	Pa
*Second Man	*Stagehands
*Elijah McNaul	Choir
*Jud	

*Can be doubled.

(Since many in the cast appear in only one scene, the producer can use the same actor to play more than one role. Thus, by judicious doubling, the play can be cast with thirteen actors.)

SCENE

Stations on the Underground Railroad from South Carolina to Pennsylvania, 1854.

An intermission is optional.

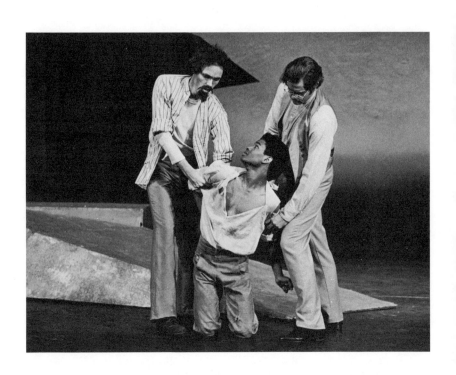

Steal Away Home

ACT ONE

*(Choir sings softly. Cue 1. "Didn't My Lord Deliver Daniel?"
The curtains open on a bare stage. Amos, twelve years old and
a slave, enters R, singing with the choir the last of the hymn
with great enjoyment.)*

AMOS. ". . . Didn't my Lord deliver Daniel,
Deliver Daniel, deliver Daniel?
Didn't my Lord deliver Daniel,
And why not-a every man?"

(He looks at audience and smiles.)

That's my favorite song. We sang it the Sunday when Preacher
Prentice came to the plantation—that Sunday when it all began.

(Comes to footlights and speaks intimately.)

Preacher Prentice was born a slave, like me; but his master freed
him. He could read and write and he had a cart and a horse and
traveled around fixing pots and pans. The white folks called
him a tinker, but to us he was the Preacher. Well, that Sunday
Obie and me sat right up close to hear him preach. After the
meeting and all the singing, Obie and me walked home, kicking
our feet in the dust like always—never thinking—never knowing that—that day—that Sunday, May 29, 1854—that that was
the day our big adventure was going to begin.

(He steps into the scene.)

I was almost to our cabin and I could smell supper cooking and
I could smell Mama's honeysuckle blooming on the gate.

(A weathered, dilapidated gate is placed at L by stagehands.)

And Obie was dawdling behind, seeing how far he could jump
on one foot.

(Calls off R.)

Obie. Come on, Obie. I'll race you to the cabin. Obie! Mama's
waiting supper for us. OBIE! I smell—benne cakes!

OBIE. *(Age ten, talkative and lively, runs in at R and dashes across the stage through gate, exiting at L shouting.)* Benne cakes! Come on! I'm hungry!

AMOS. Wait for me.

PREACHER. *(Preacher Prentice enters R.)* Just a minute, young fellow.

AMOS. Preacher Prentice!

PREACHER. I saw you at the meeting, didn't I?

(Amos nods.)

You and your brother?

(Amos nods.)

Your Pa—his name is Henry?

AMOS. Yes, sir. He belonged to Master Smithers, but they took Pa with them when they moved away five years ago.

PREACHER. *(Nods.)* Is your Mama in the cabin?

AMOS. Yes, sir.

MAMA. *(Quickly enters from L, coming through gate. Obie follows close behind.)* I'm right here, Preacher Prentice.

PREACHER. You the wife of Henry that belonged to the Smithers?

MAMA. That's right. But when they moved away from South Carolina, they took Henry with them.

PREACHER. *(Speaks in secret.)* I have something—for you.

(He looks around.)

Nobody's around, are they?

(All look. Preacher speaks in a hushed voice.)

Don't want nobody to see me or nobody to hear what I got to say.

MAMA. *(Fearful.)* Nobody here but us.

PREACHER. *(Carefully takes a folded piece of paper from inside band of his hat. Speaks cautiously.)* I got a letter for you—from Henry.

MAMA. A letter?

PREACHER. *(Carefully so no one will see, hands letter to Mama.)* He sent it by me.

MAMA. A letter from Henry!

PREACHER. Sh! Someone will hear you.

MAMA. *(Holds out letter.)* I can't read.

PREACHER. *(Reads slowly and confidentially.)* "My dear wife. Master Smithers took sick and died, but he set me free. I went north—"

MAMA. Free! Your Pa's free!

PREACHER. *(Looks around fearfully.)* Hush. "I took the name of Carpenter and live in a town called Lemhorn near the city of Philadelphia. I work and save and hope I'll have enough money to buy you and little Sally from Master Bricker.

(Reads with emphasis.)

I wish Amos and Obadiah were here to help me. God bless and keep you all. Your loving husband."

MAMA. He's going to buy little Sally and me. We'll be free with him.

OBIE. What about us, Mama? He didn't say nothing about buying Amos and me. Don't Pa want us?

AMOS. 'Course Pa wants us, but—but he don't have enough money to buy all four. Mama's first. And little Sally, she's so sickly I expect Master will sell her cheap.

OBIE. *(Beams with a comforting idea.)* Maybe he wants us—you and me—Amos, wants us—to run off! Go north and help him!

MAMA. Don't talk foolish.

PREACHER. *(Slowly and pointedly.)* Maybe—that's just what he do want.

(All look at him in surprise, Obie more surprised than the others.)

MAMA. What do you mean?

PREACHER. *(Looks around cautiously, then speaks with excitement.)* He wrote those words big. "I wish Amos and Obadiah were here to help me." It's got to mean something special.

MAMA. *(Fearful.)* You think he wants them to run away—go up north! They're just children.

PREACHER. There'd be folks that would help them along the road.

MAMA. Folks?

PREACHER. Folks on the Underground Railroad.

AMOS. The what?

PREACHER. The Underground Railroad.

OBIE. What's that?

PREACHER. It's people. People who help runaway slaves. They hide you and then send you on to the next station—and to the next and to the next—until at last you're safe and free. I figure the two of you could do it.

AMOS. Us?

OBIE. How?

PREACHER. *(All listen carefully as Preacher speaks in hushed voice but with excitement.)* Master Bricker will give you a day off on the Fourth of July.

(All nod.)

That comes on a Monday. Now, if you'd steal away Sunday morning *early*, you'd have two days' start before he knowed you was gone.

(Boys nod.)

You could slip along to the new bridge over the Pee Dee River and hide there, till I come along in my cart. Then in you'd crawl and I'd start you north on the Underground Railroad.

AMOS. What about Mama? If we run away, Master will blame her.

MAMA. If my boys were free, there wouldn't be nothing Master could do would hurt me.

(Hugs boys.)

PREACHER. He'd never know if you runned off, or if you got stolen, or got drowned, or what.

OBIE. Can we go, Mama?

MAMA. It's so far.

PREACHER. *(Nods.)* It's five hundred miles to Philadelphia.

MAMA. You're so little.

PREACHER. You think about it, and you'll decide the right way.

(Looks about to see if anyone is watching.)

Goodby. I've got a feeling I'll see you boys again—hiding under the bridge, ready to ride to freedom.

(He exits R.)

AMOS. *(Whispers excitedly.)* Can we go, Mama? Can we go?

MAMA. I don't know what to say. If your Pa wants you—

OBIE. Can we, Mama?

MAMA. Five hundred miles—

AMOS AND OBIE. Can we? Can we?

MAMA. *(Looks at them, off after Preacher, then nods her head.)* Yes. I can't stop you from going free.

OBIE. *(Bounces with excitement and shouts with joy.)* We're going! We're going!

MAMA. Hush, Obie. Quick—get inside the cabin.

(Fearful, she motions him toward cabin. Obie exits through gate, off L.)

You're going north. You're going to your Pa.

(Embraces Amos.)

It's a long way. They'll try to stop you—try to catch you, but I'm trusting in you, Amos. And I'm trusting in the good Lord.

(She exits through gate and off L.
Amos, radiant, sings the words of the song with true conviction. Choir joins him. Cue 2. "Didn't My Lord Deliver Daniel?"
Amos exits through gate and off L. The singing continues as lights dim down slightly. The singing becomes a hum as lights come up slowly. It is sunup and Mama enters cautiously from L. She enters through gate, then beckons boys, who enter L, carrying short fishing poles. Singing stops.)

MAMA. *(She is nervous and tries to keep back her tears. She speaks cautiously.)* It's time to go—before anybody's up.

(She looks about fearfully.)

You remember all I told you?

(Boys nod.)

Cut through the woods to the stream. Keep wading in the water so you'll leave no tracks if Master sets the hounds to find you. Follow the creek till it runs into the Pee Dee River. That won't be till tomorrow. Then hide—don't let nobody see you! Hide under the new bridge and wait.

AMOS. *(Not as brave as he sounds.)* We will, Mama.

(Frightened.)

Come on, Obie. It's getting light.

OBIE. *(Afraid now that it is happening.)* How far is it to—

(Has a comic difficulty pronouncing it.)

Phil—A—delph'a?

MAMA. Preacher said five hundred miles.

OBIE. *(Starts to cry.)* I'm going to miss you, Mama.

MAMA. *(Trying not to cry, gives him small sack.)* Here, take your sack. Some turnips and benne cakes.

OBIE. *(Crying.)* I ain't hungry.

MAMA. You will be.

(Nervous and fearful.)

Now—hurry before someone sees you.

OBIE. *(Sobbing, embraces Mama.)* Goodby, Mama.

MAMA. *(Crying, kisses him.)* Goodby. You mustn't cry.

(Bravely, overcoming her crying.)

Remember—keep remembering you're going to your Pa—you're going to be free.

AMOS. *(Crying.)* We will, Mama. Goodby.

(Embraces her.)

Goodby, Mama.

MAMA. Goodby.

(Kisses him, crying.)

Take care. Take care of Obie. Take care of yourself.

Amos. *(Crying freely.)* I will, Mama. Come on, Obie.

(Takes his hand and the two boys start R, both crying and rubbing their noses.)

Don't cry. Hold your head up. Keep saying—we're going to be free—free—

(They exit R.)

Mama. I can't do no more for them, Lord. They're in your hands. Help them find the way.

(Humming begins as she exits L. Cue 3. "Sometimes I Feel Like a Motherless Child." Gate is removed. Humming continues. Lights come up bright. Amos and Obie enter R, walking wearily. Singing fades out.)

Obie. I could eat some benne cakes.

Amos. Me, too.

(They sit downstage, eat, and talk with their mouths full.)

Obie. Yesterday when we left I didn't think I could ever eat again. My feet feel like they'd walked forever. But I guess your feet hurt more.

Amos. Why?

Obie. 'Cause your feet are bigger.

(Wiggles his toes.)

I keep thinking of Mama. What you reckon she's doing?

Amos. Praying that we'll be safe.

Obie. What you reckon Pa is doing?

Amos. Pa?

(A new realization.)

You know, Obie—we won't even know Pa.

Obie. But he'll know us! And when we get there we'll help him work so he can buy Mama and Sally.

Amos. And we'll have a little house—on a little farm—

OBIE. And you know what else? A little puppy.

AMOS. Remember when Master lost his puppy? He searched two days for that dog. I know he liked that dog better than he liked us, but we're worth more money.

(Fearful.)

I reckon he'll hunt harder to find us.

OBIE. *(Also afraid.)* Amos, what'll they do if they catch us?

(There is a sudden sharp sound offstage. Obie jumps up, alarmed.)

What's that! What's that, Amos?

AMOS. Hush!

(They crouch, frozen with fear. Amos slowly looks around. He whispers.)

Come on. Come on, Obie. We have to keep going.

(Fearful, they start L.)

Let's see what's around the bend in the river. Come on!

(They run a few steps, stop, and Amos points DL with joy.)

Look! There's a bridge.

OBIE. It's a new bridge!

AMOS. It's the one he said! We'll hide under it and wait until he comes.

OBIE. *(Frightened.)* Amos, what if he doesn't come?

AMOS. He said he would—and *he's* a preacher!

OBIE. *(Suddenly joyful with relief.)* Amen! Sing hallelujah.

*(Choir sings. Cue 4. "Gonna Sing All along the Way." Obie dances off L after Amos, who motions for him to hurry.
A horse and cart move on stage at R. It is a side view of a horse hitched to a cart, a one-dimensional cut-out painted front. The cart is backed by a practical platform on which are pots, pans, barrels, etc. Preacher Prentice sits on the driver's seat, driving the horse and slapping the reins.)*

PREACHER. Whoa! Whoa there!

(Horse and cart stop at R. Singing stops. Preacher looks around for the boys, but never indicates when he sees them. He sings happily as he gets down from the wagon. He carries a small jug and comes down center. He looks around and speaks in his best pulpit manner with double meaning for the boys.)

The text today is: The Lord will deliver. Noah built the Ark and the animals went in, two by two. Then Noah looked about and said to the last two, "All is well. Get on board."

(Preacher kneels and pantomimes filling jug in river. At the same time, Amos and Obie peek from L, then run quickly and hide in the cart. Preacher looks around cautiously, goes to cart, looks about once more, climbs onto cart, puts gunny-sacks over the hidden boys. He snaps the reins, shouts, "Getty-up," and the horse and cart move slowly to C. Singing starts with cart. Cue 5. "Who Built the Ark?" Preacher joggles the reins and bounces on the seat. After song, Preacher pulls on reins, frightened. Horse and cart stop at C. Boys peek out.)

PREACHER. Whoa! Whoa! There's trouble up the road. Cover up. There's a man—with a gun!

(Boys quickly cover up. A white man with a gun enters L.)

MAN WITH GUN. Let's see your pass, boy. Where's your pass?

PREACHER. My pass?

MAN WITH GUN. Whose slave are you?

PREACHER. I ain't no slave, sir. I am a freedman. Got my papers right here.

(Takes paper from pocket and gives it to Man.)

I travel around fixing pots and pans—and preaching a little.

MAN WITH GUN. *(Gives paper back.)* I've heard about you. You're the tinker.

PREACHER. Yes, sir.

MAN WITH GUN. I'm stopping everybody on the road. I'm searching every wagon that comes this way.

PREACHER. What are you hunting?

MAN WITH GUN. I'm looking for a couple of little nigger boys that run away from Bricker's place.

PREACHER. *(Innocently.)* Two runaways?

MAN WITH GUN. There's a reward out—twenty-five bucks a head.

PREACHER. *(Impressed.)* Twenty-five dollars for each boy?

MAN WITH GUN. What you got in your wagon?

PREACHER. Pots and pans, some odds and ends.

MAN WITH GUN. What's in the barrel?

(Starts to barrel in which one boy is hiding.)

PREACHER. *(Loudly, starting his game of outwitting the guard.)* Was these two boys kind of ugly-looking?

MAN WITH GUN. All the notice said was twelve and ten years old.

(Puts his hand on barrel.)

PREACHER. *(Louder, to get his attention.)* Did—did they have a fishing pole?

MAN WITH GUN. I reckon they did. They was last seen going fishing.

(Starts to lift cover.)

What's in here?

PREACHER. *(Shouts with joy.)* Well, what do you know! That must of been them I saw!

MAN WITH GUN. Be who? Saw where?

PREACHER. *(Taking his time.)* There was a couple of boys that fit that description under the bridge this morning.

MAN WITH GUN. What bridge?

PREACHER. The new bridge over the Pee Dee River.

MAN WITH GUN. How long ago?

PREACHER. Oh, some hours.

MAN WITH GUN. They might still be there. All right, you can go on. Get along!

(He starts R.)

PREACHER. *(Happily.)* Yes, sir!

MAN WITH GUN. *(To himself.)* I'll get there first.

PREACHER. Yes, sir.

MAN WITH GUN. And I'll get the reward.

(Exits R.)

PREACHER. *(Shouts in his victory.)* NO-O-O-O-O, sir!

AMOS. *(Boys pop up, eyes wide with fright.)* He—he almost caught us.

OBIE. But you outsmarted him.

PREACHER. The Lord speaks in many tongues!

AMOS. They're hunting for us!

PREACHER. *(Bitterly.)* Men, hounds, and guns.

AMOS. What are we going to do?

PREACHER. *(Also frightened.)* We're getting out of here. Quick! I'm driving to Raleigh and start you on the Underground Railroad. Now—cover up and hold on tight. We're rolling on—to the Promised Land! Getty-up!

(He slaps the reins. Boys hide. Singing starts. Cue 6. "The Old Ark's a-Moverin'." Horse and cart move quickly off L, Preacher slapping the reins and bouncing on the seat. The lights dim to night. As the cart exits L, a wing flat is placed at R. The back flat is painted with shelves and bottles of a pharmacy. The flat at an angle on the left has a window with a practical curtain. A small counter-table is placed in the room. The singing dims and stops. Mrs. Strauss enters R in the room. She is a sweet elderly lady, dressed in a robe and a nightcap, and carries a lighted candle. Preacher enters at L, silently motions for the boys. Amos and Obie, frightened, follow him.)

PREACHER. *(Speaks cautiously.)* There is a light, so they are still up. This is your first stop on the Underground Railroad. It's Mr. and Mrs. Strauss. He makes medicine. Now, quiet, and hide while I knock.

(Boys hide. Preacher looks around, then goes to room and knocks at imaginary door. Mrs. Strauss pantomimes opening it.)

MRS. STRAUSS. Why, it's Preacher Prentice. Come in.

PREACHER. Good evening, Mrs. Strauss. I've brought you two—

(Confidentially.)

two—passengers!

MRS. STRAUSS. Passengers! Oh!

(Cautiously.)

Keep watch outside. Don't let anyone see. And send in the two passengers.

(Preacher becomes a look-out, motions to boys, who slip into the room. Mrs. Strauss closes the curtains at window. The boys huddle at one side, anxious and uncertain. Preacher enters and pantomimes closing the door.)

MRS. STRAUSS. Why—they are children.

PREACHER. This is Amos and Obadiah. They are going on the Underground to Philadelphia to their Pa.

MRS. STRAUSS. All alone? And so far!

PREACHER. Goodby, boys.

AMOS. *(Afraid.)* Goodby, Preacher Prentice.

PREACHER. Remember, boys, keep going no matter what happens to you. Keep going on—to freedom.

OBIE. Goodby, Preacher Prentice. If you see Mama—

(Starts to cry.)

Tell Mama—I miss her.

PREACHER. I'll tell her, Obie, and I'll also tell her how brave you are. God bless you all.

(He exits quickly at door, looks cautiously about and slips out at L.)

MRS. STRAUSS. *(Nervous.)* Mr. Strauss is sick. Upstairs. I'm sorry he can't help you.

AMOS. *(Frightened.)* What are we going to do?

MRS. STRAUSS. I know where he keeps the Underground map. I will show you the next stop.

(She puts small map on table.)

Make sure the curtains are closed. Nobody must see you.

(Amos goes to window. She points to map.)

This is where you are—Raleigh, North Carolina.

OBIE. Where is Phil—A—delph'a?

MRS. STRAUSS. Up there.

AMOS. It's not far at all!

MRS. STRAUSS. It looks a small way on the map, but it is a long trip—beyond Richmond and Washington.

OBIE. It's going to be a long walk, Amos.

MRS. STRAUSS. You will get there, station by station. Your next stop is in Henderson at Doctor Culpepper's.

AMOS. How far?

MRS. STRAUSS. Two days walking. You will hide in the woods at night and walk by day so you can read the names of the towns.

AMOS. Read?

MRS. STRAUSS. So you won't get lost.

AMOS. We can't read.

MRS. STRAUSS. Oh. And you can't *ask* anyone directions or they'll stop you. Well! We have a problem.

AMOS. Yes, ma'am.

MRS. STRAUSS. But we will solve it.

OBIE. How?

MRS. STRAUSS. I will think. And I think better while I'm working. I'll put the covers out for you. You'll sleep here by the fire to-night.

(Takes cover from counter and puts it on floor at R.)

OBIE. *(Frightened.)* Amos, if we can't read signs, can't ask anybody, how are we going to find the way—to Phil—A—delph'a?

AMOS. We got a problem.

MRS. STRAUSS. I have the solution! But you will have to do some pre-tending.

AMOS. Pretending?

MRS. STRAUSS. You must make believe that you are Doctor Culpepper's slaves.

AMOS. Yes, ma'am. We can act like slaves real easy.

MRS. STRAUSS. You will say that he sent you to get medicine from Mr. Strauss, and you're taking the medicine back to the doctor. I will write you a pass which you can show to anyone who stops you. Now I'll fix the medicine.

(Measures from jar on counter.)

Pink pills, I think—and I will put "Poison" on the bottle. Would you like some?

(Offers them the big jar.)

AMOS. *(Alarmed.)* No, ma'am, I ain't sick!

MRS. STRAUSS. *(Laughs.)* Oh, it is not poison. It is not even medicine. It is candy.

OBIE. *(Eagerly.)* Candy?

MRS. STRAUSS. *(Enjoying her joke.)* You will be carrying a bottle of candy and no one will know the difference! Help yourself.

OBIE. Yes, ma'am.

(Boys eat candy hungrily.)

AMOS. Yes, ma'am!

MRS. STRAUSS. Now off to sleep. You must leave before sunup, slip away before anyone sees you.

AMOS. Yes, ma'am.

(Boys lie on cover. She tucks them in.)

MRS. STRAUSS. Many years ago I ran away. I ran away just like you, from my home in Europe. I wanted freedom too. People helped me. Now I can help you. Good night.

AMOS. Good night. Thank you for the medicine.

MRS. STRAUSS. So little . . . so young . . . running away to be free. Sleep well. And may your dream come true.

(Singing begins. Cue 7. "Steal Away." Mrs. Strauss writes note, quickly puts it by Amos, takes candle, and exits R. Lights dim down. Scenery is moved off. Boys exit R. Lights come up, and

the singing changes to a lively beat. Cue 8. "Oh, a-Rock-a My Soul." Obie enters R. He suddenly points to the ground and starts to run after it. Amos enters R.)

OBIE. Look, Amos. There's a snake.

AMOS. A snake? Let it be!

OBIE. Lucky I didn't step on it.

AMOS. Lucky it didn't bite you.

OBIE. It's gone. It's free.

AMOS. But we ain't. Not yet.

(Obie looks at him. Amos grins.)

This morning we have to pretend we're slaves. How're you going to act, Obie, when the first white man stops you? Let's play-like you got the pass and you're going that way, and I'm coming this way with a gun.

(He gives Obie letter and then goes to C, turns and stops Obie. He comically overacts like the Man with the Gun.)

Stop, boy, stop. Where's your pass?

OBIE. Huh?

AMOS. Where's your pass, boy?

OBIE. *(Grins and understands, then with great enjoyment overacts the slave.)* Oh, yes, sir, yes, sir. I got a pass. Yes, sir.

AMOS. Let's see it.

OBIE. Yes, sir. Yes, sir, here it is, sir.

AMOS. *(Pretends to read.)* Doctor Culpepper—

(Grunts.)

OBIE. I think you are holding the letter upside down.

AMOS. Don't get uppity with me, boy!

OBIE. No, sir. No, sir!

AMOS. You taking medicine back to your master?

OBIE. Yes, sir. Yes, sir. Special medicine for liver trouble, belly trouble, and rhu—MI—tism.

AMOS. Then go along, boy. Get along.

OBIE. Yes, sir. Yes, sir.

(Passes Amos.)

I'm getting along. Getting a long, long way from here.

AMOS. *(Laughs and shouts.)* And I'm getting along with you. Come on, Obie. We'll be at Henderson by tonight.

(Singing starts. Cue 9. "Gonna Sing All along the Way." Boys run—free—in a circle several times around the stage. As they exit, a love seat and an ornate folding screen are placed on stage L; the screen is at the right of the sofa, making the corner of the room. Miss Melissa, a pretty young lady, beautifully dressed, enters L. She looks about nervously. She is high-spirited, charming, and affectionate. Singing dims out. She pantomimes closing the curtains at an imaginary window. She calls anxiously.)

MELISSA. Come—come into the parlor. No one will see you here.

AMOS. *(Amos and Obie slowly enter L, awed by the rich surroundings.)* Is this Doctor Culpepper's house?

MELISSA. Yes, Papa is away on a sick call. Sit here.

(Nervous, but gracious.)

Now, what can we do to entertain you?

OBIE. I like to sing!

MELISSA. Sh! No. Someone would hear us.

(Looks around nervously.)

We'll read a story.

AMOS. We can't read.

MELISSA. I'll teach you! We'll play school.

(Cautious again.)

Now sit and be very quiet while I get a book.

(She exits L.)

AMOS. *(Boys look about slowly.)* Obie, we are in a parlor—a white folks' parlor—with a floor and a carpet.

OBIE. And lamps and curtains.

AMOS. And a sofa.

(They both look at it.)

OBIE. Can we sit on it?

(They look at it again and whisper.)

AMOS. Should we?

OBIE. Could we?

(They nod to each other and run to sofa, then slowly sit down and smile with the feeling of comfort.)

AMOS. It's soft.

OBIE. It's bouncy.

(They bounce gently, then faster and higher, and, as the fun increases, they even start laughing.)

MELISSA. *(Off.)* No, Nellie. I won't need you any more. Good night.

(Boys stop suddenly and stand with comic innocence. Melissa enters L with books.)

I found an old copybook. And for you Obie—

OBIE. Yes, ma'am?

MELISSA. I found a picture book of the Bible.

(Obie sits on floor with book. Amos sits on sofa with Melissa.)

Now the first thing in reading is to learn the alphabet.

OBIE. *(Points to picture in book.)* Look! They're whipping people with long whips.

MELISSA. Those are the Egyptians. They are whipping the Hebrew slaves.

OBIE. Are those slaves?

MELISSA. And that is Moses leading the slaves out of bondage.

(Doorbell rings loudly off L. Melissa is frightened and pulls the boys close to her.)

Who can that be? Nellie, see who is at the door.

(Rises.)

No. I had better go myself. Quick, boys, hide—hide and don't make a sound.

(Bell rings again and Melissa exits L. Boys look at each other. Obie points under the sofa. Amos shakes his head. They both look at screen, then nod, look off L, then tiptoe quickly to screen, each going behind it on either side.)

MELISSA. *(Off.)* Why, Edgar! How nice to see you—unexpectedly. Let me have your hat.

EDGAR. *(Off.)* I couldn't wait until morning. I simply had to come and tell you.

(He strides into the room, bursting with excitement. He is a handsome young man, educated and a Southern gentleman. Melissa follows him, nervously looking for the boys.)

It is the best of news, Melissa. It means that now we can set the date for the wedding.

MELISSA. Our wedding?

EDGAR. I am to be made a partner of the law firm. And that means a church wedding and everything you want.

MELISSA. *(They embrace.)* Oh, Edgar.

EDGAR. Of course, it also means I will have to go to Philadelphia right away.

MELISSA. Philadelphia? Did you say Philadelphia, Edgar?

EDGAR. Yes. Oh, I feel badly, too. I don't want to be away from you either. But it will only be two months.

MELISSA. How will you go—to Philadelphia?

EDGAR. I'll drive, I suppose, in the carriage.

MELISSA. Edgar . . . ?

EDGAR. What is it, Melissa?

MELISSA. Edgar, you do agree with Papa about the freeing of slaves?

EDGAR. Yes—but what has that to do with us?

MELISSA. I—I have something to tell you.

EDGAR. You sound so serious. What is it?

MELISSA. It is serious.

(With determined effort.)

I know the whereabouts of two runaway slaves.

EDGAR. What!

MELISSA. Two slaves are trying to get to Philadelphia. If they could go with you . . . ?

EDGAR. *(Astonished.)* You know the whereabouts of two runaway slaves? You are trying to help them!

MELISSA. Yes, Edgar.

EDGAR. Melissa, do you know what you are doing? What would your father say?

MELISSA. He has helped many slaves escape on the Underground Railroad.

EDGAR. Your father! But he's a born Southerner—a gentleman—a churchman. Melissa, does he know the penalties of slave-stealing?

MELISSA. Papa isn't a slave-stealer! He has freed his slaves.

EDGAR. The law says helping slaves to escape is the same as stealing them.

MELISSA. Papa thinks the law is unjust.

EDGAR. I agree. But one cannot disobey the law just because he doesn't agree with it.

MELISSA. What can you do then if the law tells you to do what you're sure is wrong?

EDGAR. Change the law! And I am certain that in fifty years slavery will be abolished.

MELISSA. Fifty years! What about the two little boys I am hiding now?

EDGAR. Hiding!

(Looks around.)

Melissa, we must turn these slaves over to the authorities at once! Where are they?

MELISSA. Authorities! Laws! That's all you know, Edgar.

EDGAR. You are in danger. You are risking your life.

MELISSA. If helping human beings is breaking the law, then I'm glad to risk my life, because I—I believe in the freedom of people.

EDGAR. This isn't like you, Melissa.

MELISSA. Yes, it is. You just don't know me. And I'm discovering that I don't know you.

EDGAR. *(Uncomprehending.)* You—you are hiding slaves.

MELISSA. You had better go, Edgar.

EDGAR. Melissa, you must obey the law. Give up the slaves.

MELISSA. I must do what I think is right. Good night, Edgar.

EDGAR. Very well. I, too, must do what I think is right.

MELISSA. What do you mean?

EDGAR. I must report them. Good night, Melissa.

(Exits L.)

MELISSA. *(Frightened.)* Edgar!

AMOS. *(He and Obie peek around the screen and come out from either side.)* Is he gone?

MELISSA. Yes. And he is going to the authorities. We can't wait for Papa. I will take you to the next stop myself—tonight!

(Calls.)

Nellie! Nellie, quick. Have John get the horses and carriage ready. Pack me a bag. I'm going to visit Cousin Emily. Hurry!

(To boys.)

I will take you as far as South Hill. That is in Virginia. The next station is a tannery. It belongs to a Quaker named Elijah McNaul. There is a box at the back door for you to hide in. He checks it early every morning before the other men come to work, and he'll get you to the next station. Now sit there.

(Gives Obie his book.)

And I'll be right back. We must hurry. Hurry before they find you!

(Exits L.)

OBIE. *(Amos looks after her, frightened. Obie points to picture in book quickly.)* Amos, look. Look at this picture again.

AMOS. It's Moses leading the slaves out of bondage.

OBIE. Yes. But look at the slaves. The slaves are white.

(They look at each other and then straight front in wonder. Singing starts. Cue 10. "Go Down Moses." The lights dim out. Boys exit L, and sofa and screen are removed. A flat painted like the side of a building and with a large box attached to it is placed DC. Lights come up. It is night. Singing stops. Amos and Obie enter R, creeping quietly and looking around, frightened at the shadows.)

AMOS. Come on, Obie, come on.

OBIE. It's so dark I can't see.

AMOS. Take my hand.

OBIE. *(Noise is heard off R.)* What's that! What's that, Amos!

AMOS. Quick! Hide—in the shadows.

(Boys separate and crouch and listen. An owl hoots.)

OBIE. *(Terrified.)* Amos! Where are you?

AMOS. It's just an owl. A hoot owl. Look! I think this is the tannery.

OBIE. I'm tired, Amos. I can't go no farther.

AMOS. It's the tannery! She said there was a box at the back.

(Comes DC.)

There it is! We're here, Obie. It's all right. We can sleep in the box tonight.

(They look around, then slowly go to the box, whispering.)

Don't make any noise when we raise the lid.

(Obie nods. They raise the lid slowly. Suddenly a figure springs up in the box and shouts.)

JOE. *(He is eighteen, another Negro slave, bitter from bad treatment, and is aggressively hostile.)* Get out! Get out! You hear me! Get out of my box!

(Joe grabs Amos by the throat and starts choking and shaking him, still shouting, "Get out.")

AMOS. *(At the same time, yells.)* Stop! You're choking me. Stop! Stop!

(He screams frantic sounds as he tries to free himself.)

OBIE. *(Hits at Joe and shouts.)* Let him loose! Let go! Let loose!

(Obie bites Joe's arm. Joe yells loudly and lets loose of Amos.)

Amos! Amos! You all right, Amos?

JOE. *(Looks at arm.)* There's blood.

AMOS. *(To Obie.)* What did you do, Obie?

OBIE. *(Facing front.)* I bit him!

JOE. What you doing here?

OBIE. Miss Melissa said to hide in the box.

JOE. You ain't going to hide in here. You ain't going to get in this box. It's mine. You hear me? Get going!

FIRST MAN. *(Off L. He is gruff and straightforward.)* I didn't hear nothing.

SECOND MAN. *(He is mean and disagreeable. The two men enter L.)* I heard something all right.

FIRST MAN. *(Coming toward box.)* Maybe a couple of tomcats meowing around.

JOE. Quick! Before they see you! Get in the box. Get in! Both of you! Hide!

(Amos and Obie quickly climb into box. They close the lid just in time.)

FIRST MAN. Well, you can see—there's nobody around in the back.

(Leans on box.)

SECOND MAN. I heard scuffling and yelling.

FIRST MAN. You was dreaming.

(Knocks his pipe on box.)

SECOND MAN. It sounded like—like niggers talking.

FIRST MAN. Whatcha mean?

SECOND MAN. *(Pointedly.)* Some folks think McNaul is hiding runaway slaves.

FIRST MAN. Hiding slaves?

SECOND MAN. On the Underground Railroad.

(Looks at side.)

I heard them all right. They was here.

FIRST MAN. The way you talk I might be standing right next to one —right now.

SECOND MAN. They're hiding somewhere.

FIRST MAN. Naw. McNaul may be a little Bible crazy, but he's not hiding runaway slaves. He ain't no criminal.

SECOND MAN. He's a Quaker.

FIRST MAN. So what?

SECOND MAN. He's different from us. And I don't trust him.

FIRST MAN. Come on. I'm going to bed.

(Exits L.)

SECOND MAN. I know I heard 'em. They was talking.

(Goes to L.)

And I'm going to tell—tell the sheriff. He'll get 'em all right. He'll catch 'em. I'd like to catch one of them runaways myself.

(Second Man exits L. There is a pause. Then slowly the lid of the box is raised and six frightened eyes look about. First Joe stands up, then Amos, then Obie.)

JOE. They're gone.

OBIE. What if they'd opened the lid—and found us!

JOE. Now get going. I'm staying here and you're getting out. So get!

AMOS. Go? We ain't got no place to go.

OBIE. If we get out, we'll get caught.

JOE. Who cares if you do!

OBIE. *(Slowly and pointedly.)* If we get caught—first thing they'll ask us is—do we know of any other runaway slaves? And I do. You. And I always tell the truth.

AMOS. We got to stay. We got to hide here.

JOE. *(Grudgingly.)* I reckon you do.

AMOS. My name is Amos. My brother's name is Obadiah.

OBIE. What's your name?

JOE. *(Angrily.)* Joe.

OBIE. Move over, Joe. You're taking more than your share.

AMOS. *(Anxiously.)* We ought to put the lid down and hide.

(He sits down in box, out of sight.)

OBIE. And go to sleep.

(Joe slinks down out of sight. Obie clasps his hands in prayer.)

Thank you Lord for helping us this far and please help us some more tomorrow. Bless Mama and Pa and Sally and Amos. Amen.

(He disappears but reappears at once.)

And bless Preacher Prentice and Mrs. Strauss and Miss Melissa. Amen.

(He disappears but reappears at once.)

And—and bless Joe. Amen.

(Joe rises up and pushes Obie down out of sight. Joe quietly lets the lid down. There is silence. The lights slowly come up to morning brightness. Elijah McNaul strides in from R. He is a large, powerful man who voices his strong convictions. He goes to box, looks around, then lifts the lid slowly.)

MCNAUL. Good morning. Welcome, pilgrims. Welcome to my tannery.

AMOS. *(Boys stand up cautiously.)* Are you—Master McNaul who is going to help us?

MCNAUL. I am Elijah McNaul. Not master. No one is a master to thee. Never let me hear thee call any man master.

AMOS. Yes, sir, Master McNaul.

OBIE. Yes, Mister McNaul.

McNAUL. *(Points at Obie.)* Thee—has some stuffing in thy head. Come. Out of the box and go inside. Thee must eat quickly before the men come to work.

(Boys climb out of box. McNaul points and boys go single file around the right of flat and out of sight behind it.)

Then thee will climb up to the loft and hide there until it is night.

(Looks up.)

So beginneth another day which the Lord hath made.

(Singing begins. Cue 11. "Heav'n Bound Soldier." McNaul exits R behind flat. The flat is turned around. The other side is painted like the top of a loft. McNaul enters from behind flat from L, followed by Amos, Obie, and Joe. Singing stops.)

McNAUL. Now up the ladder to the loft.

(He sets up an imaginary ladder. Amos looks up, then pantomimes climbing the ladder.)

Thee will stay up there until I call thee tonight.

(Joe pantomimes climbing ladder.)

Running . . . hiding . . . like frightened sparrows.

(Obie pantomimes climbing ladder.)

No man can own another man. It is blasphemy!

(Boys stand C, frightened at his voice.)

Close the trap door!

(Amos pantomimes closing door.)

Take care. Do not walk or talk or make a sound. The men below will hear thee. And remember and let it be a comfort—God has his eye on the smallest sparrow.

(Pantomimes taking down the ladder and carrying it off, as he exits L.)

OBIE. He talks like the Bible.

AMOS. *(Sits down.)* Miss Melissa said he is a Quaker.

JOE. He's white. I don't trust no white folks.

OBIE. Joe—what did you do to your face?

(*Points at long scar running from Joe's eye to his lower jaw.*)

JOE. I didn't do nothing.

(*Turns away, hiding scar.*)

OBIE. There's a big scar.

JOE. Master did it—with a whip. Cut my face open.

OBIE. He must be a wicked man.

JOE. He's a devil. All the whites are devils.

OBIE. Master Bricker wasn't a devil. He was stingy, but he never whipped us.

AMOS. But he could of. He owned us—and that ain't right.

OBIE. He was born a slave owner, just like we was born slaves.

JOE. I wasn't born a slave.

OBIE. Where was you born?

JOE. In Africa.

AMOS. Africa?

JOE. (*Slowly and proudly.*) I was born in Africa.

(*To Obie.*)

Now don't ask me why I left. I didn't have no choice.

OBIE. Why did you leave, Joe?

JOE. (*Pause. Then he relives the bitter memory.*) I was little—maybe four or five. They come to our village. They caught my mother and the baby and caught me. White folks chained us on a boat. Hid us down below so nobody could see us. It was dark and it stunk and the baby cried all the time 'cause my mother couldn't feed him and then after a time he stopped crying—and he was dead. Lots of people was dead. And then my mother died and the white folks took her away—

(*Suddenly turns on Obie.*)

What'd you ask me that for! Leave me be! Leave me be!

AMOS. *(Quietly.)* We ought to go to sleep.

(He and Obie lie down together.)

JOE. *(Sits alone.)* I've been running—running for three days. Running—running—running—

(Drops his head, exhausted.)

McNAUL. *(He hurries in at L, quickly pantomimes putting up the ladder to trap door, and calls excitedly.)* Boys! Boys! Hear me, boys!

(Boys are immediately at trap door. They speak together as McNaul continues.)

Get thee to the trap door! Open it, boys. Quick!

AMOS. It's Mister McNaul.

OBIE. Something's wrong.

McNAUL. Down! Down the ladder. It is not safe here.

(Obie pantomimes climbing down.)

Someone reported thee. Quick! Slave-catchers are coming. They will find and catch thee.

(Amos pantomimes climbing down.)

Run through the back to the river. Swim! Follow the river to Petersburg.

(Joe pantomimes climbing down.)

Go to Miss Holkum's house behind the bank. There are two horseshoes above the door.

(Boys run off L.)

Run, boys, run. Run for your life!

(Singing begins. Cue 12. "You'd Better Run," followed by spoken and clapped rhythms. McNaul exits UL. Flat is removed off UL. Singing increases in tempo. Joe runs across from L to R.)

JOE. *(Calls and motions to boys.)* Run—run!

(Joe exits R. Amos, followed by Obie, runs across from L to R.)

AMOS. Run, Obie. Run!

OBIE. *(Stumbles. Amos quickly helps him.)* My foot.

AMOS. I'll help you.

(A red glow of light is seen UL.)

OBIE. Look! A fire!

AMOS. It's the tannery.

OBIE. It's on fire!

AMOS. They're burning the loft. They're burning us!

JOE. *(Runs in at R and motions.)* Run—run!

(The stage is now red as the flames leap higher. Amos and Obie run, repeating in terror.)

AMOS. Run—run—run—

OBIE. Run—run—run—

JOE. *(Follows them.)* Run—run—run—

(They exit R as singing builds to climax. The curtains close.
   Note: *There may be a short intermission or the play may be continued, with the curtains opening immediately on the next scene.)*

ACT TWO

(Singing is heard. Cue 13. "Steal Away." The curtains open on a bare stage. Amos enters from L. He is tired and frightened. He comes to footlights and speaks.)

AMOS. We ran and we hid and we got to Petersburg. We found Miss Holkum's house with the horseshoes above the door, but they didn't bring good luck to us. She had a sickness and it was catching. She told us how to get on to Richmond, and we slept there one night at Reverend Pringle's. Then we started stealing our way to Hanover, the next station.

(Moves to L.)

We were walking along the road that night close to a stone fence.

(A section of a stone fence is placed center, at an angle. Lights dim to night.)

and we came to a couple of farm houses. The dogs heard us and they started barking, waking everybody up.

(Loud dog barks are heard off. Joe runs in DL, followed by Obie. Amos joins them.)

JOE. Come on! Before the dogs catch us!

AMOS. *(Points.)* Someone's on the porch. He's got a gun!

JOE. Hide—hide by the fence!

(Boys run to fence, crouch and hide. Jud, a farmer, enters L with shotgun.)

JUD. Who is it? Who's there? I heard you. Whatcha doing prowling around my house? Where are you?

JOE. Over the fence and run for it!

(Boys scramble over the fence.)

JUD. Stop! Stop or I'll shoot.

(He fires the gun three times in the direction of fence. Boys, at R, fall to the ground for cover and remain motionless. Jud cautiously comes to fence.)

I see you. You won't get away. I gotcha covered and I'll shoot you if you move—shoot you dead.

(Jud starts to climb wall, slips, and falls, firing gun. There is a loud gun report. He crumbles in pain and moans loudly, sits up rubbing his leg.)

Oh! Oh, my leg!

AMOS. *(Amos raises his head and looks about. Then Joe does. Then Obie.)* You all right, Obie?

OBIE. He didn't shoot me.

(Jud moans louder.)

What happened to him?

JOE. *(Looks cautiously.)* I think—he shot hisself.

JUD. My leg. My leg.

JOE. *(Boys look toward wall, then cautiously cross to the back of it. They peak over, Jud moans and rubs his leg.)* He's hurt. Now's our chance to get away. Run!

(Joe and Amos exit R, but Obie leans over the wall.)

OBIE. You—you all right, Mister?

JUD. The gun went off when I was getting over the fence. Must have shot my leg.

JOE. *(Joe and Amos enter R.)* Come on. Come on!

JUD. Get help from the next house. You can't leave me here to die.

JOE. Get help? You crazy! You was shooting at us. You was going to kill us.

(Grabs Obie.)

Come on!

OBIE. He'll die.

JOE. They ain't going to catch me just 'cause of you. Come on!

(Joe pulling Obie, exits R.)

JUD. Wait. Fetch my neighbor. I'll bleed to death.

AMOS. *(Looks at L, where Jud points at neighbor's house, then calls off R.)*

You go on. I'll catch up with you.

(He quickly turns and runs back to entrance L, knocks at an imaginary door. He knocks again. First Neighbor enters at L.)

FIRST NEIGHBOR. What you knocking for? What you want?

AMOS. Please, sir, your neighbor, he's hurt real bad—over by the fence.

FIRST NEIGHBOR. *(Grabs Amos by shoulder.)* Who are you?

SECOND NEIGHBOR. *(Enters from L.)* What's going on?

FIRST NEIGHBOR. He says Jud's hurt. Must of been the shots we heard.

SECOND NEIGHBOR. Where is he?

AMOS. By the fence. Now let me go.

(He struggles.)

FIRST NEIGHBOR. Oh, no. We're going to keep you. Get a rope. Tie him up.

(Second Neighbor exits L.)

AMOS. Please let me go. I told you where he was.

FIRST NEIGHBOR. What are you? A runaway? We'll find out tomorrow.

(Second Neighbor enters L with rope and ties Amos' hands behind him.)

That will hold you tonight and teach you a lesson. You won't be running away now. Where is Jud?

AMOS. By the fence.

FIRST NEIGHBOR. *(Goes to fence. Jud moans.)* Jud—is that you?

JUD. Oh! Thank God you've come.

(First Neighbor helps Jud up. Second Neighbor holds Amos.)

FIRST NEIGHBOR. What happened?

JUD. The gun went off—accidentally—shot my leg.

FIRST NEIGHBOR. Easy. Easy. I'll help you to the house.

(He helps Jud. They go L.)

JUD. Get the doctor from town.

SECOND NEIGHBOR. *(Pushes Amos.)* What about him?

FIRST NEIGHBOR. Put him in the shed. There may be a reward. Lock him up.

(First Neighbor exits with Jud.)

SECOND NEIGHBOR. *(Pulls Amos down L, then pantomimes opening a door.)* Get in the shed.

(Pushes Amos through the imaginary door.)

You won't steal away again. We'll lock you up till tomorrow. Then you know what will happen, don't you? You know what they'll do to a runaway slave?

(He pantomimes shutting the door, putting a peg in the latch, and exits L.)

AMOS. *(His courage and hopes are gone. He speaks softly and sadly.)* I had to help him, Mama. He was hurt. And now—I'm caught. They'll beat me. Sell me to another master.

(Starts to cry.)

I tried, Mama. I tried to get to Pa.

(Crying freely.)

But—but Obie will make it.

(Trying to stop crying.)

Please, please let Obie get away—and be free.

(Buries his head, shaking with sobs.)

I tried, Mama. I tried.

(His sobs become quieter. Obie enters L, stops, frightened but determined, looks around carefully, and moving cautiously comes to C.)

OBIE. *(Calls softly.)* Amos . . . ? Amos . . . ?

(Amos slowly raises his head.)

Amos . . . ?

AMOS. Is that you, Obie?

OBIE. Yes. Are you in the shed?

AMOS. Yes.

OBIE. You got to get out. Quick. It's almost light.

AMOS. I can't. I'm tied up and the door's locked.

OBIE. Maybe there's a loose board. I'll feel.

(He pantomimes feeling carefully around the shed.)

If I had a shovel, I could dig you out.

AMOS. There's no way out. I'm caught. But you can still get away. You go on—go with Joe.

OBIE. Leave you?

AMOS. Go on, Obie! If you stay, they'll catch you, too.

OBIE. I ain't going to leave you, Amos! I'll find a way. I'll get you out!

Amos. Go on, Obie. And keep on going—Pa's waiting for you.

Obie. He's waiting for both of us!

(He is at the imaginary door and is elated.)

Amos—Amos! The door—it isn't locked! It's just a wooden peg. I can pull it out!

(Pantomimes pulling peg out and opens door and goes to Amos. He speaks with relief, love, and joy.)

Oh, Amos.

Amos. *(Answers with the same sincere emotion.)* Obie.

(As Obie unties him).

Where's Joe?

Obie. On ahead. We hid. We saw them tie you up. We thought sure you was a goner.

Amos. So did I.

Obie. Joe tried to pull me away, but I couldn't leave you, Amos.

Amos. How did you get rid of him?

Obie. *(Proudly.)* I—bit him.

Amos. *(Freed of ropes, stretches.)* We'll catch up with him at the next stop, at Bowling Green.

Obie. Come on.

(They slip out the door and creep silently L.) It's getting light.

Amos. There's just one star left.

Obie. Amos, do you know what I think? I think maybe—there's a good angel watching and looking out for us.

(Singing begins. Cue 14. "The Angel Of The Lord." Obie holds out his hand. Amos takes it. They exit slowly at L. Fence is removed. Lights come up to morning. Singing stops. Loud shouts and repeated gunshots are heard UL. "There he goes . . . get him . . . he's heading for the house . . ." etc. Joe runs in UL, terrified and desperate, looks back; there is more shouting. He runs DL. The way is blocked. He turns, rushes to R. He is suddenly met by Old Man, who enters R, shotgun pointed at Joe. Joe stops.)

OLD MAN. Stop. You ain't running no place, boy.

YOUNG MAN. *(Enters UL.)* You get him?

OLD MAN. I got him. Tie his hands.

(Young man ties Joe's hands.)

We'll take him into town. He's a real husky one. Ought to be worth a big reward.

YOUNG MAN. They say there are three of them.

OLD MAN. Three?

YOUNG MAN. They say they shot a farmer down the road.

OLD MAN. A real mean one, huh? Shooting white folks. You got to learn your place, boy. And I reckon you will when your master gets you back. He'll take it right out of your hide.

(Gives gun to Young Man.)

Keep him covered. We'll take him to town.

(Young Man puts gun at Joe's back and guides him off R. Old Man follows.)

Step lively, boy. No more running for you. You're caught.

(They exit.)

OBIE. *(He and Amos crawl in DL. They are frightened.)* Did they catch Joe?

AMOS. Yes. Tied him up and they're taking him away.

(Off R, there are excited shouts and several gunshots. "Look out . . . He got away . . . Get him!" etc. Joe runs in from R. There are more gunshots. Joe is hit in the back. He staggers and falls. Amos and Obie hide by flattening themselves on the ground. The two men run in R.)

OLD MAN. Why did you shoot? What did you shoot him for? You stupid idiot!

(Old Man kneels over Joe.)

He's dead. You think his master's going to pay us for a dead slave? You dumb, blundering fool! Well, pick him up! We'll get rid of him.

(They drag Joe off R.)

There are two more. We'll get the other two. They can't be far. We'll get them—alive.

(They exit R.)

OBIE. *(Amos, then Obie, slowly rise up.)* What happened?

AMOS. Don't look, Obie. Don't look.

(Holds Obie close so he can't see.)

OBIE. Did they get Joe?

AMOS. Joe's dead.

OBIE. But he was just alive. I saw him running.

AMOS. He's dead. They shot him. Now they'll hunt us! We're next, Obie. We got to get to Bowling Green—before they get us! Come on! Run! Run!

OBIE. *(Nods. Singing starts. Cue 15. "You'd Better Run.")* Run!

AMOS. Run for your life!

(They exit L. A small kitchen table and a stool are placed DR. Jack Johnson, a free Negro, good-natured and unafraid, enters R and sits at table reading a book. Lights come up on room area at R. "Run" rhythms stop. Jack turns a page and yawns. Amos and Obie slip in from L, very cautiously. They hide, venture again, as they cross to R. Amos pantomimes peeking in an imaginary window, then motions Obie to follow, and they silently go to left side of room and pantomime knocking softly at a door. Jack raises his head. Amos knocks a second time. Jack goes to and pantomimes opening the door. He looks at the weary and frightened boys.)

JACK. Come in.

(Boys enter room.)

I was waiting up for you. You're kind of late getting to Bowling Green.

AMOS. How did you know we'd come?

JACK. I heard about you. But they said there were three of you.

AMOS. There was. But Joe—they shot Joe.

OBIE. He's dead.

JACK. Sit down.

(Obie sits wearily and rests his head on the table.)

The sheriff was here tonight—looking for you.

AMOS. How'd he know to come here?

JACK. Some of my good neighbors complained that I have too many night visitors.

(Innocently.)

They think I'm part of the Underground Railroad.

(Laughs.)

But they haven't caught me yet—and they ain't going to. Sheriff said you shot a white man.

AMOS. He shot hisself.

JACK. Well, they're out looking for you. And we've got to move you on fast. It ain't safe for you here. But how am I going to get the two of you out of town? They'll be combing the country for two runaway boys.

(Boys look at each other, frightened.)

It's most daylight and I'll have to go to work as usual.

(Thinking aloud.)

Now—I could take the little one with me. I sometimes take my own little boy along while I chop wood. But that leaves you.

OBIE. I ain't going to leave Amos!

JACK. Hush! You'll wake up the family.

(Nods to R. He looks at Amos.)

My other one is a girl. About your size.

AMOS. I ain't a girl.

JACK. 'Course you ain't, and they're not looking for a girl—are they?

(Beams with an idea.)

That's it!

AMOS. What's it?

JACK. You wait. I'll be right back—with a dress.

(He exits R.)

OBIE. What's he thinking?

AMOS. I don't know, but I hope it's not what I think he's thinking.

JACK. *(Enters R, holding out a dress and bandana.)* You—will be my —little girl.

AMOS. Me?

JACK. Now put on this dress.

AMOS. Me!

JACK. Put this bandana over your head. Make yourself real pretty.

(Gives Amos bandana and dress.)

Now I'll get my axe and you and me—

(To Obie.)

we'll go to the woods. We'll walk down the road, singing—like I do every morning.

(To Amos.)

Then you come along—all pretty-like in a dress—with my lunch pail. If anybody stops you, you say—real sweet like— you're taking your Pa his lunch which he forgot. Then follow the road in the woods. You'll hear me chopping and singing.

AMOS. I don't want to be—a girl!

JACK. What's wrong? You scared?

AMOS. Huh?

JACK. I figure this will be the bravest thing you've ever done, and— you have to do it all by yourself. You big enough to do it?

(Amos nods.)

And tonight I'll start you on the cattle path to Fredericksburg. The next station is at the Webber farm.

(To Obie.)

Come on—

(Pointedly.)

son. Can you sing?

(Obie nods.)

Then sing. Helps keep up your courage—and the white folks, they like to see us happy.

(Jack and Obie pantomime exiting at door and exit off L. Amos looks at dress. Then like taking bitter medicine, he braces himself, quickly puts it over his head and masculinely strides around the table. He puts bandana on his head, picks up lunch pail and sits, pulling up his skirt and crossing his legs. Singing begins. Cue 16. "Jim Crack Corn." Lights dim out on room area. Amos exits R, as furniture is taken off. Jack and Obie enter L and cross. Singing dims out as Jack and Obie sing the same song with forced cheerfulness. They see a Patrol with gun who enters R. They stop singing, look at each other, then start singing louder.)

JACK. Morning.

PATROL. Morning.

(Jack and Obie pass the Patrol, look at each other, smile, then start singing.)

Just a minute.

(Jack and Obie stop.)

You see anyone up the road?

JACK. No, sir. You looking for someone?

PATROL. We got a patrol out for two runaway slave boys.

JACK. Two runaway boys?

PATROL. They say they're dangerous.

JACK. Goodness me! What kind of dangerous?

PATROL. Shot a farmer. There's a reward for them.

JACK. Well, what do you know!

PATROL. Keep a look-out.

JACK. Yes, sir!

PATROL. They won't get by me.

JACK. No, sir! Come along—son.

(Takes Obie's hand.)

No, sir, they sure won't get by you.

(Jack and Obie look at each other and start singing and exit R. Patrol follows them to R. Amos enters L, sees Patrol and stops, frightened. Summoning up his courage, he walks toward Patrol. He stops; remembering he is a girl, he takes smaller steps.)

PATROL. *(Turns and sees him.)* Where are you goin'?

AMOS. 'Cuse me, sir—

(Raises his voice.)

'cuse me, sir.

PATROL. Yes? Speak up.

AMOS. Did you see my Papa?

PATROL. Your Papa?

AMOS. And my brother go by this way?

PATROL. He a woodcutter?

AMOS. Yes, sir.

(Raises voice.)

Yes, sir.

PATROL. They went down the road.

(Smiles.)

You his little girl?

AMOS. Yes, sir.

(Raises voice.)

Yes, sir.

PATROL. *(Pleasantly.)* And I must say you're a mighty pretty little girl.

(Amos comically smiles back at him.)

You taking his lunch to him?

(Amos nods.)

That's a nice little girl. Go along, now. Go along to your Papa. I'm patrolling the road. Two runaways going north, but they're not going to get past me.

AMOS. No, sir. No, sir. They won't get past you.

(Passes Patrol.)

PATROL. Now run along.

AMOS. Yes, sir. I'll run. I'll run. I'll run!

(Amos runs off R. Patrol exits L. Singing begins. Cue 17. "Oh, a-Rock-a My Soul." Lights come up bright. Obie enters L, running happily, pulling a small kite which is on a short string. He circles and skips and laughs. One of his bare feet has a bandage on it. A plain bench is placed DL. A box-trunk is put at L. Will Webber enters L. He is fifteen, a wholesome and manly young boy. He carries a book. Singing stops.)

OBIE. Look, Will. It flies like a bird.

(He stops, out of breath, comes to bench where Will sits.)

It's nice here on your farm. Sitting on the back porch and knowing today I'll have fried chicken again with potatoes—all I can eat—and I'll be sitting right at the table with white folks.

WILL. I'm glad thee is here. And mother says thee and Amos must stay in Fredericksburg. Stay here with us on the farm until your foot is well and thee are rested before you go on.

(Amos enters DL, in boy's clothes.)

OBIE. Look, Amos. Watch! It flies like a bird—in the sky—

(He circles with kite.)

Whee-ee-ee! I'm a bird. I can fly—in the sky.

(He exits R.)

AMOS. Obie never had no playthings before.

WILL. I brought a new book for us to read. Thee is learning to read very quickly.

AMOS. What did you write on the first page?

WILL. *(Smiles and reads proudly.)* I wrote: Will Webber is my name. Fredericksburg is my location. Heaven is my destination. Thee can write that in your first book. "Amos is my name—" But thee should have a last name.

AMOS. I never had one. But Pa—in his letter said he'd taken the name of—Carpenter.

WILL. *(Stands, and they shake hands.)* Amos Carpenter.

AMOS. How many more miles is it to Philadelphia?

WILL. About two hundred.

AMOS. We should be starting.

WILL. Mother says thee are not to walk any further.

AMOS. How we going to get there?

WILL. I said—if *I* could go to Philadelphia and visit Grandfather, I could take the train and take Obie and thee with me.

AMOS. Could you?

WILL. No. Mother said it would look very strange for a Quaker boy to have two Negro servants. And that the train stations are watched, you know, very closely by slave-catchers.

AMOS. We got to get to Pa somehow.

WILL. I wish I could help you. Oh, I wish I could put thee both in my pocket.

(Looks at trunk and smiles with a new idea.)

And I can!

AMOS. How?

WILL. I can put thee in my luggage.

AMOS. Luggage?

WILL. I can put thee in the trunk!

(Points to trunk.)

You can ride on the train all the way to Philadelphia—inside the trunk and nobody will know! Obie! Come here, and see if thee will fit!

(They pull trunk forward excitedly and raise lid.)

Get in. Try it out for size.

(Amos steps into trunk.)

Mother can put padding around the corners. We can make air holes so thee can breathe.

AMOS. *(Holds nose, raises one hand as if he is jumping into water.)*

One, two, three.

(He disappears in trunk.)

WILL. *(Obie runs in from R.)* Here, Obie, get thee in the trunk.

AMOS. *(Head appears.)* With me.

(Head disappears.)

OBIE. *(Climbs into trunk.)* What are we playing? What is the name of the game?

AMOS. *(Stands up by Obie.)* Philadelphia is—my destination!

(Amos and Obie disappear, and Will closes the lid on the trunk. Singing begins. Cue 18. "Git on Board." Mother enters DL and stands with back toward audience. She holds a cap and coat for Will, who puts them on. Then he speaks over low humming.)

WILL. Goodby, Mother. Don't worry. I won't lose my ticket and Grandfather will meet us. Goodby. I'll take good care of the trunk—and everything that is in it. Don't cry, Mother. I know it is a dangerous trip, but I'll be careful. Goodby. Goodby.

(Two stagehands enter UL and carry trunk to C. Mother waves and backs off DL. Will waves, then turns to trunk as stagehands set it down with a loud bang. Singing stops.)

Please—please be careful! There are—breakable things inside the trunk.

(Stagehands exit UR.)

CONDUCTOR. *(Calls and enters DR.)* All aboard. All aboard for Washington, Baltimore, Philadelphia, New York.

WILL. Mister, mister, can I ride in the baggage car with my trunk?

CONDUCTOR. *(Crosses to L.)* Don't make no difference to me where you ride, sonny, just as long as you pay your fare.

WILL. Oh, I have my ticket—to Philadelphia!

(Gives him ticket.)

CONDUCTOR. All aboard! All aboard!

(Conductor exits L. Singing starts slowly then gains in speed as the train moves. Cue 19. "Train Song.")

WILL. *(Stands by trunk and smiles, eyes following the passing scenery from L to R.)* We're moving. We're on our way.

(Knocks on top of trunk. There is an answering knock inside.)

Thee will soon be free.

(Singing swells, then dims as Will cautiously lifts lid of trunk and Amos and Obie peek out.)

AMOS. Look, Obie, through the crack in the door. See the trees go by.

(Their eyes move with the passing scenery.)

OBIE. So fast.

WILL. Grandfather wrote he would contact your father.

AMOS. Pa?

WILL. And tell him I am bringing two special pieces of luggage. Thee must be careful even in Pennsylvania because of the Fugitive Slave Law.

CONDUCTOR. *(Enters L.)* Hey there, sonny.

(Lid closes quickly.)

Who are you talking to?

WILL. Talking to?

(Sits on trunk.)

CONDUCTOR. There's no livestock in the trunk, is there? Let's see.

WILL. No, sir. No, sir. I—I was just—talking to myself.

CONDUCTOR. *(Crosses.)* Oh, well, I talk to myself, too. I figure I have a better conversation with myself than when I talk to some people. We're coming into Washington.

(Exits R.)

WILL. Washington!

(Knocks on trunk.)

We've come as far as Washington.

AMOS. *(Trunk lid rises. Amos and Obie nod, smile and repeat.)*

Washington.

(Lid is lowered. Will sits on trunk with arms folded. Singing swells and then dims.)

CONDUCTOR. *(Off, calls.)* Baltimore. Baltimore. All aboard!

(Singing swells and then dims. Will stands and knocks on trunk. Lid is lifted and Amos and Obie peek out.)

WILL. We just crossed a big river and I think it was the Susquehanna, so that means we're in Pennsylvania.

CONDUCTOR. *(Off R, calls.)* Philadelphia! Next stop—Philadelphia.

(Trunk lid closes quickly as Conductor enters.)

This is your station, sonny. Philadelphia.

(He exits L.)

WILL. Yes, sir. Thank you, sir.

(Singing swells and then stops. Two stagehands enter L.)

Please, will you take my trunk to my Grandfather's house. This is the address.

(He gives them a piece of paper.)

And please, please, handle the trunk—carefully. It contains two precious—gifts.

(Stagehands put trunk down at R and exit.)

Amos . . . Obie . . . we are here. Thee can lift the lid. Thee has come—to your free home.

(Will beckons off R. Pa, wonderfully real, enters DR and stands at side. Will exits R. Amos and Obie raise the lid slowly, stand, and smile to each other. They step out of the trunk, look at the free ground they are standing on, look around, then breathe deeply.)

PA. *(Steps forward.)* Amos?

(Another step.)

Obadiah?

AMOS. *(Boys look at him, at each other, and then back at him.)* Pa?

OBIE. Pa?

PA. My boys!

(Holds out his arms.)

AMOS. *(Both boys run to him, shouting.)* Pa! Pa!

(They embrace.)

We're here, Pa. We're here.

OBIE. We made it!

PA. My two big boys! Let me look at you. And you come all the way from South Carolina—by yourselves!

AMOS. *(Proudly.)* Five hundred miles.

OBIE. On the Underground Railroad!

PA. How did you do it? How did you do it!

AMOS. I think Obie said it right. It was like there was a good angel— and good people—watching over us.

(Choir starts to hum. Cue 20. "Steal Away." Preacher enters from L and crosses to R and stands.)

First there was Preacher Prentice who brought your letter and started us on the way.

(Mrs. Strauss enters R, crosses L, stands by Preacher.)

And then Mrs. Strauss who fixed candy medicine and wrote us a pass.

(Melissa enters R, crosses, stands by Mrs. Strauss.)

And Miss Melissa who drove us in her carriage to Virginia.

(McNaul enters R, stands by Melissa.)

And Mister McNaul who hid us in the loft—with Joe.

(Jack enters R and stands by McNaul.)

And Reverend Pringle in Richmond and Jack who helped us and dressed me up like a girl.

(Mother and Will enter R and stand by Jack.)

And last, Mrs. Webber on the farm and Will who hid us in his trunk and all by himself brought us—home. Together—from one to the next, to the next—

(Actors across the back in a semicircle, one by one join hands.)

they helped us—all the way. And now when we get Mama—

(Mama enters DL and stands by Pa and Obie.)

and Sally—we'll all be together—free.

(Choir sings softly, "Steal Away." Amos comes to footlights and stands at C. Singing stops. Proudly and joyfully he announces.)

My name is Amos Carpenter.
On free land is my location.
And—

(Smiles happily.)

Heaven is my destination.

(Singing begins. Cue 21. "Didn't My Lord Deliver Daniel?" The rest of the cast enter from L, cross to R, and stand behind the principals. All sing with spirit and clap in rhythm.

Curtain.)

Peck's Bad Boy

In 1882, George Peck, a Milwaukee newspaper editor, began a series of stories which appeared as editorial humor in his weekly paper, *Peck's Sun*. The stories about the despicable pranks Hennery, the Bad Boy, played on his drunken father were so successful that within months Peck's paper had a growing nationwide circulation. Within a year the first series of stories was collected and published as *Peck's Bad Boy and His Pa*, and more volumes followed.

Peck created a magical world in which the common man might rebel against the prevalent saccharine sentimentalism of the time. It is a world in which any prank, no matter how preposterous, really works, and one can laugh openly at the consequences: the pompous and overbearing victims in obvious discomfort. Through Hennery, the preadolescent practical joker, Peck pokes fun at the established and sacred institutions of family, church, and commerce, represented by priggish and hypocritical authority figures, such as Hennery's father, the clergy, and businessmen. The adult targets of Hennery's pranks, inferior beings who deserve everything they are stupid enough to take, are no match for the coarse, vigorous, and ingenious Bad Boy. Even though he is repeatedly punished for his excesses, each time he manages to rebel and remain an incorrigible but free individual.

Harris's dramatic version of *Peck's Bad Boy* has been constructed from events and characters suggested by several of Peck's stories. The play, a farce, is filled with the action of broad practical jokes and absurd schemes perpetrated and enormously enjoyed by the young hero, now named Henry. Because it is for a young audience, the play was written with an essential departure from the original source: the characterizations have been softened, so that the characters' relationships with one another are kindlier and more humane. Vulgarity and sarcasm have been eliminated; hypocrisy and cruelty, reduced to a minimum, appear only in the characterization of the swindler.

The theme, immediately and inherently evident in the opening scene as the maid describes Henry's character, is that a youth with ingenuity and imagination can outwit adult authority and usually get away with it. That thematic statement then motivates the entire plot, as Henry proceeds to test and retest its truth, either intentionally or coincidentally. Although the theme underlies his antics, neither he nor any other character states the message explicitly.

Thrusting the plot forward are a set of dramatic questions rooted in the theme. There are two major questions of plot: How will Henry manipulate his father into forswearing profanity and liquor to earn full church membership? When and how will Henry discover and stop the machinations of the swindler?

Foreshadowing of the complications not only poses further questions to be resolved, but also increases the audience's enjoyment of the chaos that results. How will Henry scare Katie, the maid? What pranks will Henry play on the deacon's wife when she comes to call? Who will step into the rabbit traps in the front yard or slip in the soft soap on the parlor floor? Who will be subjected to the sneezing powder and the red ants? To whom will Polly Parrot say what?

The entanglement of mad antics which occur in rapid succession pushes the story forward at a dizzying pace. The situations are incredible, and the impossibilities mount until all standards of normality are forgotten. These are absurd people in an illogical, unpredictable world of high hilarity.

In the center of it all is the character of Henry, the practical joker. When the complications resulting from his mischief multiply beyond Henry's control, he does attempt to warn the unsuspecting victim, even though his efforts are in vain. Through direct address, he alone of all the characters establishes a strong rapport with the audience, including them in his plans, wondering about possible outcomes, and sharing moments of delicious fun when all goes as planned.

Surrounding Henry are the other characters of the play. None is as fully drawn as the hero, who easily outmaneuvers each of them. They are either the objects of his jokes or the accomplices in his schemes. In every instance, the excessively gullible victims and assistants are more than willing to follow Henry's lead, even though everyone, except the crooked Mr. Wellington, knows he is full of tricks.

Each character is a type, perfected for the contrivances of the plot. They are a naïve, giggling, squealing maid; her lover, an easily befuddled policeman; a nearsighted, scatterbrained, and loving mother; a bellowing, quick-tempered, and easily duped father who never forgets he was a military officer; a self-assured and proper churchwoman; and a scheming, unctious swindler who fleeces the unwary.

The humor of the physical action is augmented by unexpected words and lines in the dialogue. The father's substitution of "fudge" for "damn" and the parrot's chatter are jarring and funny because they are out of context. Although the brief lines reveal little characterization, they are necessary to accomplish the action of the plot.

Peck's Bad Boy is not a musical play in the usual sense of the term, but the use of song and sound repeatedly underpin the humor and the action of the plot. Barking dogs, a doorbell ringing, a gunshot, a band playing, and a parrot who squawks timely comments throughout the play enliven the already exhilarated confusion of the household. Old songs and hymns ironically sharpen the comedy of the situations in which they are played or sung.

The play takes place in a single locale: the formal parlor of the family. The action extends beyond that room to indicate the existence of an entire home, including an upstairs, kitchen, and outside lawns. The setting is a quaint, realistic domain which contains and intensifies by contrast the ridiculous antics of the absurd inhabitants.

The comedy of the plot complications often depends on the support of technical effects, such as a talking parrot and soft soap on the stage floor. Specific costume and property pieces are necessary to project the appropriate visual images for some of the comic action. A suit of long underwear, a hornet's nest, a snake, physicians' coats, surgical instruments, and a pig's bladder are a few examples.

Peck's Bad Boy is a boisterous farce in which extraordinary characters find themselves constantly enmeshed in incredible situations. Realism and reasonable motivation have been replaced by the fantastic and ridiculous, creating a rapidly moving string of overlapping events which build to the resolution of a criminal captured and a sinner reformed.

Peck's Bad Boy

by Aurand Harris

Suggested by stories from "Peck's Bad Boy"
by George W. Peck

Katie, the hired girl

Henry, the "bad boy"

Mother, his Ma

Major, his Pa

Policeman, Katie's steady beau

Mrs. Langford, the deacon's wife

Horace Q. Winthrop Wellington, the city crook

The scene is a small town in the Midwest, 1890.
All three acts take place in the front parlor.

Peck's Bad Boy

ACT ONE

(Scene: A parlor. At back is a large center door. Behind it is an entrance hall, leading to the front door, unseen, off R, and to other rooms off L. A smaller door is DR. A bay window is at L with open French windows. A table and chair are at L. A sofa is at R. The room has a formal and proper, a quaint and carica-ture-Victorian look. There is curtain music, "Home, Sweet Home." Curtain rises. Katie, a spirited young girl, enters at back with a small feather duster. She hums and sings as she quickly dusts the table. She stops, smells flowers in vase, dusts the chair, stops, sniffs flowers again, looks about, then quickly plucks a daisy from the vase.)

KATIE. Patrick Michael O'Reilly *(She pulls petals.)* He loves me . . . he loves me not . . . he loves me . . .

POLLY. *(Parrot in a cage at L squawks in a loud voice off L.)* Silly girl. Silly girl. Silly girl. *(In panic Katie puts flower in her mouth, stuffs her cheeks, and stares straight ahead.)* Pretty Polly. Pretty Polly. Pretty Polly.

KATIE. *(Looks at cage. Relieved, takes flower out of her mouth).* Oh, you naughty, naughty bird. You gave me such a fright.

POLLY. Tickle, tickle, eat a pickle. Tickle, tickle, eat a pickle.

KATIE. Quiet, Polly. *(Dusting again.)* So much to do. Company coming to tea and the Major and the Mrs. not home yet. And Henry —goodness knows where that boy is or what he is up to. *(At footlights, to audience.)* Henry isn't a bad boy, he is just too full of fun, and always playing jokes. Last night he put bits of rubber in the macaroni—*(Laughs.)* Yesterday he tied his Pa's false teeth onto a toothless dog. *(Laughs.)* And Sunday he put a homeless skunk in the cellar, and the preacher came! Phew! Whew! *(Off R, the barking of many dogs is heard. Katie runs to hall.)* Here he comes. That's Henry, with every dog in the neighborhood barking at his heels. Listen—he'll slam the front door. *(Door slams, off.)* Watch—he'll come in with some new trick. But he won't fool me—not this time. *(Henry enters at back, whistling loudly and happily. He is a young teenager with an engaging grin, a sunny disposition, and an overflowing sense of humor. He carries a hornet's nest swinging on the end of a pole. Katie politely ignores him.)* Afternoon, Henry.

HENRY. Afternoon, Katie.

KATIE. That's a happy whistle.

HENRY. Oh, I'm working. I'm going into the whistling business.

KATIE. Whistling business?

HENRY. I'm going to hire an office and put out a sign. "Boy—to whistle for lost dogs." Think of how many dogs are lost every day! I'll whistle for them, enjoy myself, and make a million dollars. *(Whistles.)*

KATIE. *(Not looking at him.)* You'd scare them all away.

HENRY. *(Looks at her and at nest.)* Scare? I would scare who?

KATIE. Not me. Not this time. *(Henry tiptoes up behind her.)* I'm on to all your pranks. You can't trick me. No sirree. *(Henry carefully holds pole over her head, dropping the nest in front of her face. Katie screams.)*

HENRY. Don't be afraid. It's just a hornet's nest.

KATIE. Hornets! *(Screams again and runs.)*

HENRY. It's a present for Pa. He said the postman was so slow he wished he had a hornet's nest to drop in his britches. *(Pantomimes dropping it in place.)*

KATIE. Give it to me. *(Takes pole, fearfully.)* Mrs. Langford is coming. We're having tea in the parlor. *(Goes toward hall.)*

HENRY. Be careful.

KATIE. I'll put it on the porch.

HENRY. Don't shimmy them up.

KATIE. Shimmy who up?

HENRY. The hornets!

KATIE. Are there hornets INSIDE! *(Screams and runs, exiting at back.)*

POLLY. Polly wants a pickle. Polly wants a pickle.

HENRY. Hello, Polly. Pretty Polly. Pretty Polly.

POLLY. Pretty Polly. Pretty Polly. Pretty Polly.

HENRY. I've got a new word for you—desperado. Can you squawk that, Polly? Desperado. *(Takes tabloid newspaper from pocket.)* Jessie James was a desperado. Here's all about him in the *Police Reporter. (Shows paper to parrot and pronounces word slowly.)* See, des-per-a-do. Come on, increase your vocabulary, Polly. Des-per-a-do. *(He waits hopefully. Polly is silent.)* Think about it. *(Turns to back page of paper.)* And this is a LIVE criminal. "Wanted in five states." Look at his picture! He's a crook.

POLLY. He's a crook. He's a crook. He's a crook.

HENRY. That's a girl. Come on—desperado.

POLLY. He's a crook. He's a crook. He's a crook.

HENRY. *(Holds up his hand.)* Class dismissed.

POLLY. He's a crook. He's a crook. He's a crook.

HENRY. *(Waves hand.)* School is over! I brought you something— something to play with. *(Puts newspaper in one pocket, takes articles from another pocket and puts them on table.)* Now where did I put it? *(Holds up small shaker.)* No. That's a shaker of sneezing powder. *(To audience, innocently.)* You never know when someone wants to sneeze awful bad, and this powder helps them sneeze real loud. *(Sneezes as he puts shaker on table, holds up glass bottle.)* And this is Pa's old medicine bottle—full—of red ants! Look at them all running around. Little red ants crawling all over each other.

KATIE. *(Enters at back with tray on which is a cookie jar, tea cups, saucers, and plate of cookies.)* What are you putting on your Ma's best table spread?

HENRY. A bottle of my best red ants.

KATIE. Ants! Take them away.

HENRY. *(Suddenly feels his pocket and starts wiggling.)* Here's what I brought for Polly. I brought her—a little green playfellow. *(Holds up small snake.)*

KATIE. *(Her back to him, goes to sofa and fluffs pillow.)* No, Henry. Give it to me.

HENRY. Give it to you?

KATIE. Give it to me.

HENRY. You want it?

KATIE. That's what I said.

HENRY. *(Grins to audience.)* She wants it. Then I'll have to give it to her. Where? *(Katie holds out hand without looking.)* I do hereby give you—one wiggly green snake.

KATIE. Snake! *(Sees it, screams, and runs, hides behind chair.)*

HENRY. *(Chases her.)* Take him. He's yours.

KATIE. *(Rises from behind chair.)* Oh, St. Peter and St. Paul, help me! *(Crosses herself and disappears behind chair again. Doorbell rings.)*

HENRY. Someone's at the door.

KATIE. *(Rises.)* It's your Ma and Pa. *(Doorbell rings again.)* Oh, St. Peter, thank you. *(Runs to hall.)* And St. Paul. *(Crosses herself and exits.)*

HENRY. *(To snake.)* You're a lively little fellow. Look at him, wiggling like green spaghetti. He's sticking his tongue out. He's saying, "hello." Hello to you. *(Sticks his tongue out at snake.)* He's thin in the middle. I think he's hungry. Well, spaghetti-spagotly, by golly you're in luck. Katie brought in a whole jar of cookies. *(Lifts lid of cookie jar.)* Go ahead. Eat up. Have a cookie. *(Drops snake into cookie jar and puts lid on.)*

MOTHER. *(Enters at back in hallway. She is sweet and attractive and wears a loosely fitting maternity dress. She looks back off R and calls.)* Hurry, dear. Mrs. Langford will be here at four. She is very punctual. *(Calls to L.)* Katie, the Major and I are back. *(Sees Henry. She is near-sighted.)* Oh, Henry, I'm so glad you're home. Mrs. Langford is coming to tea. *(Goes to hall and calls.)* What is keeping your father? He saw a nest on the porch and went to investigate.

HENRY. A nest?

MOTHER. *(Hurries to Henry.)* Oh, such a happy day. Your father—I was so proud of him. He didn't mention the Civil War, and he didn't loose his temper. He and the preacher shook hands.

HENRY. You mean Pa has joined the church!

MOTHER. He is on probation.

HENRY. *(To audience.)* That means Pa's got one foot in the church door.

MOTHER. The preacher said, Father must prove he is sincere. And if he resists all worldly temptations, he will be—taken into the fold.

HENRY. Then Pa can go to heaven—with you and me.

MOTHER. I wouldn't think of going to heaven without your father!

HENRY. We'll get him there. Don't you worry.

MOTHER. Unfortunately he has—two weaknesses.

HENRY. Pa swears a lot and Pa drinks a little.

MOTHER. But he has promised to stop. We must help him.

HENRY. I will do anything for Pa. *(To audience.)* I'll even give him a boost through the pearly gates. *(Hand over heart.)* I solemnly swear, before I am through, Pa will swear off the bottle and Pa will swear off swearing.

MAJOR. *(Off R, shouts angrily.)* Damn it! Damn it! Oh, damn! Shoo. Go away. Damnation!

HENRY. It's Pa. And he's swearing!

MOTHER. No, Hubert. Probation! *(Looks up.)* Someone is listening.

MAJOR. *(Enters at C, swatting his face.)* Damn it! Damn it! Damn it!

MOTHER. No, Hubert, don't swear. Say—say fudge. Fudge!

MAJOR. Fudge! Fudge! Fudge!

HENRY. Is anything wrong, Pa?

MAJOR. Wrong? I'm bitten—I'm blood-sucked by a hive of damn—

MOTHER. Fudge!

MAJOR. —bees! *(Slaps his face.)*

MOTHER. *(Rushes to back.)* Katie.

KATIE. *(Off, loudly.)* I'm polishing the furniture.

MOTHER. Bring the liniment.

MAJOR. A million bees came buzz-zz-zzing out of a nest—and thought I was a sweet pea.

HENRY. A nest? Hornets?

MAJOR. Beess-ss-ss! Where is the damn—the liniment?

HENRY. I did it, Pa.

MAJOR. Did what?

HENRY. I did it for you.

MAJOR. What for me?

HENRY. The nest. I brought you a hornet's nest.

MAJOR. You!

HENRY. For the postman! You said you wanted a hornet's nest to drop inside of his—fudge—britches.

MAJOR. Oh, dam— *(Mother and Henry motion for him to stop. He tries to control himself.)* Marshmallows! Caramel! Taffy! Sourballs! Peppermint sticks! FUDGE!

KATIE. *(Breathless, enters at back with bottle in each hand and a cloth.)* Here's the liniment. Who's dying?

HENRY. Let me help. *(Takes bottle and cloth, which is saturated with brown liquid, and rushes to Major, who sits.)*

MAJOR. Quick! Oh—Oh! I feel like I have been charged by the cavalry! *(Yells and kicks as Henry smears Major's face with cloth.)* This is worse—worse than the war!

MOTHER. The bumps are turning dark.

HENRY. It's working!

MAJOR. Then put on more. More!

HENRY. *(Grins at the audience.)* MORE! *(Covers Major's face with cloth.)*

MAJOR. Help! Stop! Stop! I'm drowning! *(Spits and sputters.)* What kind of liniment is this? It tastes like—*(Spits.)* It tastes like—like polish. *(Looks at cloth.)* It looks like polish. *(Grabs bottle.)* It is! You've covered me with furniture polish! *(Rises.)*

KATIE. Furniture polish? *(Looks at bottle she is holding.)* The liniment!

MAJOR. Furniture polish! Furniture polish! Look at me! What do you think I am, the dining room table? How do I get this off?

KATIE. *(Major points at Henry. Henry points to Mother. She points to Katie.)* You don't, sir.

MAJOR. Don't! What do you mean, don't?

KATIE. It has to wear off. *(Turns and clasps her hands in prayer, looking up.)*

MAJOR. Wear off! WEAR OFF! Oh, damn.

HENRY. *(He and Mother speak together, motioning for Major to stop.)* No, Pa.

MOTHER. No, Hubert, don't swear.

MAJOR. *(Controlling himself.)* Henry! HEN-R—Y!

HENRY. Yes, Pa.

MAJOR. After I sop up this mess, I shall be back. And—you and I are going to have the HARDEST talk we've ever had—with a leather strap!

HENRY. But, Pa—

MAJOR. Not a word! Not a sound! Wear off! Oh, dam—

MOTHER AND HENRY. Fudge.

MAJOR. *(Marches center.)* Fudge the hornets! Fudge the furniture polish. *(Stops in doorway, turns and shouts.)* And damn the fudge! *(Exits L in hall.)*

MOTHER. He broke his pledge.

HENRY. I just heard the pearly gates swinging shut. *(Looks up.)*

KATIE. *(Hiccups.)* I've got the hiccups. *(Hiccups and starts to cry.)* I've got the hic-cups.

HENRY. Close your eyes, Katie. *(She does.)* Hold your breath. *(She does.)* Count to seven. *(Katie nods her head on each count, as Mother says, "One, two, three, four, five, six, seven." Henry slips behind Katie and on the seventh count, shouts.)* Boo-oo-oo-oo!

KATIE. *(Screams, jumps, then smiles.)* They're gone. You scared them out of me.

MOTHER. Scared them away.

HENRY. Scared them out of you—*(Beams with a brilliant idea.)*

That's it! That's what we'll do for Pa. We will SCARE the swearing out of Pa!

MOTHER. You can't say "Boo" to Father.

HENRY. Not a little "Boo," but a thunder of a noise. A bang that will send him to heaven. I've got it! And this will help in two ways. It will save Pa from going to . . . *(To audience.)* you know where. And will save me from getting strapped on . . . *(To audience.)* the you know what. Quick, Katie, look under my bed until you find an old—pig's bladder.

KATIE. A pig's bladder?

HENRY. I've been saving it for something worthy. And what's more worthy of a pig's bladder than Pa. Hurry. *(Katie runs out at back.)* It's hid under a slingshot that's hid under a dead pigeon that's hid under the feather bed.

MOTHER. Henry, what are you going to do?

HENRY. *(Innocently.)* Me? Nothing. *(Grins to audience.)* But Pa— Pa's going to BANG his way to the Promised Land! First, I'll blow up the bladder. *(Pantomimes comically.)* Then I'll put the bladder where Pa will hit it instead of me. You know the madder Pa is the harder he hits and I figure Pa's mad enough this time to hit hard enough to BUST the bladder—Boom! I'll act like I am dying, and you start crying. Pa will think he's killed me this time. And with my dying breath I'll make him promise never to swear again. Then we've got him—signed, sealed, and delivered to the preacher.

MOTHER. That is deceiving.

HENRY. No, Ma, it's only a little fooling on the way for the big reward at the end.

KATIE. *(Rushes in at C, holding out pig's bladder.)* Here is the bladder—ugh!

HENRY. Let me have it.

KATIE. What are you going to do with a bladder?

HENRY. Huff and puff and blow it up. *(Blows up bladder.)*

MAJOR. *(Off, shouts.)* Henry! Hen—r—y!

HENRY. Yes, Pa.

MAJOR. Are you ready?

HENRY. Ready to bust. *(Ties off balloon concealed in covering.)*

MOTHER. *(Nervously.)* Finish your work, Katie.

KATIE. *(Holds out bottle.)* There's no polish left.

MOTHER. Use the liniment. *(Katie exits quickly at back.)*

HENRY. Remember, Ma, you do your part. I'll do mine. *(Puts bladder in seat of pants.)* And Pa—will knock on the pearly gates. *(Bends over chair, back to audience.)*

MAJOR. *(Enters at back, face cleaner, and carries conspicuously a leather razor strap. He marches to C, clicks his heels in military fashion.)* Attention! *(Henry stands at attention.)* About face. Forward march. To the sofa. *(Henry marches to sofa.)* As I said to General Grant, an undisciplined soldier must be punished. Hornets, furniture polish, *(Henry grins and nods his head on each accusation.)* tripped into the fish pond, the yard dug full of rabbit traps, a skunk in the cellar, firecrackers in my cigar—Guilty! Guilty! Guilty! The time has come to face the music. *(Henry vocally "um-pa's" a march, shifting his feet in rhythm.)* Halt! *(Henry salutes.)* Prepare to receive your proper punishment. Forward. *(Henry turns to arm of sofa.)* Bend. *(Henry puts head over sofa, with bent knees.)* Extend! *(Henry straightens his knees, which causes his hips to extend.)*

MOTHER. Hubert, boys will be boys.

MAJOR. *(Removes coat and hands it to Mother, who puts it on chair back.)* A better book says: spare the rod and spoil the child.

HENRY. *(Straightens up.)* Oh, don't spoil me, Pa. Lay on the strap. *(Bends over again.)*

MAJOR. This is going to hurt me more than it hurts you.

HENRY. *(To audience.)* Truer words were never spoken.

MAJOR. For the unmanly behavior, for the tricks you have played, the embarrassment you have perpetrated—

HENRY. For heaven's sake, let her rip!

MAJOR. This I do for the good of all bad boys. Ready—aim—fire! *(Major swings a mighty blow with the strap on Henry's backside. A deafening crash is heard—drums offstage. Major is startled, Henry, comically, moans and groans and kicks, rolls on his back, etc.)*

HENRY. Oh, Pa. Oh, Pa! Oh-oh-oh, Pa!

MAJOR. What happened?

MOTHER. Something broke!

HENRY. My back! My back!

MAJOR. His back! I broke his back! *(Henry, continuing to have a hilarious time, falls, leaps, hops over sofa, etc., moans and groans, etc., during Katie's and Policeman's entrance and speeches.)*

KATIE. *(Rushes in at C as doorbell rings.)* What went off? It sounded like the Fourth of July!

POLICEMAN. *(Enters at C, from L.)* What's wrong? I heard the explosion halfway down the block!

HENRY. *(Gives a final dramatic moan and flop.)* Pa—Pa—

MAJOR. *(Kneels by Henry.)* Yes, Henry.

HENRY. If I die—

POLICEMAN. Die!

HENRY. Promise me, Pa—promise me one thing.

MAJOR. Anything.

HENRY. Promise me you will never swear again.

MAJOR. I promise.

HENRY. Then I can depart in peace.

MOTHER. *(Crying.)* Oh, Henry.

KATIE. *(Puckers her face, starts crying.)* Oh-oh-oh-oh.

MOTHER. *(Henry slowly rises, with a vacant stare.)* Henry—what is it, Henry?

HENRY. *(Waves his arms slowly.)* I . . . I feel like a bird . . . like I am going to fly . . . away.

KATIE. An angel.

HENRY. Goodby, Pa. Remember your promise—with witnesses.

MAJOR. I swear, I will never swear again!

HENRY. Amen. *(Sinks on sofa.)*

MOTHER. Henry! Henry!

KATIE. *(Cries loudly. Policeman removes his hat and holds it over his heart.)* Oh-oh-oh-oh.

HENRY. Where am I? *(Sits up.)* What's happened?

MOTHER. Oh, Henry, you're all right!

MAJOR. All right?

KATIE. All right?

HENRY. What happened?

POLICEMAN. That's what I'd like to know! What is happening here?

MAJOR. That's what I want to know! Hen-r-y! Explain your sudden recovery.

MOTHER. Don't you see, dear, by TAKING the pledge, you have GIVEN him back his life.

KATIE. A miracle! In the front parlor. *(Katie crosses herself. Policeman removes his hat again.)*

MOTHER. Come, dear, let me wash your face. *(Leads Major to back.)* Oh, Hubert, you have made me so happy, so happy. You know, I always knew you were a saint. *(She extends her hand. Major smiles at her, then looks about, doubtful and dazed. They exit.)*

HENRY. Excuse me. *(Rises and walks, squatting with legs apart.)* I have things to remove.

POLICEMAN. Why are you walking so funny?

HENRY. Because—it tickles! *(Wiggles, giggles, and exits R.)*

KATIE. *(Flirts, shyly.)* Hello, Patrick.

POLICEMAN. *(In love.)* Hello, Katie.

KATIE. I didn't expect to see you until tonight.

POLICEMAN. I was passing by—and I heard the explosion. Is everything all right?

KATIE. Oh, yes. In fact, it's been one of our quiet days.

POLICEMAN. *(Looks around.)* Katie, we're all alone. *(She nods.)* No one—but you and me. *(She nods. He takes a step with eager anticipation.)* Do you think—I could steal just one?

KATIE. *(Looks around, then nods impishly, walks to table.)* All right, but just one. *(He moves to her as she picks up cake. He puckers his mouth. She puts cookie in it.)*

POLICEMAN. *(Chewing.)* No, Katie, it's not a cake that I'm hungry for.

KATIE. Well, that's all you're going to get, Patrick Michael O'Reilly. *(Henry appears R, stands unnoticed.)* What kind of a girl do you think I am, kissing in daylight—and in the parlor!

HENRY. *(Imitates parrot's voice.)* Tickle tickle, eat a pickle. Tickle tickle, eat a pickle. *(He hides behind sofa.)*

KATIE. *(Turns to cage.)* Quiet, quiet, you naughty bird. *(Policeman quickly puts his arm around her. Dogs are heard barking.)* Someone's coming up the front walk! *(Pushes Policeman to L.)* Quick, use the side porch. Be careful in the yard. Henry has dug it up with rabbit traps.

POLICEMAN. Please, Katie, please. Just one—*(Puckers lips for kiss.)*

KATIE. *(Puts another cake in his mouth.)* Tonight—*(Romantically they both, facing front, visualize the moment.)*—when the moon is shining . . . on the back fence.

HENRY. *(Rises.)* There will be some smoochin' and moochin' on the back porch. *(Katie pushes Policeman out at French window at L. Clock chimes loudly, four times. Katie fixes herself. Mother enters at back.)*

MOTHER. Four o'clock. *(Doorbell rings.)* It's Mrs. Langford. She is very punctual. Katie, answer the door. *(Katie exits.)* Henry, promise me—no tricks, no pranks. Mrs. Langford is the DEACON'S wife. Smooth down your cowlick and put your best foot forward. *(Calling as she goes out at back.)* Hubert. Hubert, hurry.

POLLY. He's a crook. He's a crook. Desperado.

HENRY. No, Polly. And you mustn't say any Bible words. Don't yell "Satan" or "Lucifer."

POLLY. Satan and Lucifer. Satan and Lucifer.

HENRY. No-o-o! Polly! She is the DEACON'S wife.

POLLY. Devil with a pitchfork. Devil with a pitchfork.

HENRY. No! *(Looks at table.)* Oh, Jehosefat! I forgot my prize bottle of red ants. *(Picks up bottle.)*

MOTHER. *(Enters at back, followed by Major.)* Hurry, Hubert put on your coat. Let me help you. *(Holds coat for him.)* Is that your father's medicine bottle?

HENRY. Yes, Ma.

MOTHER. Give it to him.

HENRY. No, Ma.

MOTHER. Quick, put it in his pocket.

HENRY. But it's full of—

MAJOR. You heard your mother! *(They all speak together.)*

HENRY. But, Pa, it's filled with—

MOTHER. Quick, Henry.

HENRY. But, Ma—

MAJOR. PUT IT IN MY POCKET! *(Henry puts bottle in Major's coat pocket.)*

KATIE. *(Appears at back.)* Mrs. Langford is waiting. *(Exits. Mother, Major, and Henry stand in line, ready and posed—a picture of a devoted family. Katie enters.)* Mrs. Langford is here. *(Mrs. Langford enters at back. She is pious and full of vinegar and authority. Katie exits.)*

MRS. L. How do you do.

MOTHER. How do you do, Mrs. Langford. I believe you and the Major have met.

MAJOR. *(Always the ladies' man.)* Yes, indeed, I have had that honor and pleasure.

MOTHER. And let me introduce our son—Henry. *(He gives her a big wave and grin.)*

MAJOR. Salute! *(Henry salutes.)*

MOTHER. Shake hands, dear.

HENRY. *(Marches to Mrs. Langford.)* I'm glad to meet you, make your acquaintance, I hope you're well, and ain't it a lovely day. *(Shakes her hand vigorously.)*

MRS. L. *(Pulls back.)* What have you in your hand? *(He looks, is surprised.)* A cork. A cork from a bottle.

HENRY. Pa's medicine bottle! *(Looks at Major's coat pocket.)* The ants! *(Dogs bark and doorbell rings. Katie crosses in hall from L to R.)*

MOTHER. Katie. The doorbell.

MRS. L. That will be Mr. Wellington. He is selling stock—sharing his silver mine with members of the church.

KATIE. *(Appears at back.)* Mr. Horace Q. Winthrop Wellington.

MR. W. *(He enters at back. He is a city slicker, a smooth and fast talker. In his present alias, he wears an overly friendly and pious expression and speaks with a preacher's rising and falling cadence.)* Good afternoon, my good friends.

MRS. L. Major, this is Mr. Wellington.

MAJOR. How do you do. *(They shake hands.)*

MR. W. Ah, Major, I have heard about your heroic deeds with General Grant. And I have heard the high praises given to your charming wife.

MOTHER. How do you do.

MR. W. And I dare say, everyone knows—your son. *(Henry salutes.)*

MRS. L. We ladies will excuse ourselves while you men talk about money, the church, and the silver mine. *(Men nod. Mrs. L. speaks softly to Mother.)* I want to show you the little booties I am knitting for the—*(Spells.)*—b-a-b-y.

MOTHER. *(Whispers.)* I've just finished crocheting a little bonnet. *(Smiles graciously to men.)* Five minutes, gentlemen, and we shall be back for tea. *(Mother and Mrs. L. exit at back.)*

HENRY. *(To audience.)* He has a familiar look. I've seen that face before—somewhere—

MR. W. I have just come from Deacon Dinwiddie's. He bought three hundred shares in the silver mine. May he be rewarded in heaven.

HENRY. His eyes are shifty, and so is his tongue.

MR. W. As you may know, Major, it is a pure vein of silver, untapped, unmeasured—and untold in wealth.

MAJOR. So I have heard.

MR. W. When I first discovered the silver, I knew I was a chosen one —tapped on the shoulder by a Hand. *(Looks up.)* And then it came to me. I would share the mine with the church.

MAJOR. *(Eagerly.)* Most generous.

MR. W. Every faithful church member who buys a share must give half of what he gets—half of the thousands—back to the church. Of course, he will keep his half, his thousands—

MAJOR. How many shares are there left?

MR. W. Just a few hundred.

MAJOR. I have some cash in the safe.

MR. W. Another true giver. How much?

MAJOR. Only a few hundred. But I have some bonds which I can redeem. It will take a little time.

MR. W. *(Doubtful.)* I could come back.

MAJOR. It would be several thousand dollars.

MR. W. I can come back.

MAJOR. Henry, entertain Mr. Wellington while I get the cash. *(Exits DR.)*

HENRY. *(He nods to Mr. Wellington, who nods at him.)* Have a seat. Make yourself comfortable. No smoking is allowed in the parlor. But—*(Slyly.)* I can slip you—the *Police Reporter. (Gives Mr. Wellington newspaper; he looks at the back.)* There's a picture of a criminal—"Wanted in five states." *(Mr. Wellington looks at picture, gives a loud gasp, and stares straight ahead in panic, then quickly turns paper over, while Henry pantomimes shooting with two guns.)* He's a dangerous desperado—desperado.

POLLY. He's a crook. He's a crook. He's a crook. *(Mr. Wellington sits up, gasps, stares straight ahead, then slowly looks at parrot.)*

MAJOR. *(Enters DR.)* Here is the cash I have on hand, but there will be much more, much more. Are you all right, Mr. Wellington?

MR. W. *(Rises.)* Yes. *(Looks at paper, quickly puts it behind him.)* Perhaps I do need a bit of fresh air. If you'll excuse me—*(He turns, back to Henry. Henry takes newspaper, which is held out. Mr. Wellington stops, alarmed.)*

MAJOR. You must stay for tea. Hannah will be disappointed. Henry, call your mother.

HENRY. Yes, Pa. *(Tries to hide paper.)*

MAJOR. What is that?

HENRY. The *Police Reporter.*

MAJOR. You know that scandal sheet is not allowed in this house. Give it to me.

HENRY. I borrowed it. It's the only paper in town.

MAJOR. Hen-r-y! *(Major takes paper.)* I apologize, Mr. Wellington. I will burn the trash at once.

MR. W. Oh, allow me that honor. *(Takes paper.)* It will give me great pleasure to destroy it. *(Starts to rip the paper in two.)*

MOTHER. *(She and Mrs. Langford enter at back, followed by Katie with a teapot.)* Time is up. We are not going to let you take or— STEAL *(Mr. Wellington reacts.)*—another minute. Please sit down and we'll all have tea.

MAJOR. *(Gallantly.)* Mrs. Langford . . . *(Mrs. L. sits, then Major. Katie pours tea. Mr. W. puts newspaper in pocket. The paper extends out at the top.)*

MR. W. First, would it not be fitting to say a short prayer?

MOTHER. Of course. *(All bow their heads. Mr. W. coughs, opens his mouth to speak.)*

POLLY. Devil with a pitchfork. Devil with a pitchfork. *(All look at parrot.)*

MAJOR. Polly. Polly. *(All bow their heads again. Mr. W. clears his throat and opens his mouth.)*

POLLY. Satan and Lucifer. Satan and Lucifer. *(All look at parrot.)*

MAJOR. QUIET!

MOTHER. Please proceed, Mr. Wellington.

POLLY. He's a crook. He's a crook. He's a crook.

MAJOR. Stop your squawking, you FUDGE parrot. I'll wring your FUDGE neck! *(Goes to cage.)*

HENRY. He didn't swear. Open up the pearly gates. Pa's starting to climb the ladder.

MOTHER. Cakes! Pass the cakes, Katie!

KATIE. Yes, ma'am.

MOTHER. Oh, you didn't put the powdered sugar on them. *(She shakes powder from shaker over cakes.)* The powder makes them look so pretty.

HENRY. Powder? It's the SNEEZING powder!

MOTHER. Here, Katie. A-a-achew.

KATIE. Yes, ma'am. *(Quickly takes plate to Mrs. L.)* A-a-a-achew.

MRS. L. Thank you. *(Takes cake, sneezes.)* A-a-a-achew.

MR. W. *(Katie passes plate to him.)* Thank you. A-a-a-achew.

MAJOR. (Slowly starts scratching.) What the—fudge—is—crawling on me?

MOTHER. Do have another cake.

MRS. L. Thank you. *(Takes another and gives another sneeze.)* A-a-a-achew.

MOTHER. *(Takes cake and sneezes.)* A-a-a-achew.

KATIE. *(Passes plate to Major.)* ACHEW!

MAJOR. *(Takes cake.)* Thank you. *(Starts to sneeze, building it to a long and loud climax.)* A-A-A-A-ACHEW. *(Mrs. L., Mr. W., Mother, and Katie sneeze.)* Take it away. Keep away. Go away! *(He keeps sneezing longer and louder.)* A-A-A-A-A-A-A-ACHEW! *(Katie, crying and sneezing, runs to Mother, who motions her away. All sneeze and sneeze and sneeze, each sneezing louder and faster, up and down the scale, until they reach a roaring climax. There is silence. Major suddenly begins to slap himself.)*

HENRY. Is anything wrong, Pa?

MAJOR. There is something crawling—hundreds of things crawling all over me!

HENRY. The red ants!

MOTHER. Hubert, what are you doing?

MAJOR. Take my coat! *(Takes off coat.)* Take my tie! *(Takes off tie.)* Take my shirt! *(Starts unbuttoning it. Mrs. L. rises.)*

MOTHER. Hubert! What is it?

MAJOR. I am being baptized in a red sea of ants! *(Takes off shirt as he exits at R.)*

MRS. L. How mortifying! How shocking!

MR. W. Such shameless behavior.

MOTHER. Oh, I apologize. Please don't leave. Sit down again. *(Helps Mrs. L. to chair by table.)* Do—do have a cookie.

MRS. L. *(Gasping from shock.)* Yes . . . yes.

MOTHER. Out of the cookie jar.

HENRY. The cookie jar!

MRS. L. *(Puts hand into jar and pulls out snake.)* A snake! Ec-ec-eck! *(Faints in chair, throwing snake over her shoulder.)*

MR. W. She has fainted!

HENRY. Water! Water! Water! Pour on water! *(He quickly pours tea from the spout of the pot on her upturned face. Mrs. L. kicks, sputters, and comes to.)* Stand back! Give her air. Air! *(He grabs newspaper from Mr. W.'s pocket and fans Mrs. L.)*

KATIE. *(Screams off R, then runs in.)* Help! Help! Save me! Oh, St. Peter and St. Paul—strike me blind. *(Kneels in prayer.)*

HENRY. *(Points off R.)* Pa! Your pants!

MAJOR. *(Enters R wearing only long underwear, shoes, socks, and garters.)* Ants! Ants! Ants!

MRS. L. *(Sees Major and screams.)* Help! *(She faints again.)*

MAJOR. *(Slapping himself as he goes to doorway at back.)* Fudge, fudge, fudge—*(Shakes his back to audience.)* FUDGE!

(Quick curtain with loud music, "Ta-Ra-Ra-Boom-Der-Ay.")

ACT TWO

(Scene: the same. Two weeks later. Curtain music, "Home, Sweet Home." Curtain rises. Katie runs in from back, goes toward door at R.)

KATIE. Oh, what a morning! Run—run—I've never stopped running. *(Runs out DR. Doorbell rings.)* I'm coming. *(Re-enters with blankets.)* As fast as I can RUN.

MRS. L. *(Meets Katie, as she enters in hall.)* Good morning. I have come to help. I know the first day that she is back home that she will need a helping hand. How is she feeling? And how is the little bundle of joy? *(Katie nods.)* I'll go right up. I'll take these with me. *(Takes blankets and exits in hall.)*

KATIE. I'll get the others. *(To audience.)* Run up and down, up—down. I've about run DOWN myself. *(Doorbell rings.)*

HENRY. *(Rushes in from R with boxes.)* I'm back! I've got the safety pins and oil and the flannel—

KATIE. *(Points.)* Upstairs. *(Henry runs off L in hallway. Katie gives her own command.)* Run! *(She runs off DR.)*

POLICEMAN. *(Enters quietly at French window.)* Katie? Katie? *(Katie enters DR with pillows.)* Katie!

KATIE. *(She screams and tosses and catches pillows.)* Patrick Michael O'Reilly! I thought you were a burglar.

POLICEMAN. I had to tell you the news.

KATIE. *(Puts pillows on sofa.)* You're on duty. What news?

POLICEMAN. I've been promoted—Captain. Which means a big pay envelope on Saturday night—

MRS. L. *(Off, loudly.)* Ka—tie!

POLICEMAN. Which means I can—and I will—ask you the big question.

MRS. L. *(Off, calls louder.)* Ka—tie! Bring the pillows quickly.

POLICEMAN. Here. Take this. *(Thrusts a small box at her.)*

KATIE. Come back in half an hour. Be careful. Don't fall in the rabbit traps. *(Guides him to French window.)*

POLICEMAN. I'll be waiting in the bushes. *(Exits L.)*

KATIE. *(Opens box.)* A ring! An engagement ring! *(Puts on small ring.)* Mrs. Captain Patrick Michael O'Reilly. *(Grabs pillows, hugs them, and shivers.)* Yes, I will. I will, I will marry you. *(Stops.)* But he hasn't asked me yet!

MRS. L. *(Appears in hall.)* Katie, hurry upstairs. Then run to the kitchen. Boil some water for the diapers.

KATIE. Yes, ma'am. Run . . . run . . . run. *(Exits in hall.)*

MRS. L. *(To audience.)* How fortunate I came. How good it is to give a helping hand and—to take command. Henry! *(He appears in hall. She points R.)* Off to Morgan's Emporium and bring back some talcum powder, and baby lotion, and a tiny pottie-pottie. Trot along! *(She exits in hall.)*

HENRY. I'll gallop! *(He gallops to footlights.)* If you want to know what cyclone has struck this house, I'll tell you. Ma's just come back from the infirmary, and what do you think she brought for me and Pa? *(Pantomimes length of baby, rocking a baby in his arms, and then opens his mouth and cries loudly. Grins and nods.)* A little baby girl. We call her "It" because Ma wants to name her "Little June" for when she was born. Pa wants to call her "Little Hannah" after Ma. But I want to call her "Little Twurps" because she—burps. Pa's so proud he struts around as if he'd done it all by himself. *(Major is heard singing, off. "Rock-a-by-baby, on the tree top, Rock-a-by-baby, the cradle will rock.")* Here he comes now, spreading his feathers like a paycock. *(Henry stands apart at R.)*

MAJOR. *(Enters in hall, carrying flowers and singing happily.)* "Rock-a-by-baby, on the tree top . . . Rock-a-by-baby, the cradle will rock . . ."

MRS. L. *(Enters in hall.)* Quiet!

MAJOR. I brought some flowers.

MRS. L. *(Sniffs.)* They will give the baby the wheezes, the croup, and the colic. Throw them away. *(Major, disappointed, tosses the flowers away without looking. Henry catches them.)* No noise. And stay downstairs. The baby is asleep. *(Exits in hall.)*

MAJOR. Fudge. Fudge. Fudge. It's my baby, too. It's enough to make a father take a drink—and I think I will. *(Takes flask from pocket.)*

HENRY. A drink? He's going to break his pledge to the church!

POLLY. Satan and Lucifer. Satan and Lucifer.

MAJOR. *(Looks at Polly, sighs with resignation.)* Yes. I must have patience. Patience. Remember Job. He had patience—and boils. *(Sits by table.)*

HENRY. What's he doing? He's going to read the Bible. He IS in despair! I'll have to do something to cheer him up.

MAJOR. *(Reads.)* Blessed are the poor in spirit, for theirs is the kingdom of heaven—for an easy money loan, visit the City National Bank. *(He looks up, surprised; shakes his head, bewildered.)*

HENRY. He's reading what I pasted in the Bible, from the newspaper.

MAJOR. *(Reads.)* Blessed are they which do hunger, for they shall be filled—Your Meat Market pays cash for fat dogs. What—what the fudge is this?

HENRY. Pa said the Bible needed to be pepped up, so I pasted in some peppy advertisements.

MAJOR. *(Reads.)* Verily I say unto you, try Sutter's Oil for rheumatism. *(Slams book shut.)*

HENRY. I'll think how to cheer Pa up—outside. *(He tiptoes out at R.)*

MAJOR. *(Cautiously opens book again and reads slowly.)* Give us this day our daily bread—send five wrappers for your free Mama-Mama doll. *(Bangs book on table.)* Henry! Hen-r—y!

KATIE. *(Runs in from hall.)* Did you call, sir?

MAJOR. Find Henry! Send him in—ON THE RUN!

KATIE. Yes, sir—on the run! *(Runs as fast as she can DR.)*

MAJOR. *(Reaches for Bible, angrily opens it, and reads.)* The Lord is my shepherd, I shall not want—limberger cheese, two cents a smell and one smell is enough! *(Slams book shut.)* HEN—R—Y!

HENRY. *(Enters at back, holding an armful of blanket.)* Hello, Pa.

MAJOR. *(Points in front of him. Henry marches there and stops.)* Attention.

HENRY. Yes, Pa.

MAJOR. *(Points at book.)* I want to know—I want to know what the fudge—

HENRY. Sh.

MAJOR. Don't SH me!

HENRY. Sh-sh-sh-sh!

MAJOR. What is it?

HENRY. I know how you feel today, like the army is marching on without you. So I brought you—this. *(Gives him blanket bundle.)*

MAJOR. It's my Little Hannah. Coochie-coochie-coo. Come to Papa. Papa will sing you to sleepy-by. *(Turns to Henry and loudly "Sh's." Henry nods, tiptoes in rhythm to Major's singing, exits at back, giving audience a big, knowing grin and nod.)* "Rock-a-by-baby, on the tree top. Rock-a-by-baby . . ." Itsy-itsy-tootsy. "The cradle will rock." She is gurgling. She is cooing. She is— purring! "Rock-a-by-baby . . ." She's got a tail! It's a cat! *(Loud meowing is heard, off. He holds up an ugly stuffed cat.)* A meowing, scratching cat! *(Throws it out the French window.)* Scat! Scat! Henry! HEN—R—Y!

HENRY. *(Enters meekly DR, holding behind him the leather strap.)* Yes, Pa. It was just a joke—to cheer you up.

MAJOR. Cheer me up? I'm eaten up!

HENRY. Here is the strap. Here am I. Take it. Take aim. *(He bends over, facing R, away from Major.)*

MAJOR. I will! And I'll hit the target! For once and for all I am going to thrash out all the pranks and jokes you've got in that fudge head of yours. *(Raises strap.)*

HENRY. *(Straightens up.)* One thing, Pa. I have thought of one GOOD trick—a way you can outwit the burglar. *(Bends over.)*

MAJOR. What burglar?

HENRY. *(Up.)* He's robbed two houses, and I know you have all that money here for the silver mine. All that money you're going to give to Mr. Wellington. *(Bends over.)*

MAJOR. Yes? Well?

HENRY. *(Up.)* The front door and back door are locked and double-locked, but what about the side door? *(Points between his legs to L.)* You can keep a burglar outside by outwitting him.

MAJOR. I can? How?

HENRY. *(Up.)* Soft-soap him! You know how slippery soft soap is. If you'd pour a bucket of soft soap on the steps, then, when the burglar comes, he'd slip and slide and land on his—target. When you heard the noise, you'd get your gun and—charge! *(Bends.)*

MAJOR. *(Nods, agreeing with anticipated pleasure.)* Attention! *(Henry straightens up, salutes, and grins.)* Bring a bucket of soft soap from the cellar. Pour it—thick—on the steps and on the porch. Slip and slide—*(Chuckles.)* It will be a good joke on someone. *(Doorbell rings.)*

KATIE. *(Runs across back in hallway.)* I'm coming. I'm running!

MAJOR. That will be Mr. Wellington, coming for the money for the silver mines. Your father is going to make thousands of dollars.

KATIE. *(Enters at back, announces, and exits.)* Mr. Horace Q. Winthrop Wellington.

MAJOR. Come in. I've been expecting you.

MR. WELLINGTON. *(Has entered at back.)* Good morning, my good Major. I trust I am not too early. But as they say, the early bird catches—good morning, my good young man. *(Henry opens his mouth to speak, but Mr. W. continues.)* I have just been with Deacon Langford. He bought five hundred shares in the silver mine. May he be rewarded in heaven.

HENRY. *(To audience.)* I know I've seen him. His picture! But where?

MAJOR. I have my cash right here.

MR. W. Ah, another one of the faithful. How much?

MAJOR. Six thousand. I'll get the money. *(Starts R.)*

MR. W. And you, my good lad, have you been reading in the *Police Reporter* about more desperados?

HENRY. No, sir. The newspaper is—gone.

MR. W. Gone? Well! Good riddance of bad rubbish.

MAJOR. Henry! Get the soap. March. *(Major exits DR.)*

HENRY. Tramp . . . tramp . . . tramp . . . *(Speaks to audience.)* Do me a favor. Keep your eye on him. I don't trust him an inch. And why is he so troubled about the *Police Reporter*? I put the paper in a secret place, but now I have forgot where I hid it! *(Marches to back.)* Tramp . . . tramp . . . tramp . . . hep, hep, hi . . . Tramp

. . . tramp . . . tramp . . . There's more here than meets the eye! *(Exits at back.)*

MR. W. *(He picks up gold trinket from table.)* Ah. *(Weighs it in his hand, shifts his eyes to right and left, then drops trinket into his pocket.)*

MAJOR. *(Rushes in from R.)* Here is the money. I've counted it twice. Six thousand dollars.

MR. W. As a good member of the church, I trust your honesty without question. *(Takes stack of bills and, as an expert gambler, flips and counts them quickly.)*

MAJOR. When . . . how soon will the money start coming in—for the church?

MR. W. I leave for Colorado tomorrow morning. *(Gets certificates from bag.)* Two hundred and forty shares. *(Offers them to Major.)* A mere formality, but I always ask: you are a registerd church member in good standing?

MAJOR. No.

MR. W. NO!

MAJOR. I am on probation, but it will be up tomorrow.

MR. W. In that case, I can take your money today. *(Gives him shares and drops money into bag.)*

MAJOR. I could put in another thousand. My wife's savings. Yes, I'll surprise her. I'll have more money for you tomorrow.

MR. W. I can pick it up on the way to the train station. What time is it now, please?

MAJOR. *(Takes watch on fob from pocket.)* Almost noon.

MR. W. *(Shakes hands.)* Then I must be off. Good day, Major. *(Turns, toward bag, holding Major's watch, looks at it.)* It is always a pleasure to do business with such a—giving—man. *(Drops watch into bag. They go to hallway.)* I'm calling on Mrs. Tompkins. She wants to invest her insurance money in the silver mine. May she be rewarded in heaven.

MAJOR. Amen. *(They have exited in hall at R.)*

POLICEMAN. *(Appears at French window, steps inside, calls softly.)* Katie? Katie? *(He hears Henry and exits L.)*

HENRY. *(Is heard, then marches in from R.)* Tramp . . . tramp . . . tramp . . . hep, hep, hep . . . tramp, tramp, tramp . . . I haven't missed a step. *(Goes to French window. Holds up bucket.)* Here's the bucket filled with soft soap, and Pa says pour it on thick!

MAJOR. *(Enters and stays in hallway.)* Thousands of dollars! This is a day to celebrate! *(Takes out flask.)*

HENRY. Pa's going to take a drink. *(Tilts bucket so liquid pours onto floor.)* He's sliding right out of the pearly gates! *(Sees soap on floor.)* Sliding! I've soft-soaped the parlor floor!

MAJOR. *(Lifts flask.)* To the silver mine.

HENRY. *(Looks off L.)* Pa! There's a man hiding in the bushes.

MAJOR. A man!

HENRY. A burglar!

MAJOR. *(Puts flask on table.)* Call the police! I'll get my gun. This is one burglar who won't get away. *(Gets gun on wall at R.)*

KATIE. *(Enters in hall, looks to windows.)* Patrick! Go away!

MAJOR. *(Pointing gun at French window, advances.)* Company advance. Forward . . . march. Hep, hep, hep . . . Charge! Help! *(He slips on the floor, sways, cries for help, falls, gunshot is heard. He sprawls—knocked out.)*

POLICEMAN. *(Enters at French window.)* Katie!

KATIE. The Major! Is he shot?

POLICEMAN. What happened?

HENRY. Pa slipped—slipped in his own trap.

KATIE. Is he dead?

HENRY. No—just fallen into the fiery pit. And we're going to push him back up the fire escape! Take his feet. Put him on the sofa. Katie, bring the box behind the door in the other room. *(They carry Major to sofa. Katie exits DR.)* I was afraid Pa would take a drink. Everything we need is in it. Luckily, I am prepared.

POLICEMAN. What is going on here?

HENRY. *(Points to flask.)* Pa broke his pledge. Pa was going to take a drink. Pa slid backward . . . *(Looks at soap, laughs.)* and forward and sideways and up and over.

KATIE. *(Enters with large paper box.)* Here is the box.

HENRY. Unpack it. *(Katie holds up the Police Reporter.)* The *Police Reporter!* This is where I hid it! I've found the newspaper! *(Puts newspaper on chair.)*

POLICEMAN. I would like to know—

HENRY. I'll tell you. *(Picks up white butcher's coat and hands it to Policeman.)* First, put on this coat.

POLICEMAN. I am on duty!

HENRY. 'Tis a greater duty that we serve. We must return—a special delivery to the Promised Land.

POLICEMAN. WHAT IS GOING ON HERE!

HENRY. We are going to CURE Pa. We scared the swearing out of him. Now we'll scare the DRINKING out of him. *(To Katie.)* You want the Major to go to heaven, don't you, Katie? *(She nods and crosses herself.)* Then tell him to be an angel—put on his white robe. *(Henry puts on white coat, back to audience, and mustache and wig.)*

KATIE. Please, Patrick.

POLICEMAN. I am on duty.

KATIE. For me, Patrick. Please . . . *(Thrilled, he takes coat, and she helps him put it on.)*

HENRY. *(Turns and shows off his wig and mustache.)* I am ready! I have it all planned. Pa will think he is dead—died from drink. And you and I are doctors, and that we are going to dissect him.

POLICEMAN. Dissect him!

HENRY. *(Holds up saw from box.)* Saw him in little pieces! *(Major stirs.)* He's beginning to move. Quick. Katie, keep a look-out in the hall. And you—change your face, change your voice, so Pa will change his path from down to up. *(Katie runs to hallway. Policeman hooks over his ears the mustache-beard which is in his coat pocket.)*

MAJOR. Oh-oh-oh, my head . . . my head. *(Sits up.)*

HENRY. *(He and Policeman disguise their voices.)* Are you ready, Doctor Cut-a-bone?

POLICEMAN. I am ready, Doctor Spurt-some-blood.

HENRY. *(Grins and nods to audience.)* He sounds like a real doctor.

MAJOR. Where am I? Who are you—and you?

HENRY. Fortunately we arrived while the corpse is still warm.

MAJOR. Corpse?

POLICEMAN. Who was the dead man?

HENRY. He was a major in the army, had a hot temper, loving wife—and a saintly son. *(Grins to audience.)*

MAJOR. Dead man? Who is dead?

HENRY. Did you hear a voice?

POLICEMAN. There is no one here except you and me—and this dead body.

MAJOR. Dead body?

HENRY. The Major slipped, shot himself—died like that. *(Snaps fingers.)*

MAJOR. The Major? Shot himself!! Doctors—I am not dead.

HENRY. Of course you are dead!

MAJOR. I am not dead!

POLICEMAN. You are a dead corpse, and a dead corpse does not talk.

HENRY. Doctor Cut-a-bone, shall we use the hammer to crack his skull or use the saw to cut through his middle? *(Grins at audience.)*

MAJOR. Crack? Cut? I am not a corpse! I am alive!

HENRY. Listen, stiff, we paid twenty dollars for your dead body.

POLICEMAN. Dead. *(Pushes Major back on sofa.)*

HENRY. The time has come to start the dissecting. *(Grins to audience.)*

MAJOR. *(Rises.)* Dissecting!

POLICEMAN. DEAD—and stay DEAD. *(Pulls Major backward on sofa.)*

HENRY. *(Presents saw to Policeman.)* You saw first, Doctor Cut-a-bone.

POLICEMAN. *(Bows to Henry.)* No, after you, Doctor Spurt-some-blood.

HENRY. First I will saw off his head.

MAJOR. *(Rises.)* NO! NO! NO!

HENRY. Very well. I'll saw off his feet. Hold him down.

MAJOR. *(Policeman holds Major, who yells.)* Help! Help! Stop! *(Etc.)*

HENRY. *(Holding a piece of wood between Major's feet, he saws quickly. Then drops the piece of wood.)* They are off!

MAJOR. My FEET! *(Kicks and throws Policeman off.)* I am NOT DEAD!

HENRY. You will be when we're through with you. *(Nods and grins to audience.)*

MAJOR. I am alive—alive! Oh, gentlemen, surely we can talk this over—arrange something. I'll pay you.

POLICEMAN. Ah-ha, bribery. How much?

HENRY. No. Nothing can help you. The rule is: a DRUNK is not returnable.

MAJOR. Oh, let me return. I will give up drinking. I will never touch another drop.

HENRY. You will swear to that?

MAJOR. I swear.

HENRY. On your knees?

MAJOR. *(On knees.)* On my knees I swear I'll never drink again.

HENRY. Repeat that louder. It has a long way to go. *(Points up.)*

MAJOR. I will never drink again.

HENRY. Amen! Put him on the sofa. Close your eyes. Go to sleep. *(Put Major on sofa.)*

MAJOR. Go to sleep?

HENRY. The hammer.

MAJOR. The hammer!

HENRY. Tap him on the head. Put him to sleep.

MAJOR. No. No! I will go to sleep. I am asleep . . . asleep . . . asleep . . .

HENRY. *(Taking off coat and disguise, motions for Policeman to remove his and for Katie to take the box with things off.)* Are you fast asleep?

MAJOR. Yes.

HENRY. Make it faster. *(Major starts snoring, each snore becoming bigger and louder, and, each time he exhales, he shouts, "Asleep." Policeman cautiously slips out at French window. Katie exits C. Henry cautiously backs out DR, sees the* Police Reporter *on chair, tiptoes to it, picks it up, then runs off at R.)*

POLLY. Devil with a pitchfork. Devil with a pitchfork.

MAJOR. *(Sits up.)* A familiar voice. Polly? Polly?

POLLY. Tickle tickle, eat a pickle. Tickle tickle, eat a pickle.

MAJOR. Am I here? Am I—alive? I am. I AM. *(Jumps up.)* Alive! Alive! Oh, what a nightmare! *(Goes to table.)* Surely I have passed through the valley and the shadow of death. *(Picks up flask.)* Out of my life forever. Out! Out—the window. Never shall drink touch my lips again. *(Winds up and throws flask out the window. There is an immediate bang.)*

POLICEMAN. *(Off.)* Ou-ou-ouch! Right in my eye! MY EYE! *(Enters L.)* Who threw this?

MAJOR. I am proud to say I did.

POLICEMAN. I am proud to say I am the Police Captain, and I arrest you for assault and a black eye! *(Turns and shows his black eye.)*

MOTHER. *(Enters in hall, in dressing gown.)* Hubert, what is going on?

HENRY. *(Enters R.)* Pa! Pa, they are coming down the street! The Firemen's Band!

MOTHER. The Firemen's Band?

HENRY. I asked them to serenade you and the new baby! They're in the yard. *(Band is heard off L playing "He's a Jolly Good Fellow.)*

MRS. L. *(Enters in hall with baby.)* Silence! The baby is asleep! *(Music stops and voices shout off L, "Speech . . . Speech, Major . . . We want the Major . . . We want a speech.")*

HENRY. They want you to make a speech, Pa.

MRS. L. Stop the noise. Close up the window.

MAJOR. No, madam. You close up. It is the Firemen's Band and they are serenading the baby. And I am going to make a speech. *(Clears his throat and starts L.)* Friends, Romans, Cavalrymen —*(He starts slipping on the soap.)*

MOTHER. He's slipping.

HENRY. No, Ma. He's given up drink forever. Pa's flying straight to heaven.

MOTHER. Katie, help! *(Band starts playing "Hot Time in the Old Town Tonight.)*

KATIE. *(Runs to Major, who falls. She slips and falls.)* Patrick!

POLICEMAN. *(Rushes to Katie. He slips. All ad lib, trying to get up, but pulling each other down again.)* Katie.

MRS. L. Quiet! Quiet! Do something. Somebody do something.

KATIE, POLICEMAN, MAJOR. *(Struggling to get up, then sliding down again, and ad libbing.)* We can't. O-o-oh. Ooooops!

MRS. L. Then I will. *(Hands baby to Mother and strides to L, slips, falls.)* Help! *(All slip, slide, tumble over each other, ad libbing. Mother looks aghast. Henry enjoys it all and joins the band, singing loudly.)*

HENRY. "There'll be a hot time in the old town tonight."

(Quick curtain with the music continuing.)

ACT THREE

(Scene: the same. The next morning. Curtain music, "Little

Brown Church in the Dale," with church chimes. Curtain rises. Katie enters at back.)

KATIE. Faith, it's a beautiful Sunday morning. The birds are singing, and the church bells are ringing—*(Looks at ring.)* It's almost like a wedding day. Patrick will be here—OFF DUTY—very soon.

POLLY. Satan and Lucifer. Satan and Lucifer.

KATIE. Good morning, Polly.

POLLY. Devil with a pitchfork. Devil with a pitchfork.

KATIE. *(Uncovers cage.)* No, Polly, watch your tongue. This is Sunday. And the family is going to church while I mind the baby— with Patrick. The Major's probation is over. He stopped swearing and stopped drinking. He is going to join the church. *(Fearful.)* Unless—unless something else happens. Oh, surely, surely nothing will go wrong today.

HENRY. *(Enters at back, dressed in his Sunday best, including a cap; he is feeling very uncomfortable.)* Morning, Katie.

KATIE. Good morning, Henry.

HENRY. Ma wants you to fetch her gloves.

KATIE. My, you're spruced up!

HENRY. *(Stands, comically miserable.)* I'm rubbed and scrubbed and ready for church.

KATIE. Sit right there. *(Henry sits, stiffly, as if in pain.)* And don't soil or rip or tear your clothes. I must say for once you look like a proper young gentleman. *(Exits DR.)*

HENRY. I smell like a perfumed poodle. *(He looks around. Seeing no one, he raises his cap, takes out the folded Police Reporter, puts cap on, unfolds newspaper.)* If I can't play shinny, I'll read the *Police Reporter.* (*Reads excitedly.)* "Wanted in five states. Notorious swindler. Crooked promoter of oil wells, gold and silver mines." Silver mine? "Steals thousands." There is his picture. *(Looks closely.)* I've seen him . . . Yes! . . . He looks like . . . I think he is . . . I'm sure he is . . . HE IS! He's Mr. Wellington. He's a crook!

POLLY. He's a crook. He's a crook. He's a crook.

HENRY. You tell 'em, Polly. Katie! Katie, come quick!

KATIE. *(Runs in DR.)* What is it?

HENRY. He's coming here this morning. *(Gets gun from rack.)* I'll cover him with the gun and you grab his money bag.

KATIE. Me? Who? What money bag?

HENRY. Who? Horace Q. Wellington. Here's his picture in the *Police Reporter*. He's a crook.

POLLY. He's a crook. He's a crook. He's a crook.

HENRY. And a thief!

KATIE. Mr. Horace Q. Winthrop Wellington is not stealing. He is GIVING money to the church.

HENRY. You have to help me catch him, Katie.

KATIE. Indeed I will not help you. He is a man of the church.

MOTHER. *(Enters back, sees Henry pointing gun.)* Henry! Henry, what are you doing?

HENRY. Getting a bead on a desperado.

MOTHER. Put that gun up at once. You know you are not allowed to play with it.

HENRY. Play? No, Ma, this is REAL.

MOTHER. AT ONCE.

HENRY. *(Puts gun up.)* I found his picture. "Wanted in five states." Look.

MOTHER. No, dear, I have no time for any games. Today your father is going to join the church. Katie, lay out his dress uniform. *(Katie exits DR.)*

HENRY. It's Mr. Wellington! See.

MOTHER. I don't have my glasses. *(Gets book from table.)* I want to carry the family Bible.

HENRY. Ma, listen to me. I'm trying to help—to save Pa's money. *(Points to book she holds.)* That is the Almanac.

MOTHER. *(Exchanges books.)* Oh, thank you. You see, dear, you are a big help.

HENRY. Please, Ma, listen to what I'm saying.

MOTHER. Hurry, we mustn't be late for church. Not THIS morning. Oh, what a happy day this is going to be. *(Exits at back.)*

HENRY. She won't listen. Katie won't listen. Nobody listens to me. *(Major is heard singing, off.)* Pa! Pa will. He'll do something. It's his money.

MAJOR. *(Singing happily and lustily.)* "Onward, Christian Soldiers, marching as to war, with the cross of Jesus going on before." *(Enters at back.)*

HENRY. Pa, I want to talk to you.

MAJOR. *(Smiling with a new contentment.)* Yes, Henry.

HENRY. Pa, I want you to listen to what I say. I want you to HEAR me.

MAJOR. Of course, Henry.

HENRY. Pa, you are being robbed, bamboozled!

MAJOR. Robbed?

HENRY. By a criminal. Mr. Horace Q. Crooked Wellington.

MAJOR. Mr. Wellington?

HENRY. Here is his picture. He's a crook. A CROOKED crook.

MAJOR. *(Laughs.)* No, Henry. This is one of your tricks. I am not going to be fooled this morning.

HENRY. It's not a trick.

MAJOR. Oh, I enjoy a little joke, too—but not his morning. Today I am marching with a new army. *(Sings happily.)* "Onward, Christian soldiers . . ."

HENRY. Pa, listen. It's no trick. It's no joke. It's the truth.

MAJOR. Hen—r—y! This is Sunday and I forbid you to tell any tall tales! And I forbid you to read that scandal paper. Take it to the kitchen and burn it! Attention. March! *(He sings happily and marches off DR.)* "Onward, Christian soldiers, marching as to war, with the cross of Jesus . . ."

HENRY. He won't listen. No one listens to me. *(Dogs bark off.)* That's the dogs. He's coming up the front walk. *(Doorbell rings.)*

KATIE. *(Runs across in hallway.)* I'm coming. I'm running.

HENRY. He's here—with the stolen money. And there is nobody to stop him. Nobody—*(Grins.)* But me! I'll do it! I'll do it for Pa and for the church. *(Salutes.)* I'm marching, Pa—*(Marches in one spot.)* Tramp, tramp, tramp . . . Fast as I can . . . tramp, tramp, tramp—

KATIE. *(Appears.)* Mr. Horace Q. Winthrop Wellington—

HENRY. And I always get my man!

KATIE. And Mrs. Langford are here. *(Mr. W. enters at back, followed by Mrs. L.)*

HENRY. Mrs. Langford! She can read!

MR. W. *(Annoyed.)* Where is the Major? The train leaves in fifteen minutes.

MRS. L. *(Brushing herself.)* All the dogs in the neighborhood are in your yard. Someone is going to be bitten.

HENRY. *(At R, to Mrs. L.)* Pst. Pst.

KATIE. *(At L, to Mr. W.)* Excuse me, sir, but I have my savings all tied up here in my handkerchief.

MRS. L. What is it?

HENRY. Look. Read. *(Points to picture.)*

KATIE. I want you to put it in the silver mine, for me and for Patrick —and for the church.

MR. W. How much?

KATIE. All my savings—twenty-five dollars.

MRS. L. Who is it?

HENRY. Him! Look!

MR. W. That will be one share. But as the Bible says—*(He stops, not knowing.)*

KATIE. Yes?

MR. W. *(Solemnly.)* From a little acorn grows the mighty oak. *(Katie nods and crosses herself and takes certificate. He drops handkerchief into bag.)*

HENRY. He's a crook! A thief! *(Mrs. L. begins to study the picture and read seriously, then looks at Mr. W. and at picture, while Henry points and pantomimes.)*

MAJOR. *(Enters DR.)* Good morning, Mr. Wellington, good morning.

MR. W. Mrs. Langford is driving me to the train and we have just a moment. I have forty certificates left—one thousand dollars, I think you said. *(Holds out certificates.)*

MAJOR. One thousand it is, and here it is. *(Mr. W. flips through the bills, counting them. Major looks at certificates.)* What a surprise this will be for my wife.

MRS. L. It is! It is the same man.

MR. W. Goodby, Major. I must be going.

MRS. L. *(With great authority.)* Just a minute!

HENRY. Go get him! *(Gives her a push.)* And I'll get the police and all the dogs! *(Exits DR.)*

MRS. L. Henry is right. This is your picture, an exact likeness. A scar on your right cheek and a mole on your chin.

MR. W. What are you talking about?

MRS. L. You! Notorious swindler!

MAJOR. Mr. Wellington!

MRS. L. Call the police!

MR. W. Police!

MAJOR. I demand an explanation.

MR. W. *(Suddenly whips out gun and becomes tough and menacing.)* Stay where you are! Put up your hands—higher! One move and I'll give you an explanation—with this gun.

MRS. L. Do something. You are a Major.

MR. W. Pipe down!

MRS. L. Don't tell me—

MR. W. *(Aims gun at her.)* Shut up. *(She retreats.)* On your knees. You church-loving people like to kneel, so on your knees.

MAJOR. Sir?

MR. W. Bend! *(All kneel, facing front.)* And start saying your prayers that I don't shoot you. *(Cautiously he gets bag and starts toward window. At the same time, Henry, disguised as a burglar —hat, handkerchief over mouth, long coat, etc., enters DR. He carries a bag like Mr. Wellington's. He advances slowly with toy gun.)* Now I will take my bag . . . take my leave of this hick town . . . and say to all of you, goodby. *(Turns to go.)*

HENRY. *(With gun against Mr. Wellington's head, speaks in disguised voice.)* Drop that bag.

MR. W. What the . . . ?

HENRY. There's a gun at your head and my finger is itching on the trigger. Drop that bag! *(Mr. W. drops bag.)* And your gun. Drop your gun! *(Mr. W. does.)* One move and I'll paint your brains on the wallpaper. On your knees. Bend! *(Mr. W. kneels.)* Now I will take the money and say goodby.

MOTHER. *(Enters at back.)* Henry! Take off that hat and put up that toy gun.

MR. W. Toy gun? *(Quickly gets his gun.)* You little fool, try to trick me, uh? *(Knocks gun out of Henry's hand and pushes him toward Mother.)* This is no kid game, and this is no toy gun.

HENRY. *(Pulls off hat and mask.)* I'll fight you—with my fists!

MR. W. Fight? Take that! *(Hits Henry in the stomach. Henry falls.)*

MOTHER. Henry!

MR. W. On your knees, sister.

MOTHER. Mr. Wellington!

MR. W. *(Flourishing gun.)* On your knees or I'll give YOU a slug—of lead.

MAJOR. Bend, Hannah, bend. *(Mother kneels. Henry sits up.)*

MR. W. On your knees, you little troublemaker. Now I've got the last laugh—on you. Kneel! *(Henry kneels.)* Everyone stay on his knees—eyes in front—and don't move. Or I'll shoot daylight straight through you. *(Picks up Henry's bag.)* This is Sunday, so while you are kneeling, I want to hear you sing a hymn—real loud—and KEEP singing it until you come to—amen. SING! *(Mrs. L., nervous, sounds a note, then starts singing, "Throw Out the Life-line." All join in singing: "Throw out the Life-line! Throw out the Life-line! Someone is drifting away. Throw out the Life-line! . . ." Mr. W. quickly backs out at French window. As soon as he is gone, Henry interrupts the singing.)*

HENRY. He's gone. *(Goes to French window.)* Get your gun, Pa. I'll set the dogs after him! *(Whistles loudly and calls and shouts, "Sic 'im, go get him," etc. A few dogs bark, off.)*

MRS. L. My money. Gone!

MAJOR. Ruined! It's enough to make a man LEAVE the church.

HENRY. No, Pa. It makes you want to JOIN the church. SOMEBODY out-tricked Mr. Horace Q. Slicker.

MAJOR. Out-tricked him?

HENRY. He took the empty bag and left—his money bag. *(Tosses out bills.)* Hundreds of dollars . . . thousands of dollars.

MRS. L. My money.

MAJOR. My money.

KATIE. *(Henry tosses handkerchief to her.)* My handkerchief!

HENRY. *(Many dogs are heard barking loudly off L.)* The dogs! The dogs are on his trail! *(Rushes to window.)* They've found him. He's running back THIS way. *(Major and Mother rush to window.)*

MAJOR. He fell.

HENRY. He fell into my rabbit trap!

MAJOR. He's lost his gun! *(Gunshot is heard off.)*

MOTHER. The dogs are eating him up.

HENRY. The dogs are chewing him!

MAJOR. He's coming this way.

HENRY. Get your gun, Pa! *(Major gets gun from wall at R, Henry follows him. Dogs bark louder.)*

MR. W. *(Runs in from L, shirt torn and bloody.)* Help! The dogs are ripping me apart!

HENRY. *(Grabs gun from Major. Aims it at Mr. W.)* Stop!

POLICEMAN. *(Enters at back, gun drawn.)* I heard the shooting. What's wrong?

MAJOR. Arrest that man.

MRS. L. He's a thief.

POLICEMAN. *(Holding gun on Mr. W.)* Put your hands behind you. Behind you! *(Mr. W. does.)* Henry, put the handcuffs on him.

HENRY. Me?

MAJOR. Yes, Henry, you. You have saved us all.

HENRY. *(Gives gun to Major, takes handcuffs from Policeman, and talks tough to Mr. W.)* Hold 'em out! Hick town, uh? You thought you could double-talk, double-cross me, uh? Well. I have handcuffed and double-locked you! Now WHO has the last laugh!

MR. W. You won't get away with this.

POLICEMAN. Come along. I'm taking you in. *(Policeman and Mr. W. start.)*

KATIE. Patrick, be careful! I want to be a bride before I am a widow.

POLICEMAN. Katie, will you marry me?

KATIE. Oh, yes—yes!

POLICEMAN. And seal it with a kiss.

KATIE. You're on duty!

POLICEMAN. March! *(Mr. W. and Policeman exit at back. Church bells ring.)*

MOTHER. Church! It's time for church!

MRS. L. *(Still on knees, eagerly picks up bills. Henry, on knees, helps.)* I'll take the money to the preacher. He will give it back!

MOTHER. Hubert? You are—are going to church? And be saved?

MAJOR. I have been saved.

MOTHER. *(Joyously.)* Oh, Katie, my hat, my gloves, and the Bible— and burp the baby. *(She hurries out back, followed by Katie. Major exits DR, singing "Onward, Christian Soldiers.")*

MRS. L. I've never been late in my life, and I always give the choir the pitch. *(Rises. Sounds a note.)* Ah-ah-ah. *(Exits at back singing and waving the money high and happily.)* "Glory, glory, Hallelujah! Glory, glory, Hallelujah! Glory, glory, Hallelujah! His truth is marching on."

POLLY. Hallelujah! Hallelujah!

HENRY. *(To audience.)* Everything has turned out all right. Mr. Horace Q. Thief is safe behind bars. And Pa—with a little help—has hopped on the heaven express!

POLLY. Hallelujah! Hallelujah!

MAJOR. *(Enters DR wearing fancy military coat and hat. Marches to C.)* Mother! I am ready to join a new and greater army.

MOTHER. *(Enters at back wearing a beautiful flowered hat.)* Yes, dear. I am ready to march with you. *(Stands by his side.)*

MAJOR. To the church—and hurry! *(Offers his arm. Exit music begins, "Little Brown Church in the Dale." They go to doorway at back. Stop.)* Hen—r—y.

HENRY. Yes, Pa. I'm coming—right behind you. *(Major and Mother exit. Henry runs to back.)* This time I'll make sure they LOCK the pearly gates! *(He salutes and marches off at back.)*

(Quick curtain with music continuing to play.

Curtain calls follow immediately. Mr. Wellington first and Policeman behind holding him by the collar, enter from L, stop at C, bow, Policeman smiling, Mr. W. frowning and hissing. Policeman raises stick and they run off at L.

Music changes to "Battle Hymn of the Republic," and Mrs. L. enters from R, walks quickly to C, bows, opens hymn book, and exits L, singing loudly.

Music changes to a Wedding March. Katie, in a bridal veil and carrying flowers, and Policeman enter from R, cross to C, face audience, and bow. Policeman quickly steals kiss. Katie gasps and smiles. They exit L.

Music changes to "Home, Sweet Home," Major and Mother enter from R. He is pushing a Victorian baby carriage. They bow at C. A small child in carriage, wearing baby cap, suddenly sits up, waves her arms, and cries loudly. Major and Mother quickly push carriage and exit at L.

Music changes to "Ta-Ra-Ra-Boom-Der-Ay." Henry runs in from back, waves, and bows. He sings with music and encourages audience to sing with him. He motions to the L and to the R. The cast enters, forming a final curtain line. They sing, dance, and make a last rousing moment before the final quick curtain.)

Yankee Doodle

Yankee Doodle is a musical revue created from events of 151 years of American history. Accomplishments of the famous and the forgotten become an entertaining and absorbing theatrical chronicle of the United States from 1776 to 1927.

Because the script is a revue rather than a play, it is not constructed in the conventional method of inseparably bound elements of dramatic form. The six elements of theme, plot, character, dialogue, song, and spectacle, however, are present and to an extent shape the work.

The theme is stated in the opening song by the entire cast and, soon after, repeated by the Drummer. America was and is its people, both great and small. On the basis of that statement the play moves ahead as a collection of "makers and shakers" who are brought forth to tell the story of the United States. A reprise of the opening song closes the work so that the theme is restated in the conclusion.

Since there is no circumscribed plot that builds in intensity, entangles itself with complications, and is finally resolved, the content is presented in a series of unrelated scenes. The particular historical events have been selected with attention to their dramatic potential, so that the past is revealed in action. Even when accompanied by narration in speech or song, the dramatic action carries the weight of the meaning. Accurate, although pared down to the essentials, the scenes and shorter references merely suggest either a period of history, an individual American, a group, or an event. The known and important are made more interesting by their combination with the trivial and amusing. The choice of Lindbergh's historic trans-Atlantic flight for the conclusion is arbitrary; however, the dramatic excitement inherent in the event makes it a triumphant and joyous celebration on which to end.

To sustain audience interest, the scenes, especially in their juxtaposition, exhibit great variety of pace, mood, length, and number of characters. Quickly moving comedy may follow or precede slower, more deliberate dramatic scenes. For example, the moving Molly Pitcher scene, which encompasses not only the fear and sorrow of death in war, but a determined retaliation, is preceded by a comic one-liner mocking death from Benjamin Franklin and followed by the light-hearted song of exploration by Lewis and Clark.

Scenes vary in length as well as in the number of characters included. A single statement indicates the signing of the Declaration of Independence. A brief two-person exchange dramatizes the Mexican-American cowboy in the Southwest. Four characters enact the mass production of early valentines, and nine present several past residents of the White House. The entire cast assists in telling Johnny Appleseed's story.

Since the development of characterization in a musical revue is not essential for meaning, characters reveal themselves as individuals only in terms of their contributions to America. The relative unimportance of characterization in the work is evident from the fact that there are over one hundred roles of people and objects (which may be played by a cast of twelve). The only character present throughout the work is the Drummer, a master of ceremonies, but he, too, has no identifiable characterization, for he is merely a spokesman. He exists to narrate when necessary, to impart historical facts, and to create occasional transitions between scenes.

Dialogue, written in terse, compact lines, augments the dramatic action. Historical facts are abundantly interspersed throughout the play, either spoken directly to the audience by a character or inherent in the dialogue of the action. Occasionally both methods of revelation occur at once. For example, in the segment about Thomas Edison, actors who play characters in the scene drop their roles momentarily during the action to enlighten the audience with some pertinent comment.

When lines of dialogue have been constructed from literary sources, such as Longfellow's "Paul Revere's Ride" and "Casey at the Bat" by Ernest Thayer, a work is never quoted in its entirety, but has been condensed to the lines which convey action. The source is always one likely to be recognized and appreciated by the young audience.

The lines of historical personages have been written with particular consideration for accuracy. When possible, famous, short quotations of a single sentence are used, such as "Give me liberty, or give me death!" In longer lines, when a character, such as Davy Crockett or Susan B. Anthony, explains his or her part in forming America, the words have been written to suggest the personal speech of the speaker.

Examples of special speech patterns which are typical of American society make the sound of the dialogue even more varied and authentic. There are hawkers at a fair; cheerleaders; a sportscaster; words recorded on an early, halting phonograph; and abbreviated, staccato messages from a teletypewriter.

In the scene between the Drummer and the tramp clown, dialogue serves to emphasize the immediately forthcoming conclusion of the play. Such a signaling device is a necessary replacement for the conventional resolution of plot.

Whether the lyrics are based on familiar or original tunes, song enlarges the emotional mood of the scene throughout the play. In a scene such as the building of the transcontinental railroad, the music increases the tension and excitement. In the Harriet Tubman scene, music emphasizes first a feeling of poignant sadness about her fate, and then a celebration of her triumph. When the music is a song, the lyrics and their accompaniment concur in feeling, as in the rousing "Yankee Doodle, We Salute!" and the jocund music of the Clermont scene.

A few simple hand properties and costume pieces and special lighting in the finale of the Edison scene enhance the meaning of the action, but spectacle is primarily a matter of mime. Visual requirements as dissimilar as horses, a mountain, scissors, and a baseball bat are given reality by actors in movement on a bare stage, so that the pace of the play proceeds uninterrupted by scenic demands.

Yankee Doodle is a musical salute to the United States from 1776 to 1927. This panorama of American history unfolds in scenes of action that are flavored with surprise, suspense, patriotism, pathos, and especially humor. Through mime, dance, singing, and acting, the names and contributions of over one hundred selected Yankee Doodles represent the vast diversity of people whose combined efforts created a nation.

Yankee Doodle

A Musical Revue

Spotlighting Early Makers and Shakers of the U.S.A.

by Aurand Harris

Music by Mort Stine

A galaxy of early Yankee Doodles

(Twelve actors, by doubling in several parts, can play all the characters, wearing a basic costume and changing only a hat or a jacket or carrying a prop. A complete list of all Yankee Doodles in the play appears on pages 365–366.

The U.S.A. from 1776 to 1927.

An intermission is optional.

Note: This version of *Yankee Doodle* differs in two instances from the original play script: the Harriet Tubman scene is a new addition, and the location of the Elijah McCoy sequence has been changed.

Yankee Doodle

ACT ONE

(A red, white, and blue Drummer marches down the aisle, beating a drum. On the bare stage, he stands in a spot of light.)

DRUMMER. The play is—YANKEE DOODLE.

(He beats the drum, or there is a fanfare, off. Cue 1.)

The place is—the U.S.A.

(Drum or fanfare.)

The cast is—

COMPANY. *(Enters. Sings. Cue 2.)*

Rich man, poor man, painter, preacher,
Doctor, lawyer, merchant, teacher.
Anyone, any occupation,
Who helps to make and shake our nation.

Beat the drum
Rat a tat tat,
Blow the bugle
Toot ta too toot,
Yankee Doodle, Yankee Doodle, Yankee Doodle,
We salute.

You'll find them—
From Oskaloosa to Tuscaloosa,
From Kalamazoo down to Waterloo,
Anyone who hails from any location
Who helps to make and shake our nation.

Beat the drum
Rat a tat tat,
Blow the bugle
Toot ta too toot,
Yankee Doodle, Yankee Doodle, Yankee Doodle,
We salute.

Drummers, and hummers, and mummers, and plumbers, and
Sailors, and whalers, and jailers, and tailors, and

Yankee Doodle's daughter and son,
Yankee Doodles everyone.

You'll find them—
From Oskaloosa to Tuscaloosa,
From Kalamazoo down to Waterloo,
Anyone who hails from any location
Who helps to make and shake our nation.

Beat the drum
Rat a tat tat,
Blow the bugle
Toot ta too toot,
Yankee Doodle, Yankee Doodle, Yankee Doodle,
We salute.

From Oskaloosa to Tuscaloosa,
Yankee Doodle, Yankee Doodle, Yankee Doodle, Yankee
    Doodle,
Yankee Doodle, Yankee Doodle, Yankee Doodle, Yankee
    Doodle,
We salute.

(Chorus dances off.)

DRUMMER. We will begin at the beginning. The thirteen English Colonies are ready to fight for freedom. In Boston two patriots, Paul Revere and Billy Dawes, have a plan.

REVERE. *(Paul Revere enters L when his name is said. Billy Dawes enters R.)*

"... If the British march ...
Hang a lantern aloft in the belfry arch ...
One, if by land, and two, if by sea;
And I on the opposite shore will be,
Ready to ride and spread the alarm ...
For the country-folk to be up and to arm."

(Dawes nods and runs off.)

DRUMMER. *(Revere pantomimes.)*

"On the opposite shore walked Paul Revere ...
Now gazed at the landscape far and near ...

(Actor enters R, stands with back to audience.)

But mostly he watched with eager search
The belfry-tower of the Old North Church . . .
And lo! as he looks, on the belfry's height

(Actor raises left arm, holds it high, then spreads and moves his fingers.)

A glimmer, and then a gleam of light!

(Revere pantomimes following scene.)

He springs to the saddle, the bridle he turns . . .

(Actor raises right arm, holds it high, then spreads and moves his fingers.)

A second lamp in the belfry burns!
A hurry of hoofs . . . through the gloom and the light,
The fate of a nation was riding that night."

REVERE. *(Revere pantomimes riding his horse. First, Second, and Third Farm People move into position at R, C, and L, and stand with backs to audience. First Farmer is the actor who was the church steeple.)*

The British are coming! The British are coming!

FARMER. *(At R, turns and yawns and stretches.)*

What is it you shout?

REVERE. The British are coming!

FARMER. *(Awakes immediately.)*

The British!

REVERE. Be up! Be armed! Be about!

(Farmer stands at attention with imaginary gun. Revere rides to C.)

DRUMMER. "It was twelve by the village clock,
When he crossed the bridge into Medford town."

REVERE. The British are coming!

WIFE. *(Turns, facing audience.)*

The Redcoats?

REVERE. They come with the morning sun!

WIFE. John! Wake up! John, get your gun!

(Husband turns and faces audience, stands at attention with imaginary gun.)

DRUMMER. "It was one by the village clock,
When he galloped into Lexington."

REVERE. The British are coming! The British are coming!

FATHER. *(At L, turns and faces audience.)*

Who shouts in the night?

REVERE. Paul Revere. The British are near!

FATHER. Allan!

ALLAN. *(Turns and faces audience.)*

Yes, Papa.

FATHER. Man and boy, today we fight for what we believe is right.

(Father and Son stand with imaginary guns. Revere rides off at L.)

DRUMMER. "It was two by the village clock,
When he came to the bridge in Concord town . . ."

DIAMOND. *(A bright, young boy quickly enters L.)*

My name's Will—William Diamond. I was the drummer boy at Lexington. Just a handful of us, against hundreds of them. Our captain, John Parker, said, "Stand your ground! Don't fire unless you're fired upon! But, if the British want war, let it begin here." Someone fired the first shot. And the fight for freedom began.

(He steps in line with the others and stands at attention.)

DRUMMER. "So through the night rode Paul Revere . . .
A cry of defiance and not of fear.
A voice in the darkness, a knock at the door,
And a word that shall echo forevermore!"

ALL. Freedom!

(All the Minute Men pose in a battle picture.)

DRUMMER. "Their flag to April's breeze unfurled . . .
They . . . fired the shot heard round the world."

(A loud roll on the drum and a boom is heard, off.)

And—Yankee Doodle is born!

(Cue 3. Drummer sings as others march in drill formation.)

Father and I went down to camp
Along with Captain Gooding
And there we saw the men and boys
As thick as hasty pudding.

Yankee Doodle, keep it up,
Yankee Doodle dandy,
Mind the music and the step
And with the girls be handy.

And there was Captain Washington
Upon a slapping stallion
A-giving orders to his men,
I guess there was a million.

DIAMOND. *(Or one of the other men may sing.)*

And there I saw a little keg,
Its head was made of leather,
They knocked upon it with little sticks
To call the folks together.

ALL. Yankee Doodle—

(They stomp three times.)

Yankee Doodle—

(They stomp three times.)

Yankee Doodle—

(They stomp three times.)

Yankee Doodle Dandy.

(All exit with music, except Drummer, who stands C.)

DRUMMER. Yankee Doodle is you and you and you. All the men and women who give their time, their talent, their lives to make America a great U.S.A.!

(Points.)

George Washington. First in war, first in peace, first in the hearts of his countrymen.

WASHINGTON. *(Quickly appears at L.)*

I do solemnly swear that I will faithfully execute the office of the President of the United States.

(Exits.)

DRUMMER. *(Points R.)*

Thomas Jefferson, who wrote the Declaration of Independence.

JEFFERSON. *(Quickly enters R.)*

We hold these truths to be self-evident: That all men are created equal . . . with certain inalienable rights . . . life, liberty, and the pursuit of happiness.

(Exits.)

DRUMMER. *(Points L.)*

John Hancock, the first to sign his name to the Declaration of Independence.

HANCOCK. *(Quickly enters L.)*

I wrote my name large so King George may read it without his spectacles.

(Exits.)

DRUMMER. *(Points R.)*

Patrick Henry, who spoke for the people.

HENRY. *(Quickly enters R.)*

Give me liberty or give me death.

(Exits.)

DRUMMER. *(Points L.)*

Benjamin Franklin, Mr. Ben of Philadelphia.

FRANKLIN. *(Enters L.)*

I did a few things to help: Gave them a hand with the constitution, went to France and persuaded the King to send us troops, and I wrote a book, *Poor Richard's Almanack.*

(Reads from book.)

"Early to bed, early to rise, makes a man healthy, wealthy and wise."

(Exits.)

DRUMMER. *(Points R.)*

Francis Hopkinson, the designer of the American flag.

HOPKINSON. *(Enters R.)*

A new country must have a new flag—a symbol for the world to see. I designed a flag—red, white, and blue.

(Exits.)

DRUMMER. *(Drums beat, bugle blows. Abraham Swartwout, a soldier, enters, followed by talking, excited crowd. They freeze.)*

The Ninth Massachusetts Regiment arrives at Fort Schuyler bringing ammunition and supplies—and a report.

SWARTWOUT. *(Holds up imaginary newspaper.)*

Item: Congress has adopted a resolution for a national flag. Thirteen alternate stripes of red and white; thirteen stars, white in a blue field.

(Crowd cheers. Someone shouts, "We want a flag. We want a new flag." Others shout, "Red, white and blue . . . red, white and blue.")

MAN. White! White! Take my shirt.

(Takes off shirt.)

WOMAN. Red! Red! Take my petticoat.

(Turns and quickly pulls her red petticoat down.)

SWARTWOUT. Blue! Take my uniform.

(Takes off coat.)

Let history say that I, Captain Abraham Swartwout, for my country gave the coat off my back!

ALL. *(Crowd cheers and sings. Cue 4. They wave a homemade flag.)*

Yankee Doodle needs a flag,
Yankee Doodle Dandy,
Yankee Doodle *makes* a flag
And it's a Jim-Dandy!

Yankee Doodle keep it up,
Yankee Doodle Dandy.
Mind the music and the step,
Yankee Doodle Dandy.

(Crowd exits L.)

FRANKLIN. *(Quickly enters R, speaks to audience.)*

I have just written another proverb: One egg today is better than a hen tomorrow.

(Laughs.)

And listen to this one. Three may keep a secret, if two are dead.

(Exits R.)

DRUMMER. The Revolutionary War goes on. Fighting at Fort Ticonderoga, the Battle of Brandywine, of Trenton, and of Monmouth.

MOLLY. *(Off, distant booming of cannons is heard. Molly Pitcher enters L.)*

All day the men fire the cannons . . .

(Boom.)

In the heat and dust . . .

(Boom. Men enter, weary, kneel and fall to the ground as she speaks.)

I carry them water. "Water," they call. "A pitcher of water." "Here comes Molly with her pitcher . . . Bring me a pitcher, Molly." Molly Pitcher they call me. I stand by my husband, John. "Water," he calls as he falls in the heat and the dust. His cannon is still. I take his place and I fire the cannon. I fire at the British! I fire at the Hessians! I fire until the sun goes down and the battle of Monmouth is won!

(Boom.)

FIRST SOLDIER. *(Four Soldiers quickly run in and stand at either side of her.)*

Dan Morgan wins at Saratoga and at King's Mountain.

(Boom. A fallen soldier rises and stands at attention.)

SECOND SOLDIER. George Rogers Clark wins at Fort Vincennes.

(Boom. Another fallen soldier rises.)

THIRD SOLDIER. John Paul Jones wins at sea.

(Boom. Another fallen soldier rises.)

FOURTH SOLDIER. George Washington wins at Yorktown!

(Boom. All fallen soldiers rise.)

ALL. The war is over!

(Boom.)

MOLLY. Yankee Doodle wins! The States—thirteen united—begin! And watch them grow!

(All cheer and march out. Cue 5.)

FRANKLIN. *(Enters.)*

I did a few more things to help. I started a university, a fire company. I invented a heating stove and bifocal spectacles.

(Pantomiming holding a string and looking up at a kite.)

And—I discovered one night by flying a kite that lightning and electricity are the same.

(Loud claps of thunder are heard. He makes a loud sizzling sound, jumps, and runs off.)

DRUMMER. America spills over the mountains. President Jefferson buys the Louisiana Purchase. Two explorers make a map.

(Meriwether Lewis and William Clark enter, sing, and do a soft-shoe dance, pantomiming action to fit the words. Cue 6.)

LEWIS. I am Lewis.

CLARK. I am Clark.

BOTH. Ready and about to start,

With brave men, men the best,
Blaze a trail out west.
We'll explore where no man
Has ever been before,
Make a map, make a mark, make a chart—Who?
Lewis and Clark.

In a boat, row, row, row,
On the Missouri River go.

(Indian Chief enters.)

Indian Chief dressed
In leather with a feather
Comes this way
Raise our hand, bow and stand,
Greetings say together.

INDIAN. Hi up, hi up, hi up—ho.

LEWIS. Howdy-do.

CLARK. Hello.

BOTH. For a feast we take a seat,
Head of rattlesnake we eat.
Pipe of peace
Pass to each,
Puffs and puffs and puffs.
Council meet on a hill,
Call it Council Bluffs.

INDIAN. *(Rises, holds out arms.)* Hi up, hi up, hi up—ho.

LEWIS AND CLARK. Goodby. We go.

(Indian exits.)

Need a guide to lead the way
Beyond the unexplored West.

(Sacajawea enters.)

Found a guide, leave today,
For she is the best.
Indian maid, unafraid,
Sacajawea,
Lead us, guide us, show us—do.
We follow you.

(She, in front, pantomimes.)

River fork, we go where?
Mountains high, pass is there.
Grizzly bears! Shoot with gun,
Off the grizzlies run.

Rocky Mountain, straight ahead,
Horses load and ride,
Getty-up, getty-up, getty-up—over
The Great Divide.

(Sacajawea exits.)

End of journey, ocean ahead,
Columbia River, paddle fast.
Plant the flag
Of the U.S.A., end of trail at last,
Mission done, West is won
Now for everyone.
We did it, we did it, we did it—it's done.
By Lewis, by Clark.

(Exit L.)

FULTON. *(Enters R.)*

The new United States is growing and traveling fast. It needs a steamboat. I, Robert Fulton, will build one. The *Clermont.*

(One at a time, eight actors enter. Each, on his right side, wears a large letter on a big square. The letters spell C-L-E-R-M-O-N-T. The actors always face L and line up slowly, letters "E" and "O" supplying the comedy by never being in the right place in line and changing many times during the dialogue.)

It is 150 feet long, 13 feet wide, and draws 2 feet of water. There is an anchor on the bow—

("T," first actor, enters and stands at far L. One side of his square is pointed like the bow of the ship. There is also a short rope with an anchor.)

and a rudder on the stern.

("C," second actor, enters, and stands at the end at R. He has a rudder on his square.)

There is a tall smokestack that funnels the smoke from the fire under the boiler.

("R" enters and stands in a center position. He wears a four-foot-long stovepipe hat and gives a long whistle sound, "Whoo-whoo-whoo.")

There is a mast in the front and a mast on the back, but there are no sails; only the new American flag catches the breeze.

("L" enters carrying a mast. "N" enters carrying a mast with an American flag. Both stand in their proper places.)

The boat moves by the turning of two paddle wheels, one wheel on each side of the boat.

("M" enters moving his arms slowly like paddle wheels and stands in his right place. "E" and "O" enter, trying various wrong places in the line.)

It takes four months to build. There were others who built a steamboat—Fitch, Rumsey, Stevens—but I, with my business partner, Robert Livingston, built the first successful commercial steamboat.

(Proudly points at the now assembled line.)

The *Clermont*.

(Spells out letters.)

C-l-e-r-m-o-n-t.

(Letters "E" and "O," who are in the wrong places, quickly change and stand in correct positions.)

On August 17, 1807, all is ready. Black smoke pours out of the chimney.

(A painted piece of "smoke" flips up from "R's" stovepipe hat and he gives a "whoo-whoo-whoo.")

Steam hisses from every valve.

(All actors make loud sound effects.)

The anchor is raised.

("T" pulls up the anchor.)

Bells ring. Ropes are eased off. The engine starts. The paddle wheel turns—and the boat moves!

("M" circles his arms slowly. All actors make loud sound effects. "Chug-chug, splash-splash, toot-toot," hisses of steam, and the boat moves slowly to L. Cue 7. Fulton runs and jumps "aboard," moving off with the boat and shouting above the sound effects and soft music.)

Up the Hudson River to Albany at five miles an hour. On the rivers, over the lakes, across the ocean, steamboats chug and change the world!

(All exit L, as Franklin enters R.)

FRANKLIN. *(Waves off L and imitates, "Toot-toot.")*

Little Bob Fulton. I knew him as a boy. Now he's built fifteen other steamboats, invented a torpedo, an air gun, and a submarine. Yes, little Bob grew up to be Mr. Fulton. From little acorns grow mighty oaks.

(Excited with a new proverb.)

That's very good! I must write that down in my Almanack!

(Franklin exits quickly, repeating loudly, "From little acorns grow mighty oaks . . . from little acorns . . ." Cue 8. Pat and Mike enter L, dancing an Irish jig and pantomiming digging with a shovel. They stop at C.)

PAT. I'm Pat.

MIKE. I'm Mike.

PAT. We are digging the Erie Canal.

MIKE. An important ditch history will say—

PAT. Because it will make New York the biggest city—

BOTH. In the U.S.A.

(Music. Shoveling, they dance a fast jig as they exit.)

DRUMMER. By river, by canals, by forest trails America moves west. And the Yankee Doodles lead the way. Daniel Boone blazes a trail and helps settle Kentucky.

BOONE. *(Enters R.)*

If you want to see what's beyond the mountains, come along. We'll settle a town or two, join an Indian tribe, and be a captain in the army. Bring your gun, 'cause we're opening up the Wilderness Road.

(He exits L, as Pike enters R.)

DRUMMER. Lieutenant Zebulon Montgomery Pike, explorer of the Louisiana Purchase.

(Four actors may enter, form a circle, arms locked, making a mountain.)

PIKE. With a party of soldiers, I set off to explore the great American desert.

(Looks through spyglass.)

Looking in my glass, I see the highest mountain in the range. On my map, I draw the "Grand Peak." Later they name it for me, Pike's Peak. And when the wagon trains start rolling west, they'll sing, "Pike's Peak or Bust."

(He exits L as James runs in at R.)

DRUMMER. Edwin James, a geologist and botanist.

JAMES. *(Runs to C or behind the actors who make the mountain and who slowly bend down as he pantomimes climbing up the mountain.)*

I—am the first man—to climb to the TOP—of Pike's Peak!

(He runs off L, as Dilworth enters R. Actors who make mountain also exit.)

DRUMMER. Mary Jane Dilworth, one of the hundreds of Mormons who travel west for religious freedom.

DILWORTH. From Pennsylvania, to Illinois, to Iowa we travel on. Until our President, Brigham Young, says this is the place, and we settle the City of the Saints by the Great Salt Lake. The children come to school for the first time. I, age sixteen, am the first teacher. We begin by singing . . . "Come, come, ye Saints, no toil, no labor fear, But with joy wend your way. Though hard to you this journey may appear . . ."

(She exits as she starts singing. Crockett enters R.)

DRUMMER. Davy Crockett, pathfinder and coonskin congressman.

CROCKETT. When I was eighteen, my wealth consisted of a rifle—I called her Betsy—one suit of clothes, which I had on, and a horse not all paid for.

(Two actors run in, performing like a horse. The front one neighs and the back one kicks. The back one removes his arm from the front one, leaving Crockett standing between them.)

I figured I was rich enough to get me a wife, and I had her picked out—Polly. We got hitched, and later we, with our two boys, headed west.

(He and "horse" trot to side.)

Someone said, as a joke, I should run for Congress. Well, I did, and the joke was on them. I won. So I took my coonskin cap and I went to Washington. But now there's fighting at the border of Texas.

(Two actors who were the horse quickly stand at attention like soldiers.)

I'm on my way to help them out. To fight it out—at the Alamo.

(Gunfire is heard. Several actors run in, kneel, fire imaginary guns. All exit.)

DRUMMER. And—there is one Yankee Doodle who is different from the others. A Yankee Doodle who goes west without a gun. He carries only a sack of apple seeds.

JOHNNY. *(John Chapman enters and speaks to audience in "Story Theatre" fashion.)*

Once upon a real time—during the first year of the Revolutionary War—John Chapman was born in the State of Massachusetts. As a boy he walked in the woods and *(Walks and mimes.)* looked up at the trees. "They are my friends," he said.

(Actor-tree enters, stands with back to audience.)

Of all the trees, his favorite was one apple tree. An old, old apple tree.

(Tree turns around. He wears a long green beard.)

A bent and gnarled—

(Tree crooks his arm.)

ancient apple tree.

(To audience.)

"Everyone should have an apple tree," John said.

FRANKLIN. *(Appears quickly and writes.)*

"An apple a day keeps the doctor away." That's a good one!

(Exits happily.)

JOHNNY. When John was eighteen he set off for the West. He said goodby to his favorite apple tree.

(John raises his hand. Tree waves, then exits R.)

And he walked toward the setting sun. He walked across the Allegheny Mountains . . .

(Mimes walking up, body tilted backward.)

walked UP the east side . . .

(Mimes walking down, body bent forward.)

and DOWN the west side. And he walked until he came to Fort Pitt. There he settled on a farm, but there were no apple trees. So he went to the cider mills.

(Pantomimes the following.)

And he scooped and he scooped up sacks and sacks full of apple seeds, and planted them. He watered and cared for them.

(Actor enters and sits low, back to audience.)

He watched the seeds begin to grow. Slowly . . . and the first year there appeared a green shoot.

(Actor raises hand with green glove.)

The next year, a bigger seedling.

(Actor raises other hand with green glove.)

And it grew and grew until, in five years, there stood an apple tree.

(Actor has slowly risen to full height.)

And, lo and behold, in the spring a tiny green bud appeared.

(Actor opens his fist, which holds a big pink blossom.)

"A miracle," he said. "That happens every spring." And where the blossom had been, there, starting to grow, was a little round apple.

(Actor puts a red balloon to his mouth and blows it up, or holds a red circle of cloth he takes from his sleeve.)

The apple grew and it grew, bigger and bigger, until it was a beautiful big red apple. "It is a miracle," he said. "That happens every fall."

(Actor exits.)

Then he knew what he must do. "I will go west, not with a gun, but with sacks of apple seeds. I will plant them and they will grow—and every year a miracle will happen." As he traveled, planting orchards, he became a living legend. And they called him Johnny Appleseed.

FIRST INDIAN. *(Indians creep in.)*

The Indians also watched and listened. They heard him talk to the animals.

SECOND INDIAN. They saw him walk through the snake country without shoes. They saw him plant seeds—and trees grow.

THIRD INDIAN. They knew he was brave because he carried no gun.

ALL INDIANS. "Magic," they said, and bowed low to the white medicine man.

JOHNNY. But Johnny held out is hand and said, "Friend."

SECOND INDIAN. "Come," the Indian said, and in their village they made a celebration.

FIRST INDIAN. *(He sits R. Second Indian sits at L. Johnny sits in center facing audience.)*

They gave him beads of sharp teeth and shining shells.

THIRD INDIAN. They gave him moccasins of soft skins.

SECOND INDIAN. *(Standing behind Johnny.)*

The Chief crowned his head with a circle of bright feathers and called him "Brother."

JOHNNY. Friend of the Indians, friend of the settlers, he tried to keep peace between them. When he heard the war drums beat,

(War drum beats. He rises and comes to front.)

he ran thirty miles to bring soldiers to Fort Mansfield. When the Indians saw they were outnumbered they slipped quietly away.

(Drum stops. Indians slip out.)

On he went, and more and more of his orchards bloomed in the wilderness.

(Actors enter quickly and quietly, scatter over the stage, and stand with backs to audience. Johnny walks among them.)

"I'll come back," he always said. "I'll come back in the spring." And he did, pruning and tending his trees. As he grew old, he was asked, "Are you not lonely, always walking alone?" He held out his arms to the woods. "I have a thousand friends." When he was seventy he took his last walk. He became ill with the winter plague, pneumonia, and was nursed in the house of William Worth. One morning William said, "The old man is dead."

(Music. Cue 9. Actors over music, chant, "I'll come back." Music continues softly.)

Every spring his trees burst into pink and white clouds of beauty.

(Actors move their arms like branches and chant over music, "I'll come back. I'll come back.")

Every fall the branches are heavy with red and golden apples. A miracle that happens every year.

(Actors, above their heads, spread brilliant red fans which they hold. They chant with the music, "I'll come back. I'll come back. I'll come back.")

Johnny Appleseed went west without a gun.

(A few notes more of music, and then Johnny exits. Music stops.)

DRUMMER. The year is 1849. Gold is discovered in California and there is a rush!

(Music. Cue 10. Actors shout and exit.)

A transcontinental railroad is needed. Theodore Judah makes a map. President Lincoln grants the money. Two railroads, one starting from California, one starting from Nebraska, will meet and join the country together.

SINGERS. *(Three singers enter singing. Cue 11.)*

I've been working on the railroad
All the live-long day,
I've been working on the railroad
Across the U.S.A.

(They continue humming.)

DRUMMER. January, 1863, the Central Pacific starts building from the west.

(Two workers enter L, pantomiming hitting spikes, laying tracks, etc.)

Hundreds of Chinese workmen build trestles, tunnels, and bravely do the impossible—hanging in baskets, blasting cliffs with dynamite. So many are killed the phrase becomes common, "Not a Chinaman's chance."

(Two other workmen enter from R, pantomiming pumping a railroad car, etc.)

The Union Pacific starts building from the east. General Dodge organizes the workmen and runs the crews like an army. They lay ties, fight the hostile Indians, and eat buffalo meat shot by William Cody, who makes a new name for himself—Buffalo Bill. Trains follow on the tracks. From the west puffs the engine Jupiter.

(Two actors enter. First one wears a cowcatcher and smoke-stack hat. Second holds on to the first and waves a red lantern behind. The train whistles and shuffles.)

SINGER. *(Speaks through a megaphone over music.)*

Through Sacramento Valley . . . choo-choo-choo . . . up the mountain . . . down and around . . . Reno . . . Elko . . . choo-choo-choo . . . Utah border is in sight!

(Train stops at R.)

DRUMMER. From the east chugs Engine Number One Ten.

(Two actors enter, wearing the same train costume. They whistle and shuffle.)

SECOND SINGER. *(Speaks through a megaphone over music.)*

Clickety-clack, along the Platte . . . Rocky Mountains high ahead.

(Train goes slowly over mountain.)

Chug—chug—chug . . . Laramie . . . Salt Lake Desert . . . clickety-clack . . . See the other train on the track.

(Music stops. Trains stand on either side.)

DRUMMER. It is a race to see which of the two can reach the other first. Get set. Ready. Go!

(Fast music. Both trains "chug" and "choo," hiss steam, clang bells in a race about the stage. Music stops.)

The Central Pacific wins!

(Holds up hand of engine. Other train hisses steam in defeat.)

The two meet at Promontory, Utah. Governor Leland Stanford lifts the hammer to hit the last, golden spike.

(Stanford, one of the workers, steps forward proudly and mimes.)

He swings. He misses. Thomas Durant of the Union Pacific lifts the hammer.

(Durant, one of the workmen, steps forward and pantomimes.)

He swings. He misses.

(A workman steps forward and pantomimes.)

A workman, standing by, swings and with practiced rhythm drives the last, golden spike. East joins West.

(The two Engines shake hands.)

The states are united!

(Fast music. All get in lines between the engine and the caboose lantern, forming two long trains. The trains "hiss," "chug," and pick up speed, circling the stage. They start to come together in a crash. Drummer quickly pantomimes throwing switch. One train continues and chugs offstage. The second train stops short, avoiding a collision. Music stops. Second train whistles, chugs, and starts to move ahead slowly, but only the first three actors. Fourth and caboose lantern are left standing. Fourth actor whistles and toots loudly. Front of

train stops, looks around, then backs up, making a jolt when connecting. Train starts again slowly. All follow. Music starts and builds. Train chugs off fast and loud. Drummer waves goodby.)

America. Land of dreams. Land of promises. Settlers come from all countries, following the rainbow to find the pot of gold. People doing their part to help America start.

(Drummer exits. Music in a lively tempo. Cue 12. Four actors, a white man, black man, woman, and comedian enter, singing.)

ALL. We are Yankee Doodles
From every state
Who have helped to make
Our country great.

For a portrait we should sit,
And our name
Should be writ
In the Hall of Fame,
In the Hall of Fame.

(Each turns his back to audience except when he speaks. Music continues, underscoring the speaking.)

FIRST. The North spoke with a twang,
The South with a drawl,
I helped America
To have one speech for all.

My name, Noah Webster,
Is still said in schools,
Where my dictionary
Still spells the words and rules.

SECOND. *(Faces front, speaks.)*
On Lake Michigan
I built a trading post.
Indians trusted me;
I was friend to most.

Jean Baptiste Pointe Sable,
I traded furs by pack.
In Chicago
The first settler was black.

THIRD. *(Faces front, speaks.)*

> Women have always nursed
> And cared for the ill;
> But only men could be
> Doctors until . . .

> I did become . . .
> And history will tell . . .
> The first woman doctor,
> Elizabeth Blackwell.

FOURTH. My name is Marvin Stone
    From Washington, D.C.

(Holds up soda glass prop with two drinking straws.)

> I made the drinking straw
> For my girl and me.

(Third, a girl, joins him and they sing, dance, and sip.)

> In the good old summer time,
> In the good old summer time,
> Sipping sarsaparilla *(Sips.)*
> with a straw that's mine.
> You sip, *(Sips.)* she sips, *(Sips.)* then sip together, and
> That's a very good sign
> That's she's your tootsey wootsey
> In the good old summer time.

(Turn their backs to audience.)

FIRST. *(Faces front, speaks.)*

> While visiting in the South
> It came to my attention
> To take the seed from cotton,
> So I made an invention.

> The cotton gin, which
> Changed the economy,
> Was invented by me,
> Eli Whitney.

SECOND. *(Faces front, speaks.)*

> I worked my way through school,

Became a teacher myself,
And wrote books you'll find
On a library shelf.

Booker T. Washington
I sign my name with pride,
And try to help the black
And white live side by side.

THIRD. *(Faces front, speaks.)*

I stand for women's rights,
Even how they dress.

(Unties and takes off wrap-around skirt.)

So, Amelia Bloomer
Exchanged long skirts for less.

And in public wear
Despite humorous rumors,
What's been named for me,

(Reveals her walking bloomers.)

Emancipated—bloomers.

FOURTH. *(Faces front, speaks.)*

Some like to chew it fast, *(Does.)*
Some like to chew it slow, *(Does.)*
Some like to chew it smack. *(Does.)*
Some like to bubbles blow. *(Does.)*

Juicy fruit and mint.
More flavors to come!
I, Mr. Semple,
Patented chewing gum!

ALL. *(Face front, exit singing.)*

We are Yankee Doodles
From every state
Who have helped to make
Our country great.

For a portrait we should sit,
And our name
Should be writ

In the Hall of Fame,
In the Hall of Fame.

(Exit.)

DRUMMER. *(Enters.)*

Yankee Doodle works: William Kelly turns iron into steel; Hyman Lipman puts a rubber eraser on the pencil. Yankee Doodle plays: P. T. Barnum opens his museum and starts the American ballyhoo.

(Acts.)

Step right up and see the smallest man alive, General Tom Thumb.

(Drummer again.)

And—America laughs at its first great clown—Dan Rice.

CLOWNS. *(Three clowns run in, turning flip-flops, and perform as cheerleaders.)*

Rah, rah.
Rah, rah, rah.
Give a cheer—
One, two.
Give a cheer—
For who?
Dan Rice.
Say it twice.
Dan Rice. Dan Rice.
Greatest clown in the town!

P-I-G spells pig.
He's got a pig that does a jig!

(Clown dances like a pig.)

He's got an elephant
That can dance and lope

(Clown pantomimes elephant.)

And can walk on a high tightrope.

Who can tell a funny joke?
Dan Rice.

Who can sing a funny song?
Dan Rice.

Who is Mr. Strong?
Dan Rice.

Say it twice.
Dan Rice. Dan Rice.
Rah. Rah. Rah.

NAST. *(Thomas Nast enters.)*

My name is Thomas Nast. I am an artist.

(Holds up pencil and pad.)

I have come to make a drawing of the famous clown Dan Rice.
A sketch for the *Harper's Weekly*, showing him dressed in his
new red, white, and blue costume.

(Clown points off L. Nast looks off L and sketches on pad.)

FIRST CLOWN. He's got a costume. He's got a costume.

SECOND CLOWN. What a beaut!

THIRD CLOWN. It's a flag made into a suit.

NAST. *(Speaks as he draws.)*

A high tall hat on his head.

CLOWNS. Head, head, head.

NAST. Whiskers growing on his chin.

CLOWNS. Chin, chin, chin.

NAST. A suit of white and red.

CLOWNS. Red, red, red.

NAST. With stars and stripes sprinkled in.

CLOWNS. In, in, in.
A walking flag,
A walking flag
Is his suit.
Start the band
And salute!

(Clowns march, pantomiming playing various instruments.)

A boom and a boom and a boom, boom, boom.
And a root and a toot and a rootee-toot-toot.

(As they circle L, Uncle Sam in full costume enters L and follows them. He stands C.)

Mister Whiskers—we salute!

(Clowns kneel and salute him.)

NAST. No, not Mr. Whiskers. He is—he will be a symbol—Mr. United States—Mr. U.S.—us!

CLOWNS. U.S., U.S.,
　Yes, yes, yes,
　U for uncle,
　S for Sam.
　Sis boom bah, sis boom bam!
　We've got an UNCLE—
　UNCLE SAM!

　Clap your hands, clap, clap.
　Tap your feet, tap, tap.
　UNCLE SAM can't be beat!

(Uncle Sam walks slowly DC as Clowns continue.)

　Zip! Zoom! Zah!
　Alacazoop! Alacazam!
　Rah! Rah! Rah!
　UNCLE SAM!

(Uncle Sam points finger at audience. All exit with music. Cue 13.)

DRUMMER. The United States has a flag, the star-spangled banner. The United States has a symbol, Uncle Sam. The United States wants a national anthem, a song to sing together.

(Francis Scott Key enters and stands in profile at back.)

In the War of 1812, Francis Scott Key is held on board a British ship while the British are making an attack on Fort McHenry.

(Light effect begins, red glow, rockets bursting, smoke, etc., with the booming sound of cannons growing louder.)

Through the night Francis Scott Key stands on the deck watching the cannons' red glare. Only when the bombs burst in the air can he see proof that the stars and stripes are still there. He starts to write a poem, and later it is set to music, and "The Star-Spangled Banner" is proclaimed our National Anthem.

ALL. *(Music. Cue 14. "The Star-Spangled Banner" is played with dramatic effects. The entire cast appears and sings proudly.)*

Oh! Say, can you see, by the dawn's early light,
What so proudly we hail'd at the twilight's last gleaming!
Whose broad stripes and bright stars, thro' the perilous night,
O'er the ramparts we watched were so gallantly streaming:
And the rockets' red glare, the bombs bursting in air,
Gave proof thro' the night that our flag was still there.

(Cast advances downstage, waving flags they have had behind their backs.)

Oh! Say, does that star-spangled banner yet wave
O'er the land of the free and the home of the brave.

(Short intermission. Or the play may be continuous. If so, the actors can exit on "Yankee Doodle" music or "Stars and Stripes Forever," by John Philip Sousa.)

ACT TWO

DRUMMER. *(Enters.)*

Presidents! Presidents!
Elected in a democratic way.
Presidents! Presidents!
Highest office in the U.S.A.

SINGERS. *(Four singers enter and sing. Cue 15.)*

They've been—
Republicans, Democrats, Federalists, and Whigs;
Dressed in—
Knee pants, ruffles, spats, tall hats, beards, and wigs.
They've been—
Quiet Quakers, city makers, and romantic suitors,
Indian fighters, legal writers, marble shooters.

DRUMMER. Presidents! Presidents!
Elected for a four-year stay.

Presidents! Presidents!
Highest office in the U.S.A.

There was—

FIRST SINGER. *(Sings, as Andrew Jackson enters in coonskin cap and mimes.)*

President Andrew Jackson, born in South Carolina,
An orphan at fourteen, a soldier at fifteen in a coonskin cap.
Cut on a cheek by a British sword, a scar was left.

(Jackson looks into imaginary mirror.)

Looking in a mirror, he said—

JACKSON. My face looks like a map.

FIRST SINGER. In the War of 1812 he made a name for himself.
They called him "Old Hickory." He was tough and lean,
When he led his troops to victory in New Orleans.
Elected him President for the people true.

JACKSON. Let the people rule, instead of a few.

FIRST SINGER. And that's what he did as President in 1832.

JACKSON. *(Sings as he hangs his cap on Drummer's head and exits.)*

When I hung my hat in the White House.

DRUMMER. *(Sings.)*

When he hung his hat in the White House.

(Speaks.)

Presidents! And their wives!
Set the style and fashion of the day.
Presidents! And their wives!
First Family of the U.S.A.

There was—

SECOND SINGER. *(Sings as Dolley Madison enters, elegant with a hat with a feather. She mimes and dances.)*

Dolley Madison, a charming, witty social caller,
Who was younger than her husband and four inches taller.
She danced at all the balls dressed in a formal gown;
Just to see her, people broke the windows down.

(She admires hat in imaginary mirror.)

While her husband ten amendments put together,
She, on her hat, put an ostrich feather.
A social hostess, she rules supreme,

(Pantomimes tasting with a spoon.)

Served a new frozen dessert—

DOLLEY. I think I'll call it "ice cream."

SECOND SINGER. And she did, as First Lady, with honor and esteem.

DOLLEY. *(Sings as she hangs her hat on one of the Drummer's upheld hands and exits.)*

When I hung my hat in the White House.

DRUMMER. *(Sings.)*

When she hung her hat in the White House.

(Speaks.)

Presidents! Presidents!
Great ones making history every day.
Presidents! Presidents!
Highest office in the U.S.A.

There was—

THIRD SINGER. *(Sings as Abraham Lincoln enters, wearing a stovepipe hat.)*

Abraham Lincoln, a poor boy who rose to fame.
"Honest Abe," they called him; he was true to his name.
Some one said he was a very common-looking cuss.

LINCOLN. Yes, surely the Lord must love us; he made so many of us.

THIRD SINGER. He freed the slaves. The Emancipator he was called for that.

(Lincoln takes off hat.)

He kept important papers in his stovepipe hat.
A little girl wrote—

LINCOLN. *(Reads letter taken from hat.)*

"Why don't you let your whiskers grow?

Then the ladies will tease their husbands to vote for you, you know."

THIRD SINGER. He thanked her and began a beard, which all his pictures show.

LINCOLN. *(Sings.)*

When I hung my hat in the White House.

(Hangs his hat on the other upheld hand of the Drummer and exits.)

DRUMMER. *(Sings.)*

When he hung his hat in the White House.

(Speaks.)

Presidents! Presidents!
It's the great American way.
Presidents! Presidents!
Highest office in the U.S.A.

There was—

FOURTH SINGER. *(Sings, as Theodore Roosevelt enters, wearing glasses and a Spanish-American War hat. He looks in imaginary mirror.)*

Theodore Roosevelt, a rich but sickly boy,
Looked at himself and said—

ROOSEVELT. Pipestem legs and four eyes.

FOURTH SINGER. But with exercises which he did all his life,

(Roosevelt starts pantomiming various exercises, boxing, rowing, tennis, lifting weights, running, skipping rope, diving, swimming, etc., which he continues without stopping until he exits.)

His health became robust; he won a boxing prize.
He was a cowboy, led the army in a war.
Then for President he was the pick,
Saved our forests, built the Panama Canal.
His rule was—

ROOSEVELT. *(Holding imaginary weight overhead.)*

Speak softly, carry a big stick.

(Continues exercising faster.)

FOURTH SINGER. And he did as President and it did the trick.

ROOSEVELT. *(Sings, put his hat over the coonskin cap on Drummer's head and exits.)*

When I hung my hat in the White House.

DRUMMER. *(Sings.)*

When he hung his hat in the White House.

SINGERS. *(Sing, as they circle Drummer, and each takes a hat from him and exits.)*

Presidents and First Ladies too
Proudly hang their hats day and night
In that famous house that's painted white
On Pennsylvania Avenue.

(Drummer exits.)

TUBMAN. *(Harriet Tubman enters as the cast, offstage, hums "Steal Away Home.")*

I was born a slave. I can show you the scars where I was whipped. My prayer was always—let me, Harriet Tubman, be free.

(Cast enters and enacts in pantomime Tubman's experiences as she relates them.)

One night I told the cabin-folks I was going to run away north. I dared not speak the words aloud, so I sang them.

(Sings.)

Steal away, steal away,
Steal away to Jesus.
Steal away, steal away home.
I ain't got long to stay here.

They heard and understood; to steal away meant to escape from slavery. When the North Star was shining bright, I slipped away on the Underground Railroad.

(Cast hums "Steal Away Home.")

I hid in the attic of a Quaker lady's house. I was hidden in a potato hole for a week with a free black family. I was covered in a wagon and driven north by a farmer whose words I could not understand. I was buried safely in a haystack when the slave hunters came with their hounds and guns. I was rowed in a boat up the Choptank River. And at last—at last I crossed the freedom line into Pennsylvania. I felt like I was in heaven. I was free!

(Cast continues to pantomime action.)

Now that I knew the way, I knew what I must do. I must go back. I, like Moses, must lead my people out of slavery. Let my people go—on the freedom train. Nineteen trips I made. Three hundred slaves I delivered up to freedom—always guided by the North Star and my trust in God. Oh, let it be written and remembered that I, Harriet Tubman, never ran my train off the track and I never lost a single passenger!

(Cast exits clapping and singing "Didn't My Lord Deliver Daniel?")

Didn't my Lord deliver Daniel,
Deliver Daniel, deliver Daniel?
Didn't my Lord deliver Daniel,
And why not-a every man?

ESTHER. *(Esther Howland enters, carrying a large, beautiful valentine.)*

I received a valentine from England. "To Esther Howland, Worchester, Mass., U.S.A." I made a few valentines and sold them, and sold some more, and soon I had a factory. I hired several of my friends to help.

(Three actors enter, stand in line, backs to audience and work, pantomiming cutting, folding, pasting.)

In my attic at a long table each person did his work. One cut, one pasted, one folded—and I, using the first assembly line— was first to manufacture a valentine.

FIRST HELPER. *(Turns and faces audience.)*

Fair is the lily,
White is a dove.
But the fairer is
The girl I love.

(He turns his back as Second Helper faces audience.)

SECOND HELPER. I love you once,
  I love you twice;
  I love you better
  Than cats love mice.

(He turns his back as Third Helper faces audience.)

THIRD HELPER. As sure as grass grows round the stump,
  You are my darling sugar lump.

(He turns his back. Music. Cue 16. Girl runs across from L to R, followed by Boy. They stop C. Music stops.)

BOY. Mary Ann is pretty.
  Mary Ann is smart.
  Mary Ann is the girl
  Who's won my heart.

(Music, Boy runs after Girl, who runs off R, as First Helper waltzes with Esther three measures. Music stops.)

FIRST HELPER. Butter is butter.
  Cheese is cheese.
  What's a kiss
  Without a squeeze?

(He squeezes her. Music starts. They waltz. Second Helper taps First on shoulder. Second Helper dances with Esther three measures. Music stops.)

SECOND HELPER. Roses are red,
  Pickles are green;
  My face is funny,
  Yours is a scream.

(Music starts. They waltz. Third Helper taps Second on shoulder. Third Helper dances with Esther three measures. Music stops.)

THIRD HELPER. You can fall from the mountain,
  You can fall from above,
  But the best way to fall
  Is to fall in love.

(Music starts. They dance three measures and are in line with the other Helpers as Boy runs in R, followed by Girl. Music stops. They stop in C.)

GIRL. A kiss is a germ
  Or so it's been stated.
  But—kiss me quick,
  I'm vaccinated!

(Music starts as Girl chases Boy off L. Music stops.)

THIRD HELPER. *(All four stand in line. Third holds valentine.)*

Valentines, valentines,

(Hands valentine to Second Helper.)

SECOND HELPER. Saying few words, but true.

(Hands valentine to First Helper.)

FIRST HELPER. Valentines, valentines,

(Hands valentine to Esther.)

ESTHER. Saying—

ALL. I love you.

(Exit with music.)

DRUMMER. *(Enters, blowing a referee whistle.)*

Yankee Doodles make history in the world of sports! Presenting
—the All Time, All Star Athletes! The great American Champions!

(Blows whistle.)

In baseball! The first great batter in baseball history—Ty Cobb!

(Music. Cue 17. Cobb runs in, pantomiming swinging an imaginary bat, hitting balls, etc. Music stops. Drummer blows whistle.)

In boxing! With bare knuckles or with boxing gloves, the early champion of the ring—John L. Sullivan!

(Music. Sullivan runs in, shadow boxes, shakes hands over his head, the winner. Music stops. Whistle blows.)

Champion of the ladies. Queen of sports. In basketball, track, golf, baseball, swimming, and football—the First Lady is—Babe Dedrickson Zaharias!

(Music. Zaharias runs in, mimes various sports. Music stops. Drummer blows whistle.)

In marble shooting! While shooting a game of marbles John Tyler is informed that President Harrison has died, and that he, Vice President, is the new President of the United States. A marble shooting champion—President John Tyler.

(Music. Tyler walks in and tips his dress hat in victory. Music stops. Whistle blows.)

In horse racing. The first jockey to be the winner of Kentucky Derbies is—Isaac Murphy!

(Music. Murphy, black, enters and mimes racing on a horse, then gives a wave as the winner. Music stops. Whistle blows.)

The All Around Greatest Athlete, in track, in football, in baseball, Olympic winner and a native American Indian—Jim Thorpe!

(Music. Thorpe runs in and mimes throwing a forward pass, which he runs and catches. Music stops.)

At the Olympic Games the King of Sweden says,

(Points to Thorpe, who steps forward.)

"You, sir, are the greatest athlete in the world."

And Thorpe answers, "Thank you, King."

(Drummer blows whistle.)

And last on the great Yankee Doodle Team is the famous, the all-time, old-time favorite—Casey at the Bat!

(Music. Cue 18. The seven athletes take positions, making a small baseball diamond: Pitcher, catcher, first and second and third basemen, umpire; and Drummer and other actors are batters. A Reader appears at the side and recites the poem while the ball game is played in pantomime. All the action is in slow motion. Music stops.)

READER. "It looked extremely rocky
For the Mudville team that day;
The score stood two to four
With but one inning left to play.

If only—if only Casey
Could get a whack at that,
They'd put even money now,
With Casey at the bat.

(First batter goes to plate.)

But Flynn preceded Casey,
And likewise so did Blake,
And the former was a puddin'
And the latter was a fake.

(Pitcher warms up, winds up, throws imaginary ball. Batter strikes, hits, runs to first, all in slow motion.)

But—Flynn let drive a single
To the wonderment of all.

(Second Batter is up. Ball is pitched. He hits it, runs to first, then slides to second. Flynn slides to third and holds baseman around the legs.)

And the much-despisèd Blakey
Tore the cover off the ball.

And when the dust had lifted
And they saw what had occurred,
There was Blakey safe at second,
And Flynn a-huggin' third.

Then the crowd began to yell
And arose from where it sat;

(Casey enters, strutting with comic confidence.)

For Casey, mighty Casey,
Was advancing to the bat.

There was ease in Casey's manner
As he stepped into his place,
There was pride in Casey's bearing
And a smile on Casey's face.

And when responding to the cheers
He lightly doffed his hat,
No stranger in the crowd could doubt
'Twas Casey at the bat.

Ten thousand eyes were on him as
He rubbed his hands with dirt, *(Casey mimes.)*
Five thousand tongues applauded when
He wiped them on his shirt.

Then when the writhing pitcher ground

The ball into his hip, *(Pitcher mimes.)*
Defiance gleamed from Casey's eye,
A sneer curled Casey's lip.

And now the leather-covered sphere
Came hurtling through the air,
(Ball is pitched.) And Casey stood a-watching it
In haughty grandeur there.

Close by the sturdy batsman
The ball unheeded sped;
"That ain't my style," said Casey.
"Strike one," the umpire said. *(Umpire mimes.)*

"Kill him! Kill the umpire!"
Shouted someone on the stand. *(Umpire reacts, Casey lifts
    hand.)*
And it's likely they'd have killed him
Had not Casey raised his hand.

With a smile of Christian charity
Great Casey gave a grin;
He quieted the rising tumult,
The game began again.

He signaled to the pitcher *(Casey signals.)*
And once more the spheroid flew; *(Ball is pitched.)*
But Casey still ignored it,
And the umpire said, "Strike two." *(Umpire mimes.)*

"Fraud!" cried the maddened thousands,
And the echo answered, "Fraud!"
But one scornful look from Casey
And the audience was awed.

They saw his face grown stern and cold,
They saw his muscles strain, *(Casey gets ready.)*
And they knew that Casey wouldn't let
The ball go by again.

The sneer is gone from Casey's lips,
His teeth are clenched in hate.
He pounds with cruel vengeance
His bat upon the plate.

And now the pitcher holds the ball,
And now he lets it go,

(Pitcher throws, Casey swings, twisting completely around, facing audience with a surprised look on his face.)

And now the air is shattered
By the force of Casey's blow! *(All freeze in a moving position.)*
But there is no victory shout—
Mighty Casey has struck out!

(Casey opens his mouth in bewildered amazement. Black out. Music. Cue 19. All exit.)

DRUMMER. *(Lights come up on him.)* America grows to twenty, thirty, forty-eight states. Cyrus McCormick invents the reaper. John Deere, a steel plow. Joseph Glidden fences the West with barbed wire. From south of the border comes the Mexican vaquero.

(Music. Cue 20. Cowboy enters, pantomiming riding a horse.)

With his ten-gallon hat—

COWBOY. Sombrero!

DRUMMER. His chaps—

COWBOY. Chaperas!

DRUMMER. His handkerchief—

COWBOY. Bandana!

DRUMMER. And he becomes a Yankee Doodle cowboy!

(Music increases. Cowboy dance-mimes riding a bucking horse, then twirling his lasso and roping a steer. He waves his hat and rides off.)

Cities grow. Elisha Otis makes an elevator that goes up and up, and William Jenney designs a building that scrapes the sky. Yankee Doodle takes a land and makes it into a nation.

(Drummer exits. Music. Cue 21. Four actors, the same who were in Hall of Fame in Act One, enter singing.)

ALL. We are Yankee Doodles
From every state
Who have helped to make
Our country great.

For a portrait we should sit,

And our name
Should be writ
In the Hall of Fame,
In the Hall of Fame.

(Each turns his back to audience except when he speaks. Music
continues, underscoring the speaking.)

FIRST. *(Speaks.)*

Talk, talk, talk,
I studied sounds we get,
And taught the deaf to speak
With a special alphabet.

Later, I, Alexander
Graham Bell, alone
Let everybody talk
By inventing the telephone.

SECOND. *(Faces front, speaks.)*

My name is Daniel Williams
I found there was a lack,
So I started a hospital
For doctors who were black.

A man was stabbed in the heart—
I was the first to do
A successful heart operation,
And the man pulled through.

THIRD. *(Faces front, speaks.)*

I did not believe in slavery;
I did what I could do.
Uncle Tom's Cabin, a book,
I wrote stating my view.

It was blessed by some;
Others cried, "Not true."
Harriet Beecher Stowe—
I did what I had to do.

FOURTH. *(Faces front, speaks.)*

I never gave up till I found
By trial and error and luck

How to vulcanize rubber
That didn't come unstuck.

The Rubber Man they called me,
And Charles Goodyear, too.
Then tires were made from rubber

(Flirts with Girl, Third Singer, who turns around.)

For a bicycle built for two.

(Music blends into "Daisy Bell." Man in front and Girl behind pantomime riding a bicycle and sing.)

Daisy, Daisy,
Give me your answer, do!
I'm half crazy
All for the love of you!
It won't be a stylish marriage,
I can't afford a carriage,
But you'll look sweet
On the seat
Of a bicycle built for two! *(They turn around.)*

FIRST. *(Faces front, speaks.)*

I didn't build the first,
But the popular automobile.
Henry Ford, that's me,
Put you behind the wheel.

The Tin Lizzie, the Flivver,
Its fastest speed is slow,
But I with mass production
Put America on the go.

SECOND. *(Faces front, speaks.)*

Fighting snow and ice,
Racing toward our goal,
Admiral Peary and I
Reach the North Pole.

I, ahead, planted
The American flag unfurled;
I, Matthew Henson,
Stood first on top of the world.

THIRD. *(Faces front, speaks.)*

In the Civil War
Soldiers I healed
And searched for the missing
On the battlefield.

I, Clara Barton,
In trouble and loss,
Started for all
The American Red Cross.

FOURTH. *(Faces front, speaks. He holds two hand puppets, which he manipulates.)*

I am Wilbur. I am
Orville Wright—Right! *(Puppets nod to each other.)*
Famous brothers who made
The first powered flight.

Took off at Kitty Hawk,
Flew a minute—then slid.
But we proved that man can fly
Because WE DID.

ALL. *(Face front, exit singing.)*

We are Yankee Doodles
From every state
Who have helped to make
Our country great.

For a portrait we should sit,
And our name
Should be writ
In the Hall of Fame,
In the Hall of Fame. *(Exit.)*

McCOY. *(Elijah McCoy and Drummer enter. McCoy holds a red, white, and blue wheel which he can turn in one hand and an oil can in the other.)*

The wheels of America turn. *(He turns wheel.)* And every wheel needs oiling. I, Elijah McCoy, son of a runaway slave, invented a drip cup,

(Pantomiming with can.)

which oils the wheels while they run. Everyone wants my invention, the real thing. I, Elijah McCoy, help the wheels of America move.

(Spins wheel.)

Oh! Some say from my name comes the popular phrase the *real McCoy. (Exits.)*

ANTHONY. *(There are boos, whistles, and catcalls off. Susan Anthony enters, holding a sign: "Women's Rights.")*

I stand for Women's Rights! Equal rights with men! I, Susan Anthony, went to the voting polls. I was arrested. I was handcuffed and fined. I may be handcuffed today, but I will fight tomorrow and tomorrow for women's rights! The law must be changed. There must be an amendment! Women must have the right to vote!

(Off, boos, cheering, clapping are heard as she exits.)

DRUMMER. *(Pointing to her over cheering.)*

Protesters and reformers guard our social and civil liberties. Yankee Doodles with courage and vision lead the way!

ANTHONY. *(Music. Cue 22. She marches in holding a sign: "Women Can Vote.")*

Congress PASSES the Nineteenth Amendment! Women have the right to vote! Uncle Sam may be a man, but gentlemen please note this: The Statue of Liberty is not a he, She is a MISS! *(Exit. Music stops.)*

DRUMMER. Yankee Doodle has a fair and invites the world to meet me in St. Lou—ie!

(Music. Cue 23. Ernest Hamwi enters R with a sign, "Waffles," crosses to L and sets down sign. At the same time another man enters L with sign, "Ice Cream," crosses to R, and sets sign down. They nod in passing to each other. Music dims out.)

HAMWI. *(Pantomimes making a waffle.)*

O . . . stir the batter, thin as mush . . .
Pour the batter in a rush . . .
And make and bake a waffle
That is de—lic—ious!

MAN. *(Pantomimes filling a dish of ice cream.)*

> Ice cream. Ice cream.
> Any flavor that you wish . . .
> Chocolate, cherry, raspberry . . .
> Treat yourself and eat a dish!

(Crowd enters from all sides and rushes to ice cream stand, shouting, "Ice cream, ice cream.")

HAMWI. *(Looks wistfully at ice-cream customers, who freeze in position.)*

> Make a waffle . . . bake a waffle . . . that's de—lic—ious.

(Hopefully offers his wares.)

> Buy a waffle . . . try a waffle . . . that's de—lic—ious.

MAN. *(Crowd moves, surrounding him, and shouts, "Ice cream. Ice cream." He breaks through them, comes downstage. Crowd freezes in position.)*

> Ice cream! Ice cream! They all shout for ice cream. And I have run out of dishes!

(He returns to his stand, again surrounded by the crowd, which moves and shouts, "Ice cream, Ice cream." Then crowd freezes.)

HAMWI. I have waffles nobody wishes. He has customers, but no clean dishes. A waffle? A dish? What can I do . . . to combine the two?

(Beams with an idea, then mimes.)

> If I bake a waffle . . . that is paper thin . . . and take the waffle while it's hot . . . and begin . . . to twist it one revolution, so . . . HO HO, I've got a solution!

(From his sleeve he twists in his hand and holds a cone.)

MAN. *(Crowd moves and shouts, "Ice cream, ice cream." Man breaks through them and comes downstage. Crowd freezes.)*

> On my knees I pray, let me find a way to do AWAY with dirty dishes!

HAMWI. Sir!

MAN. *(Hopefully.)* Yes, Mr. Hamwi?

HAMWI. I have the answer to your prayer.

MAN. How? What? Where?

HAMWI. There! *(Holds out prop cone.)*

MAN. *(Takes it.)* What is that?

HAMWI. It is a waffle shaped like a cornucopia.

MAN. True, but what do I do?

HAMWI. On the top—you flop ice cream. While the bottom—you enfold and hold in your hand.

MAN. Ah . . . the waffle-holder is an added treat.

HAMWI. And . . . it is . . . a dish . . . that you can eat!

MAN. Make way. Ice cream makes history today!

> *(He quickly returns to stand, back to audience. Crowd "Oh!" and "Ah!" as he mimes dipping ice cream. He faces audience holding a cone heaped high with ice cream. He holds the prop high and admires it.)*

> A work of art, no doubt about it! But the name—cornucopia—is too high-flown! *(To Hamwi.)* Mr. Hamwi, you have invented the . . . ice cream . . . CONE!

ALL. *(Crowd, facing audience, holds up ice cream cone and sings.)*

> Meet me in St. Louis, Louis,
> Meet me at the Fair.
> Don't tell me the lights are shining
> Any place but there.
> We'll eat ice cream creamy dreamy
> In a cone that's munchy crunchy,
> If you will
> Meet me in St. Louis, Louis,
> Meet me at the Fair. *(All exit.)*

DRUMMER. Yankee Doodle is a thinker, a creator, an inventor. Lewis Waterman makes a fountain pen. Scott Joplin writes ragtime music. And the greatest inventor of his time is Thomas Alva Edison.

(Drummer exits.)

EDISON. *(Thomas Edison enters. The scene is played in Story The-*

atre fashion. Edison first acts like a young boy, becoming older as the scene continues.)

Once upon a time in Ohio, a boy was born named Thomas Alva Edison. His first words were "Why? How? What makes it so?" When he was six he wanted to know how a chicken was hatched. To find out he went into the barn and sat on a dozen eggs. *(Squats.)*

NANCY. *(Enters.)* Nancy, who looked after him, found him sitting on a nest. "What are you doing?"

EDISON. "I am hatching chickens."

NANCY. But all he got was scrambled eggs.

EDISON. *(Rises.)* Edison wondered: If birds can fly, why can't I? He reasoned: Birds eat worms.

(Pantomimes digging and holding up a worm, then puts it between his hands like a sandwich.)

NANCY. He offered me a strange-looking sandwich which he begged me to eat. *(Eats and swallows.)*

EDISON. "Now, Nan, you can fly."

NANCY. "Fly? Why?"

EDISON. "Because—you ate a worm."

(Nancy gasps, puts her hand over her mouth, and runs off.)

When he was seven he attended a one-room school. One day when he came home he asked, "Mother, what does ADDLED mean?"

MOTHER. *(Who has entered.)* "Addled means . . . mixed up . . . confused. Why?"

EDISON. "When I ask a question at school the teacher says I'm addled, that my head is shaped too big, and that I'm not bright."

MOTHER. "Of course you're bright."

EDISON. "And all the children laugh when I ask—why?"

MOTHER. "There will be no more school for you. You will study at home. You and I will find all the answers to all your questions."

(She exits.)

EDISON. Edison never attended a school again. On his tenth birthday his favorite present was *The Book of Natural and Experimental Philosophy. (Excited.)* "I'm going to build a chemistry laboratory and try every experiment in the book!" he said. And he did. When he was thirteen he worked as a newsboy on the Grand Trunk Railroad, selling his papers up and down the aisle. *(Pantomimes selling.)* "*Detroit Free Press.* Latest news from the battle front. General Robert E. Lee wins at Chancellorsville." One day at Fraser Station he jumped off the train to sell his papers. *(Pantomimes.)*

TRAINMAN. *(Enters, waves, signals.)* "All aboard. All aboard," the conductor called.

(He stands, body moving with the movement of the train.)

EDISON. The train started and he ran to catch the moving cars. *(Pantomimes.)* He grabbed the railing of the baggage coach, but he could not pull himself up. He hung above the moving wheels. "Help! Help!"

TRAINMAN. The brakeman inside saw him. *(Pantomimes.)* "Watch out for the wheels!" He grabbed the boy's head at his ears and pulled him to safety.

EDISON. "You saved my life." *(Trainman nods, smiles, and exits. Edison rubs his ears.)* "My ears. Something popped . . . and they ring . . . I can't hear." It was the beginning of total deafness. Later he said, "I don't mind that I can't hear. All the noise would interfere with my inventions." When he was seventeen he made his own telegraph machine, modeled after Samuel Morse's, and became a roving telegraph operator.

(Actor enters, comes to Edison, kneels, holds one hand out, and puts the other above his head.)

He sent the news by dots and dashes from different cities. New Orleans. Dash-dash-dot-dash-dash—

(Edison taps dots and dashes on the extended hand of actor.)

ACTOR. *(Moves his hand above his head.)* Cyrus Field lays cable across the Atlantic Ocean.

EDISON. Indianapolis. Dot-dash-dot-dash-dash—

ACTOR. Mark Twain writes new book, *Celebrated Jumping Frog.*

EDISON. Louisville. Dot-dash-dash-dot-dot—

ACTOR. Sarah Hale persuades President. Thanksgiving is a national holiday.

EDISON. In New York he invented a stock ticker for the Stock Exchange.

(Actor becomes a stock ticker, holds out his hands and moves his head.)

LEFFERTS. *(Enters.)* General Marshall Lefferts looked at the ticker and said, "I will buy it. How much money will you sell it for?"

EDISON. Edison had never sold an invention. Dare he ask a hundred dollars?

LEFFERTS. "I will pay you thirty thousand dollars."

EDISON. Edison could only swallow.

LEFFERTS. "All right, I'll give you FORTY thousand dollars."

EDISON. He nodded and held out his hand and received his fortune.

(Lefferts exits with stock-ticker actor.)

Forty thousand dollars rich! "Now I can spend all my time experimenting and inventing." And he did. He invented the phonograph.

KRUESI. *(Enters with actor who was the ticker.)* John Kruesi, one of Edison's helpers, carried in a strange machine which he had built according to Edison's design. "Here it is, but what is it for?"

(Actor sits.)

EDISON. "It is a talking machine."

KRUESI. "A talking machine!"

EDISON. He spoke into the mouthpiece, which was connected to the cylinder by a pointed pen *(the finger of the actor)*, which would follow a special groove as he cranked it. "It will record what I say. Then it will say it back to me." He took a deep breath, turned the crank and shouted, *(Cranks actor's extended arm. Actor moves his finger, which is pointed down and which is the pen, slowly sideways.)* "Mary had a little lamb, Its fleece was white as snow, And everywhere that Mary went, The lamb was sure to go." Edison moved the cylinder back to the starting point. *(Moves actor's finger back.)* "Now we will see if it will talk." *(Edison turns a switch. Actor begins speaking mechanically, "Mary had a little lamb, Its fleece was white as snow.")*

KRUESI. "It talks! It's your voice!"

(He lifts actor's finger. Voice stops. He puts actor's finger down. Voice repeats, "White as snow . . . white as snow." Kruesi moves actor's finger, and voice finishes poem as Kruesi talks. "Everywhere that Mary went, The lamb was sure to go.)

"It's saying your words! Mr. Edison, you have invented a talking machine." John Kruesi was amazed, and so was the world!

(He exits, guiding the actor off before him. Actor repeats, ". . . sure to go . . . sure to go . . . sure to go.")

EDISON. Thomas Alva Edison made a thousand inventions. One was a practical incandescent lamp.

(A single bare light bulb on a cord drops down. Stage lights dim down.)

To the ages of darkness and shadows, lit only by torches, lamps, and candles, Thomas Edison was a bringer of light.

(Single light lamp goes on, shining alone in the darkness.)

He lights the world with an incandescent glow.

(On the back drop, a glow of colored light begins. Soft music is heard. Cue 24.)

Fifty years later, the wizard of science was honored with a Golden Jubilee.

(Edison speaks slowly with dramatic pauses, as a light show begins on the backdrop. Patterns of beautiful colors and light designs appear and change. Music underscores speech.)

At dusk, around the world, myriads of lights glowed in every country. Towers and arches twinkled in the darkness, colors in fantastic designs flashed in the sky, celebrating a golden age of light.

(He salutes.)

Yankee Doodle turns night into day!

(He turns, runs to the back, stands with back to audience, slowly raises his arms, silhouetted against the colored lights.

The music and the light show build to a climax. Black-out, and the music stops. Edison exits.)

DRUMMER. *(Enters.)* A year and another year goes by, and every Fourth of July Yankee Doodle celebrates another birthday.

CLOWN. *(A comic tramp clown enters, carrying a large cake with one lighted candle. He sings.)*

"Happy birthday to you. Happy birthday—"

DRUMMER. *(Takes the cake.)* And so every year brings new things for Yankee Doodle to do.

CLOWN. *(Nods and sings.)* "Happy birthday to you . . ."

DRUMMER. *(Stops him.)* And every year when the old year is through—

(Clown blows out the candle.)

Yankee Doodle leaves the old year behind—like an old hat—

(Clown takes off his hat, looks at it, and lets it fall. There is a sound effect.)

or an old shoe.

(Clown takes off one shoe, looks at it, then happily lets it fall. There is a sound effect. Drummer steps forward and enthusiastically describes the years. He is unaware of the clown, who with great fun starts removing his clothes.)

The first year left behind was 1776. Thomas Paine writes for America's independence in his patriotic pamphlet *Common Sense.*

(Clown comically drops his other shoe. Sound effect.)

The year 1804 is left behind. Thomas Jefferson sets a new style. He is the first President to wear long pants.

(Clown drops his scarf. Sound effect.)

The year 1828 drops behind. John James Audubon paints pictures of American birds so real they could fly off the page.

(Clown comically drops his big coat. Sound effect.)

The year 1860 comes and goes. The Riders of the Pony Express deliver mail from Missouri to California in seven days.

(Clown with fun drops one bright stocking. Sound effect.)

The year 1886. John Pemberton mixes a tasty soft drink and the world sips Coca Cola.

(Clown drops other stocking. Sound effect.)

The year 1900. Doctor Walter Reed controls yellow fever, and the Panama Canal can be built.

(Clown happily drops his necktie. Sound effect.)

The year 1917 goes by. The United States enters World War I. Yankee Doodle fights with General Pershing "Over There."

(Clown drops his shirt. Sound effect.)

The year 1924 is left behind. Luther Burbank grows five hundred different kinds of cherries on ONE tree.

(Clown with abandonment drops his pants. Sound effect.)

The year 1927 comes—

(He turns and see Clown, who is happily unbuttoning his long red underwear.)

Stop. Stop. We go no further. 1927 is the last year we leave behind. 1927 is the year our play stops. After a World War and political scandals, the people want a hero.

(Clown reacts comically.)

And out of the blue there comes a new Yankee Doodle. Charles A. Lindbergh flies the world into a new age of air and space. Yankee Doodle is doing dandy!

(They salute each other, quickly gather up clothes, and exit as Newsboy enters, shouting.)

NEWSBOY: Extra! Extra!
Read all about it!

(Eight actors hurry in with newspapers.)

Lindbergh ready to fly.
One hop.
New York—Paris.
Nonstop.
Charles Lindbergh ready to try!

(Actors, in a line, face audience. Each holds newspaper so it

masks his face. On cue each quickly lowers his paper, speaks, and quickly raises his paper again.)

THIRD. Roosevelt Field. Dark and misty.

FIFTH. Runway: muddy—slippery.

SIXTH. Engine churns. Propeller turns.

SECOND. Take off ready. Hold stick steady.

FOURTH. Off the ground. Begins to rise.

NEWSBOY. Lindbergh in the air. Lindbergh FLIES! *(Faint airplane sound begins.)*

FIRST. Over Connecticut.

SECOND. Rhode Island below.

THIRD. Past Cape Cod.

FOURTH. Three thousand miles to go!

FIFTH. Nova Scotia.

SIXTH. Newfoundland in sight.

SEVENTH. Over the ocean.

NEWSBOY. Lindbergh flies off into the night!

FOURTH. Will he make it?

FIFTH. Can he make it?

SECOND. All alone.

THIRD. One-motor plane!

FIFTH. No radio!

SIXTH. No parachute!

SEVENTH. Only compass!

EIGHTH. Flying Great Circle route!

FIRST. In the air—

SECOND. Six hours—seven hours and more.

FOURTH. Ten hours—eleven hours—

SIXTH. Never been done before!

FOURTH. Will he make it?

FIFTH. Can he make it?

NEWSBOY. Extra! Extra! Lindbergh sighted over land!

FIRST. Over Ireland.

SEVENTH. Over England.

EIGHTH. Coast of France is near.

NEWSBOY. Lindbergh lands! Thousands cheer!

FIRST. *(The following is very fast.)* He made it!

SECOND. He made it!

THIRD. He made it!

FOURTH. Three thousand miles flown!

FIFTH. He made it!

SIXTH. He made it!

SEVENTH. He made it!

EIGHTH. Made it all alone!

ALL. *(Lindbergh, wearing helmet with goggles, is carried in on the shoulders of two actors. It is a big finale with lights, cheers, falling balloons, and streamers. All sing. Cue 25.)*

Charles Lindbergh is the one
Hurray to him we say—ay.
A dandy Yankee Doodle of
The good old U.S.A.—A.

Yankee Doodle takes his place,
He's a Yankee hero,
Flying high into space
A Yankee Doodle hero.

(An enormous American flag is illuminated at the back. All turn and face it and salute. Then face audience and sing.)

Beat the drum
Rat a tat tat,
Blow the bugle
Toot ta too toot,

Yankee Doodle
We salute.

Drummers, and hummers, and mummers, and plumbers, and
Sailors, and whalers, and jailers, and tailors, and
Yankee Doodle's daughter and son,
Yankee Doodles every one.

Beat the drum
Rat a tat tat,
Blow the bugle
Toot ta too toot,
Yankee Doodle, Yankee Doodle, Yankee Doodle,
We salute.

(Curtain.
For a curtain call, all sing "Yankee Doodle" and encourage
the audience to sing with them.)

THE YANKEE DOODLES OF THE PLAY

Susan B. Anthony
Johnny Appleseed (John
 Chapman)
John James Audubon
P. T. Barnum
Clara Barton
Alexander Graham Bell
Elizabeth Blackwell
Amelia Bloomer
Daniel Boone
Luther Burbank
George Rogers Clark
William Clark
Samuel Clemens (Mark
 Twain)
Ty Cobb
William Cody (Buffalo Bill)
Davy Crockett
Polly Crockett
Billy Dawes
John Deere

William Diamond
Mary Jane Dilworth
Grenville Dodge
Thomas Durant
Nancy Edison (Cousin)
Nancy Edison (Mother)
Thomas Alva Edison
Cyrus Field
John Fitch
Henry Ford
Benjamin Franklin
Robert Fulton
Joseph Glidden
Charles Goodyear
Sarah Hale
Ernest A. Hamwi
John Hancock
William Harrison
John Hays
Mary Hays (Molly Pitcher)
Patrick Henry

Matthew Henson
Francis Hopkinson
Esther Howland
Andrew Jackson
Edwin James
Thomas Jefferson
William Jenney
John Paul Jones
Scott Joplin
Theodore Judah
William Kelly
Francis Scott Key
John Kruesi
Robert E. Lee
Marshall Lefferts
Meriwether Lewis
Abraham Lincoln
Charles Lindbergh
Hyman Lipman
Robert Livingston
Cyrus McCormick
Elijah McCoy
Dolley Madison
James Madison
Dan Morgan
Samuel Morse
Isaac Murphy
Thomas Nast
Elisha Otis
Thomas Paine
John Parker
John Pemberton

John Pershing
Zebulon Montgomery Pike
Walter Reed
Paul Revere
Dan Rice
Theodore Roosevelt
James Rumsey
Jean Baptiste Pointe Sable
Sacajawea
William F. Semple
Leland Stanford
John Stevens
Marvin C. Stone
Harriet Beecher Stowe
John L. Sullivan
Abraham Swartwout
Jim Thorpe
Tom Thumb
Harriet Tubman
John Tyler
Booker T. Washington
George Washington
Lewis Waterman
Noah Webster
Eli Whitney
Daniel Williams
William Worth
Orville Wright
Wilbur Wright
Brigham Young
Babe Dedrickson Zaharias

ACKNOWLEDGMENTS

Songs and poems by the following Yankee Doodles are used in the play:

Charles O'Donnell and Bobby Heath, "Pony Boy."
Ren Shields and George Evans, "Good Old Summer Time."
Hughie Cannon, "Waltz."
Harry Dacre, "Daisy Bell."
Kerry Mills, "Meet Me in St. Louis."
Henry Wadsworth Longfellow, "Paul Revere's Ride."
Ralph Waldo Emerson, "Concord Hymn."
Ernest Lawrence Thayer, "Casey at the Bat."

Appendix 1. The Plays of Aurand Harris

Children's Theatre	High School	Adult	Publisher	Date
Once upon a Clothesline			Row-Peterson[a]	1945
	Ladies of the Mop		Row-Peterson[a]	1945
	The Moon Makes Three		French	1947
		Madam Ada	French	1948
Seven League Boots			Baker's	1948
	The Doughnut Hole		French	1948
		Missouri Mural	Unpublished	1948
Circus Day[b]			French	1949
		Lo and Behold	Unpublished	1949
Pinocchio and the Indians			French	1950
	And Never Been Kissed		French	1950
Young Alec			Unpublished	1950
Simple Simon			Anchorage	1953
	We Were Young That Year		French	1954
Buffalo Bill			Anchorage	1954
		Hide and Seek	Unpublished	1955

[a]Originally published by Row-Peterson; currently distributed by Baker's Plays, Inc.
[b]Circus Day (1949) was revised and published in 1960 as Circus in the Wind.

The Plain Princess	Anchorage	1955
The Flying Prince	French	1958
Junket	Anchorage	1959
Circus in the Wind[b]	French	1960
Pocahontas	Anchorage	1961
The Brave Little Tailor	Anchorage	1961
Androcles and the Lion	Anchorage	1964
Rags to Riches	Anchorage	1966
Pinocchio and the Fire-Eater[c]	McGraw-Hill	1967
A Doctor in Spite of Himself	Anchorage	1968
Punch and Judy	Anchorage	1970
Just So Stories	Anchorage	1971
Ming Lee and the Magic Tree	French	1971
Steal Away Home	Anchorage	1972
Peck's Bad Boy	Anchorage	1974
Yankee Doodle	Anchorage	1975
Star Spangled Salute	Anchorage	1975
Robin Goodfellow	Anchorage	1976

[c]Although first published in 1967, this brief playlet for classroom use was written during Harris's years in Gary, Indiana, 1939–1941.

Appendix 2. The Playwriting Awards and Honors of Aurand Harris

Play	Year	Award
Once upon a Clothesline	1944–1945	Seattle Junior Programs
Circus Day (Red Letter Day)	1945	John Golden Playwriting Contest
Seven League Boots (Hop-o'-My-Thumb)	1945–1946	Seattle Junior Programs
Madam Ada	1947	The Midwestern Writers Conference
The Woods Colt (Missouri Mural)	1948	Stanford University Miles Anderson Award
Young Alec	1950	Seattle Junior Programs
Simple Simon	1951–1952	Seattle Junior Programs
Hide and Seek	1956	Johns Hopkins University Marburg Prize
Pocahontas	1956–1958	Seattle Junior Programs
The Flying Prince	1958	Birmingham Junior Programs
The Flying Prince	1958–1960	Seattle Junior Programs
Pocahontas	1960	Junior League of New Jersey
Pocahontas	1960	Birmingham Junior Programs
Androcles and the Lion	1962–1964	Seattle Junior Programs
The Brave Little Tailor	1962	Birmingham Junior Programs
Rags to Riches	1966	North Shore Music Theatre, Beverly, Massachusetts
Rags to Riches	1967	Horatio Alger, Jr., Newsboy Award of the Horatio Alger Society
"For Aurand Harris's Continued Contributions to the Field of Children's Drama in the Writing of Superior Plays for Young Audiences"	1967	Charlotte Chorpenning Award of the Children's Theatre Association of the American Theatre Association
Creative Writing Fellowship	1976	National Endowment for the Arts, Washington, D.C.

Photo Credits

Aurand Harris at Grace Church School, 1974 (page 2)

Androcles and the Lion (page 30)

The Department of Drama, The University of Texas at Austin
March, 1966

Directed by Coleman A. Jennings
Costumes by Paul D. Reinhardt
Choreography by Shirlee Dodge
Scenery by Robert R. Blackman
Lighting by Bennet Averyt
Musicians' costumes by Judith Burke
Songs by David Earnest and Tom Wells
Incidental music by Tom Wells

CAST:
Prologue: Ira Moore
Androcles: Michael Wolfe
Pantalone: Manzy Mooney
Isabella: Suzanne Anderson*
           Cheri Kearl*
Lelio: Robert Black*
       Joe Neal*
Captain: Don Stoll
Lion: Ira Moore
*Played alternate performances.

Assistants to the Director: Michael Wolfe and Nan Elkins Kazmar
Stage Manager: Nan Elkins Kazmar

Photography by Walter Barnes

Androcles and the Lion (page 38)

The Department of Drama, The University of Texas at Austin
October, 1976

Directed by Coleman A. Jennings
Scenery by B. J. Fredrickson
Lighting by James F. Franklin
Costumes by Barbara Fisher
Musical direction by Bob Jones
Choreography by Michael Sokoloff
Voice coach, Rosalie Blooston

CAST:
Androcles: Gene Barkley Alford
Lion: Louis Moloney
Pantalone: Mike McKinley
Captain: Eduardo Silva

Isabella: Cynthia Bock
Lelio: Jeff Broyles

Assistant to the Director: Rachel Winfree
Stage Manager: Rebecca Spann

Photography by Stanley Farrar

Rags to Riches (pages 88 and 96)

The Department of Drama, The University of Texas at Austin
February, 1971

Directed by Coleman A. Jennings and Jagienka Zych
Musical direction by James Thomason-Bergner
Costumes by Gary Burton
Lighting by Vincent Landro
Scenery by Augustina Kymmel

CAST:
Ragged Dick: O. Neal Smith
Policeman: Rob Ramsey
Mickey Maguire: George O'Conner
Mark Menton: Charles Bergner
Mr. Greyson: David Deacon
Mrs. Flanagan: Georgia Clinton*
                Stephanie Voss*
Mother Watson: Janet Braun*
                Francine Hemphill*
Roswell: Mark Harelik
Ida Greyson: Jacque Browning
Citizens: Ann Armstrong, Michael Face, Ricardo Garcia, Ghent Howell, Pamela
    Johnson, Bill Leigon, Jill Mize, Cameron Sevier, David Silber, Lee Skinner, Anita
    Wilkins, Janet Braun, Georgia Clinton, Francine Hemphill, Stephanie Voss
Demon/Butler: Ghent Howell
Heroine/Maid: Lee Skinner
*Played alternate performances.

Assistants to the Director: Ricardo Garcia and Pamela Johnson
Stage Manager–Technical Director: Leonard J. Wittman

Photography by Dale Kennedy

Punch and Judy (page 148)

The Atlanta Children's Theatre
December, 1976

Produced and directed by Charles L. Doughty
Choreography by Charly Helms
Musical direction by Paul Ford
Scenery and costumes by Ruth Ann Maddux
Lighting by William B. Duncan

CAST:
Toby: Ray Stephens
Punch: Mark Young

Judy: Nancy Jane Clay
Professor: Patricia Landon
Hector: Eric Price, Rob Zapple
Doctor: John Dance
Policeman: Rob Zapple
Guards: Reid Pierce, William B. Duncan
Hangman: William Colquitt
Ghosts: Patricia Landon, John Dance, William Colquitt
Devil: Eric Price

Production Stage Manager: D. Wayne Hughes
Company Manager: Bix Doughty

Photography by Steve Oliver

Punch and Judy (page 156)

The University of Kansas Theatre for Young People
Spring, 1974

Directed by Jed H. Davis
Musical direction by Janet Erickson
Choreography by Richard Rees
Scenery and costumes by Terryl Asla
Lighting by Tom Rowe
Properties by Ruth Gennrich
Make-up by Andrea Southard
Special music by Mike Huebner

CAST:
Punch: Michael C. Booker
Judy: Roxy Callison
Toby: Beth Johnston
Professor: Myke Fox
Hector: Jamie Dibbins, Dan Walters
Doctor: Dan Rawlings
Policeman: Dan Walters
Guard: Jamie Dibbins
Hangman: Myke Fox
Ghosts: Roxy Callison, Dan Rawlings
Devil: Jamie Dibbins

Assistant to the Director: Richard Rees
Technical Assistant: Gary Andrew
Stage Manager: Glenn Bickle
Company Manager: Terryl Asla

Photography by Andrew Tsubaki

Steal Away Home (pages 206 and 210)

The Department of Drama, The University of Texas at Austin
November, 1975

Directed by Coleman A. Jennings
Music by the Gospel Choir of the Ebenezer Baptist Church, Allyne Lewis, Director
Scenery and properties by Bob Briggs

Lighting by Michael Drew Roberts
Costumes by Allana Patterson

CAST:
Amos: Anthony Joiner
Obie: Roland Brown, Jr.
Preacher Prentice: Dock Lee Jackson, Jr.
Mama: Demetrius Roy
Man with Gun: John Brooks
Mrs. Strauss: Amber Walker
Miss Melissa: Sidney Weaver
Edgar: Peter Pope
First Man: Don S. Butler
Second Man: Peter Waldron
Joe: Dock Lee Jackson, Jr.
Elijah McNaul: Scott Ward
Jud: Raymond Benson
First Neighbor: Don S. Butler
Second Neighbor: John Brooks
Mrs. Johnson: Yolantha Harrison
Patrol: Scott Ward
Will: Michael H. Meyerson
Mother: Amber Walker
Conductor: Raymond Benson
Porters: Don S. Butler, John Brooks
Pa: Sherman D. Wilson

Assistant to the Director: Betsy Smith
Stage Manager: Mary Clark

Photography by Stanley Farrar

Peck's Bad Boy (page 260)

The Goodman Children's Theatre of The Art Institute of Chicago
January–March, 1975

Directed by Kelly Danford
Costumes by Richard Donnelly
Scenery by Brad R. Loman
Lighting by Neal J. Yablong
Musical accompaniment by David Coleman and Kelly Danford

CAST:
Katie: Mary Beth Cobleigh
Henry: Richard Porter
Mother: Susan Monts
Major: Geoffrey Shlaes
Patrick Michael O'Reilly: William Kenzie
Mrs. Langford: Concetta Tomei
Horace Q. Winthrop Wellington: Martin Levy
Understudy: Susan LaFollette

Assistant to the Director: Geoffrey Shlaes
Stage Manager: La Vetta L. Clemans

Photography by G. E. Naselius

Yankee Doodle (page 304)

The Department of Drama, The University of Texas at Austin
World Première, November, 1974

Directed by Coleman A. Jennings
Choreography by Lathan Sanford
Musical direction by Christopher W. Jarvis
Costumes by Moppy Vogely
Scenery by James F. Franklin
Lighting by Susan Hallman
Properties by James Pringle

CAST:
Laura Bucklin*
Christopher Bulot
Richard Craig
Doug Franklin
J. Alex Guthrie
Tom Harrison
Kevyn Colleen Jones*
Cindy Kahn†
Christopher McIntyre
Rick Porter
Pat Robertson
Beverly Robinson†
John Lee Spanko
Gary A. Williams
*/†Played alternate performances.

Assistant to the Director: Terri Daggett
Stage Manager: Rodney Gordon

Photography by Ralph Hawkins

Yankee Doodle (page 308)

The Department of Drama, The University of Texas at Austin
Bicentennial Professional Touring Production, February–May, 1976
Presented in cooperation with the Texas Commission on the Arts and Humanities,
the National Endowment for the Arts, and the University of Texas at Austin
President's Associates Fund

Directed by Coleman A. Jennings
Choreography by Lathan Sanford
Musical direction by Christopher W. Jarvis
Costumes by Moppy Vogely and Allana Patterson
Scenery by James F. Franklin
Lighting by Dennis Higgins
Properties by James Pringle

CAST:
Sherry Bashaw
Brian Carpenter
Richard Craig
Bunny Dees

Eric Henshaw
David Huffman
Dock Lee Jackson, Jr.
Daniel P. Jones
Deborah Malone
Rick Porter
Mark Rodgers
Scott Ward

Touring Production Staff:
Tour Manager: Sharon Watkins Bown
Company Manager: Catherine O'Brien
Technicians: Allana Patterson, Michael Drew Roberts
Conductor/Pianist: William Reber
Percussionist: Robin Wayne Binford

Photography by Stanley Farrar